"After over four decades as an associate pastor, I enthusiastically commend this book as the most comprehensive, practical, and valuable tool for staff members that I have ever read. It speaks powerfully to a critical and urgent issue in the church today."

DR. BILL FLANAGAN,
retired Presbyterian minister

"Finally, a book that honors the calling of ministry staff members and instructs them on how to be effective! We have ignored the vital contributions of ministry staff and senior leadership teams far too long, focusing upon the role of the senior leader as if he or she has led alone. Doug provides practical, wise advice for new and experienced staff alike. Having served as a senior leader and a ministry staff member for over thirty years, I wish a resource like this had been available decades ago. It might have helped me to avoid many unnecessary mistakes in my ministry!"

CRAIG WILLIFORD,
President, Denver Seminary

"For the pastor or associate who wants to work effectively on a team, *The Ministry Staff Member* is like having an experienced, mature mentor sitting beside you sharing clear, concise, and intensely practical counsel. Doug has 'been there.' It shows on every page. Read this book."

DR. BILL RUDD,
Senior Pastor, Calvary Church,
Grand Rapids, Michigan

"I have only one complaint about this book. I needed it thirty years ago when I stepped into uncharted territory first as a pastoral staff member and later as a senior pastor. Dr. Fagerstrom is a spiritual leader who has spent his life turning godly vision into effective and fruitful ministry. It's no surprise to me his handbook for ministry staff members is so wise, practical, and real-world helpful."

DR. JERRY SHEVELAND,
President/CEO,
Baptist General Conference

"Fagerstrom has provided a gift for every ministry team. Pastoral teams should study this book together to help one another equip and be equipped, encourage and be encouraged, empower and be empowered for ministry."

JEFFREY D. HALSTED,
Senior Pastor, Calvary Baptist Church,
Grand Rapids, Michigan

Also by Douglas L. Fagerstrom

The Single Adult Ministry Handbook

Single to God

Single to Single

Drama in Worship, Volumes 1–6

Worship and Drama Library, Volume 14

THE MINISTRY STAFF MEMBER

A CONTEMPORARY, PRACTICAL HANDBOOK TO
EQUIP, ENCOURAGE, AND **EMPOWER**

DOUGLAS L. FAGERSTROM

ZONDERVAN™

GRAND RAPIDS, MICHIGAN 49530 USA

ZONDERVAN.COM/
AUTHORTRACKER

We want to hear from you. Please send your comments about this book to us in care of zreview@zondervan.com. Thank you.

ZONDERVAN™

The Ministry Staff Member
Copyright © 2006 by Douglas L. Fagerstrom

Requests for information should be addressed to:
Zondervan, *Grand Rapids, Michigan 49530*

Library of Congress Cataloging-in-Publication Data

Fagerstrom, Douglas L.
    The ministry staff member : a contemporary, practical handbook to equip, encourage, and empower / Douglas L. Fagerstrom ; forewords by Leith Anderson and Ed Dobson.
        p. cm.
    Includes bibliographical references.
    ISBN-13: 978-0-310-26312-8
    ISBN-10: 0-310-26312-3
    1. Church officers—Handbooks, manuals, etc. 2. Church management—Handbooks, manuals, etc. 3. Christian leadership—Handbooks, manuals, etc. I. Title.
    BV705.F34 2006
    253'.2—dc22

                                                                                                                2005030105

Interior design by Ruth Bandstra

Printed in the United States of America

06 07 08 09 10 11 • 18 17 16 15 14 13 12 11 10 9 8 7 6 5 4 3 2 1

This book is dedicated to

Donna, my wife,

my exuberant cheerleader,

faithful prayer warrior,

and constant encourager

as we work tirelessly,

serve constantly,

and worship authentically ... together!

Contents

PART 4: Serving Others

PART 5: Leaving a Legacy

PART 6: Managing Life and Ministry

PART 7: Practical Advice for Senior and Governing Leaders

Foreword by Leith Anderson

Born October 27, 1728 to a day laborer in Yorkshire, England, James Cook was one of seven children. He worked in a nearby fishing village and fell in love with ships and the sea. At age seventeen he took an apprenticeship with a family-owned shipping business that specialized in transporting coal. Cook not only learned about ships but personally studied mathematics and navigation. After nine years as an apprentice he enlisted in the Royal Navy in 1755 and served on *HMS Eagle*, a gunship headed for North America. Quickly rising through the ranks, he was given command of a survey ship even though he was an ordinary sailor and not an officer. His first assignment was to map the estuary of the Saint Lawrence River in Quebec.

Cook's next assignment was mapping the coast of Newfoundland. His reputation quickly spread as a careful cartographer. In three major explorations Captain Cook and his crews circumnavigated the world and explored all seven continents. Bays and inlets are named for him from Canada to Chile and from Alaska to Australia. But he did more than explore the world for the British navy; he drew the maps for others to follow. According to biographer Nathan Kerl, "The surveys were so accurate and complete that they were in use until the beginning of the twentieth century."

This book is a map—not by a seasoned sea captain but by a seasoned church leader; not of the seven continents but of the Christian ministry. Like James Cook, Doug Fagerstrom has held a variety of ranks and fulfilled a multitude of roles before becoming captain/president of a theological seminary. His experiences and study of the practical side of church ministry is evident on every page. What you are about to read is a map for ministry—showing the dangerous coastal rocks to avoid and explaining how to raise the sails and sail with God's wind. Doug tells how the church's crew is to recruit, relate, stay safe, and explore new horizons. You can read from cover to cover as you would a typical book, or you can turn the pages as you would reference an atlas, focusing on the information you need for your current journey. And, like any good navigator's atlas you will find that some pages are for waters you've already sailed, some are for stormy days only, and all are valuable for a successful journey.

No experienced sailor would think of taking a long journey without the maps and experience of those who have gone before. Here is a lifetime of experience from a leader who has gone ahead and been kind enough to bless those who follow.

Bon voyage!

Leith Anderson
Wooddale Church
Eden Prairie, Minnesota

Foreword by Ed Dobson

Prior to coming to Calvary Church as senior pastor, I served for twelve years as the associate pastor of Thomas Road Baptist Church in Lynchburg, Virginia. I have been both a ministry staff member and a lead pastor. Both roles are unique and bring their own set of challenges. As an associate pastor, I was much quicker to jump to conclusions and give my advice. As senior pastor, I found that decisions are not as clear as I once thought, and besides, I was not responsible for each decision.

I worked together for many years with Doug Fagerstrom. He was one of the key staff members on our ministry team at Calvary Church and much of our growth can be attributed to his leadership and vision. He is more than qualified to write this book, filled with helpful advice and practical suggestions about serving as a staff member, dealing with staff members, and building team spirit. This is not a book of theory; it is a book about living out ministry together in the trenches of everyday life.

Every senior pastor should read this book. Every ministry staff member should read this book. And everyone who cares about the church, whether layperson or vocational minister, should read this book. It's by far the best guide available for pastoral ministry in a local church setting.

Ed Dobson
Pastor Emeritus
Calvary Church
Grand Rapids, Michigan

Acknowledgments

*Remember your leaders, who spoke the word of God to you. Consider
the outcome of their way of life and imitate their faith.*

Hebrews 13:7

I want to give thanks for the four senior pastors who God brought into my life over thirty-one years of ministry. I could not have written this book without them. They shaped my life as a ministry staff member. They demonstrated servant leadership, modeled godliness, taught the Bible, and mirrored the person of Jesus Christ through their faithfulness to God, their families, and others. This book is as much about them as it is about me.

- Pastor Bob Savage taught me the joy of ministry (1972–1975).
- Pastor Chuck Ver Straten taught me to pray through the ministry (1975–1979).
- Leith Anderson taught me to how to lead in ministry (1979–1986).
- Ed Dobson taught me to love God and the people in the ministry (1990–2003).

My wife, Donna, and I are most blessed to have known these men, their wives, and children. Our prayer is that we will follow their examples, imitate their faith, and share God's truth, no less than they.

In addition, the ministry staff members who worked with me since 1972 are my heroes in ministry. I would try to list their names but there are so many, I fear missing just one. It was my privilege to serve Jesus Christ alongside each and every one of them. The providence of God allowed me to learn and mature through them. The different lessons I learned from each is still causing me to grow and be more like Christ. Fellow colleagues, men and women, thank you.

I want to express my sincere thanks and appreciation to Paul Engle and Greg Clouse at Zondervan. They shared my passion for this book, encouraging and helping me through each page and paragraph. Their ideas and comments were invaluable! Paul and Greg, thank you.

Acknowledgments

To God, I give thanks. He called me to be his son and his servant. It is most humbling to think through all of my stories and moments in ministry. I will be forever blessed. God, thank you.

A ministry staff member,
Doug Fagerstrom

Why Read This Book?

I remember the first time, as an associate minister, I was privileged to perform the sacrament of baptism. After the service, a rather prominent leader in the church critically approached our senior minister and pointedly and purposefully asked, "Did the baptisms performed by Doug this evening count?" That question reported back to me was devastating news. I could not believe the ignorance (my thought at the time) of that comment. It was insensitive. It hurt. As an associate, I was perceived differently; there was an honest lack of understanding of my role and relationship to the body of Christ. My credentials were not really recognized and it did not even seem to matter that I was ordained. I was a ministry staff member, *not* the senior or lead minister.

Throughout the years, members of the congregations where I served as a ministry staff member would ask questions such as, "When are you going to become a real pastor?" or, "When are you going to get your own church?" or, "How long will you be with us?" After a while, I learned that most people, including many ministry staff members themselves, have differing views of what it means to be a ministry staff member. For some, it is a "stepping-stone" to a senior leadership role. For others, it's a resident internship to discover if this is what they really want to do for the next thirty-plus years. Very few understand that a person in ministry could be called by God to just that place and would be content to serve as an associate for their entire ministry life. Given such unfocused definitions, it's no wonder that people often have a weak perception of the ministry staff member.

The Ministry Staff Member is designed and developed to paint a clear picture of the role and responsibilities of volunteers and paid staff members in every area of Christian ministry. It was written to encourage a church congregation or parachurch ministry to appreciate and honor *all* those who serve; to inspire renewed confidence in ministry staff members serving Jesus Christ and the family of faith with the gifts and competencies that God has given; and, most of all, to foster unity among those who work alongside one another in the body.

When I think of "staff members" in the Old Testament, I think of men and women such as Joshua, Caleb, Ruth, Esther, and Elisha. I think of their courage, of their impact on thousands in their day and the millions who have followed their example. I am reminded how God uniquely used them unlike any other in their time. When I read the New Testament, I think first of Jesus and his twelve "ministry staff members." Then my mind goes to Paul, Barnabas, John Mark, Lydia, Martha, Silas, and Timothy. I begin to imagine how they struggled, shared, sacrificed, and served. And the more I think of them, the more the twenty-plus "one another" exhortations of the New Testament come alive as characteristics that must have surely marked the spirit of their lives.

The role of a ministry staff member cannot be communicated without considering the underlying character qualities of submission and humility. The greatest model is Jesus Christ. He was submissive to the Father, giving up the splendor of his heavenly throne and glorious "rights" as he served among us (Philippians 2:6–7). He is our example, our model to imitate, the One every ministry staff member can follow.

It all comes down to obedience to what God has asked us to do. For some it is to serve as a volunteer. For some it is to serve as a senior or lead minister. For some of us, our act of obedience is service as a ministry staff member. And that is God's idea. As I wrote this book, I was constantly aware of my thirty-one years of service as a ministry staff member. I wore many hats and had many titles related to youth ministry, music, adult ministries, single adult ministry, and administration. Through every topic in this handbook I saw my own failures and weaknesses. I was reminded how at times I failed people and did not always honor God. Yet I found moments in my memories to thank God for wonderful coaches, mentors, and people he brought into my life and ministry. I would not delete one year of my experience as a ministry staff member.

What Will You Discover in *The Ministry Staff Member*?

Inside *The Ministry Staff Member* are anecdotes, dialogue, and action points from seasoned ministry staff members' experiences. The ideas are practical and useful because they have already been tested and tried. They do more than make sense. They work. And applied carefully and prayerfully, they can work for you too.

The short stories you read in each chapter are real. Of course, the names, places, roles, and situations have all been changed. Yet each character comes from real-life ministry experience. No matter where you are in ministry, you will likely find some of the narratives to be rather familiar.

Introduction

The Scripture passages referenced or quoted in each chapter are God's truth and principles for effective ministry and leadership. Read each text carefully, either as you go along or later. Read the context. Discover the greater narrative. And find the joy of God working in the lives of ordinary men and women.

The sidebars are simple, quick reference tools to grab out of the ministry toolbox at any time. Each one features well thought-out principles that can provide the kind of support and advice that may trigger the right response for your ministry goals and objectives. Use them. Share them with others. Teach them to your colleagues and ministry staff members.

This book applies to every staff person engaged in ministry. That includes:

- Youth pastors and children's ministry leaders
- Youth campus leaders, including Young Life and Campus Life directors
- Collegiate ministry directors, including InterVarsity, Campus Crusade for Christ, and Navigator staff
- Single adult ministry and senior adult leaders
- Christian education directors and adult ministry leaders
- Women's and men's ministry staff leaders
- Associate pastors, teaching pastors, mission pastors, and visitation pastors
- Music directors, worship leaders, choral and orchestral directors
- Business managers, facility managers, technicians, and information system managers
- Executive pastors, lead pastors, chefs, custodians
- The countless volunteers who work diligently and faithfully...
- ... and of course, your title and role that is not listed above

Chapters 31 – 35 are written specifically to the senior pastor, senior leader, lead pastor, executive director, and the governing board members. While each ministry staff member will do well to know the content of these chapters, there are certain responsibilities which fall on the ministry leaders' shoulders. The staff members serving in your ministry are your responsibility before God and others. Treat them as gifts from God. Treat them as you would desire to be treated.

God desires that we pursue godliness (1 Timothy 4:7; 6:11). It is our training objective. From godly living, no one is exempt, including the volunteer, the parachurch executive director, the senior minister, and the ministry staff member. It means reflecting and imitating the person of Jesus Christ in every area of our lives, so that when other people look at us they begin to think of him. There can be no higher goal.

I trust that this book will be an ongoing resource, one you pull off the shelf and use often to help you, other staff members, and volunteers with whom you will share the ministry.

So, enjoy the journey. The land of the ministry staff member is filled with adventures. The course may not always be well charted, but the Guide has promised to lead you to growth and maturity. The discoveries will be many, the nights and days may be long. But, at the end, you will celebrate with the King of kings and Lord of all. And may you hear from others, in time, "Well done, you have been a good and faithful ministry staff member."

With love and respect for all ministry staff members,
Doug Fagerstrom

PART 1

Establishing Your Ministry Identity

The First 100 Days

Plans fail for lack of counsel, but with many advisers they succeed.

Proverbs 15:22

It's the start that stops most people.

I t was Carl's first day as the associate pastor of Bethel Community Church, a day he and his wife, Liz, had dreamed about for nearly four years. As he unpacked the five badly beaten boxes of used seminary books, reality slowly gripped his emotions.

On one hand, he was elated to be in the 150-square foot office next to the senior pastor. On the other hand, he felt a bit fearful. Old voices began to interrupt his new joy: *Will you succeed? Will the people really like you? What will you do after you have placed your small and inadequate library on five of the fifteen office shelves?*

Carl snapped out of his reverie and quickly tried to recall the seminary class on "how to begin your first ministry." What were those three award-winning principles to being a success? He finished putting his books on the shelves and sat for the first time in his office chair. After praying he walked out into his new world and began to introduce himself to the rest of the staff. "Where can I find a cup of coffee?" he asked.

How Carl begins in ministry may well determine how he concludes. The beginning days may be a time of great joy or unbearable anxiety. A rough *start* may bring an early *stop*.

Carl is not unlike most first-time associates. His experience is limited and he is flooded with a sea of emotions and ideas. He is a passionate idealist who

Suggestions for Leadership to Welcome the New Staff Member

- Create a "welcome" sign and present a small gift in the "new office."
- Gather staff and/or volunteers together on the first day for refreshments. Perhaps schedule a lunch with a few "key" people or the entire staff.
- Send the new staff person's job description to appropriate leadership. *(Make sure that everyone shares the same performance expectations of the new staff member.)*
- Place in the new staff member's office more-than-adequate supplies, building keys, and an area map if they're new to town. Remember to purchase a nameplate for their door.
- Provide membership and volunteer lists with phone numbers, email, and street addresses.
- Provide helpful policy guidelines, needed business forms, and ministry procedures that will allow smooth sailing and prevent early disasters.
- Provide a calendar and discuss important meetings or events that the staff member is expected to attend over the next few months.
- Give the new staff member suggestions of people to call for appointments.
- Pray together.
- Maintain daily contact in person or by phone for the first few weeks.

wants to change the world, to make a difference, and to honor God. He is just not quite sure where to begin.

The Supervisor Is Key to a Good Start!

The senior minister, lead pastor, or an assigned ministry leader who has just taken responsibility for the Carls and the Carlas in ministry can be most helpful at the start. He or she would do well to take time in the early days of a staff member's ministry to introduce the new staff member to other staff and ministry participants. They can go on a leisurely and complete tour of the facility and surrounding vicinity. They can have lunch together. They can meet with other ministry leaders in the community. They can take a day to plan, pray, and prepare for those first days of the staff member's ministry.

These early and simple beginning steps can make all the difference in the world. And, if married or with children, don't forget to include the ministry staff person's spouse and children during this time of transition. Remember, they may not know anyone in the community. Also, they do not have the day-to-day opportunity to become acquainted with people like the staff person.

I remember my initial days with Pastor Bob during my very first ministry experience at age twenty-two. Nearly every day of my first few weeks, Bob would include me in his hospital visits, home visits, and lunch meetings. And when a regular lunch was not scheduled he would take me home for an onion sandwich—his favorite, never mine! As we spent time together and he told me stories about the church, I learned valuable lessons. We became a team and nothing ever broke that bond of mutual respect and admiration. What Bob did was so simple yet incredibly thoughtful and unusually helpful to me.

Take Personal Responsibility

God has called you, the ministry staff member, to this new role. You have been given a charge to serve others, new responsibility, and in most situations, leadership with authority. Without question, if you have been "given much … much is required." Take your new role seriously, not expecting others to perform to your expectations or even to the suggestions in this handbook. Consider the following to create a healthy start:

Keep your spiritual life in alignment with God. Leith Anderson once said, "Prayer is alignment with God." I like that definition. We need to keep our lives in sync with God's will, his Word, and his work. People in ministry depend on us, as Eugene Peterson said, "to point others to Jesus." And that is where we need to live—in Jesus, in Christ, in line with God. So, confess, live a life of ongoing repentance, and model Christ.

Do your job. *Stick to the knitting.* This rather popular organizational phrase carries a lot of weight. People hired you to do "your job." Do it. Don't worry about others' jobs and responsibilities, unless you have permission and passion to assist and help make them a success. Don't get in the trap of criticizing the work of others. Leave your comparative and competitive spirit far behind you. Fulfill the job description that you committed to. It is not your prerogative to just start doing what you want to do or like to do and ignore the role given you by the ministry that hired you.

Become a part of the team. Don't hide in your office. Don't pretend behind your PC. Engage in the lives and ministry of others while you do your job. Pray for others. Share your life and ministry with others. Encourage one another.

Work hard. That is biblical. People hired you to work, not just "hang out" with them. While some hangout time has value, you still have a job to do. I remember a friend years ago who, after being hired in ministry, was expected to go golfing, fishing, and boating with the people in the ministry to the extent he hardly had time to do his job. It was not long before he resigned from that ministry. Try not to settle for average. You will be the first to know when you are not giving your best. Before long, others will notice the same.

Focus on people, not performance. "The focus of my ministry is people, people, people." I have heard it repeated by church planters, seminary

Sample Schedule of Your First 100 Days

In your first 100 days, you hope to build strong alliances and support from your new constituency. With each step, relationships are being established and built. It is people over programs. Programs come later.

While the following is very hypothetical, it may serve as a good overview to prioritize and create an intentional focus for your start.

Days 1–21

Get to the know the ministry staff, board, and key volunteers. Read two or three books in your related area of ministry and read available documents on the ministry's history and current status. Establish new personal disciplines of prayer and fasting for the ministry.

Days 22–35

Create several small-group forums to learn about the current ministry as well as people's dreams and needs. Follow up with one-on-one meetings. Initiate numerous lunch and dinner "gatherings" with ministry participants. Establish times to pray with these people.

Days 36–49

Learn about similar ministries in your region. Get to know the leadership of those ministries. Identify and take key leaders on one or two "vision trips" to these similar ministries in your geographic area. Go with the intent to learn and create a new dialogue with your ministry team.

Days 50–72

Develop a basic training program for new and current leaders. Encourage current and future leaders to read the same books and magazines and view the same videos that have impacted your ministry values and objectives. Create a dialogue with your people about core values (see chapter 2).

Days 73–94

Present the biblical core values for the ministry to ministry leaders and participants as well as boards, committees, other staff, and your target audience.

Days 95–100

Create one new event which brings people together to give a taste of a new vision for the future. Pray together.

presidents, associate pastors, and youth ministers. Jim Griffith says it well: ministry is a "contact sport." Do everything you can to connect with people, and it is amazing how your "performance" will connect in a meaningful way.

Don't try to be superhuman. You are not the Messiah. Resist the feeling that you have to change the world tomorrow. Besides, you can't. The church of Jesus needs you, but they don't want a Mr. Madison Avenue, Miss Know-It-

All, or Slick Sam or Sue. They want a godly person who reflects Jesus, while committed to their biblical values and mission.

Leadership Challenges for a Healthy Start

Learn the Culture

Every ministry has its own personality, beliefs, and "tribal customs." The new staff member will do well to learn the ministry's DNA sooner than later. You will do well to discover if your new ministry culture values people over programs, or small groups over preaching, hard work over creativity. Know the differences. Know the community values.

A friend in ministry shared with me how he was informally mentored by an "old-timer" in the church. Once a week, the longstanding member would take my friend out to lunch and share the rituals, peculiar customs, and values of the people in the community. Each week offered valuable lessons for a long and healthy ministry, lessons that might otherwise have been learned the hard way through stumbling and blind offenses. Ask questions about the culture and history around you, especially if you are from "out of town."

Win People Over Right Away

Go to people. Don't wait for them to come to you. Forget email and memos during your first few months. Pick up the phone. Talk. Walk down the hall. Visit.

Let people in the ministry know that you are genuinely interested in their lives and their ministry role. Encourage them to share their greatest ministry joy. Inquire about the ministry's history or how you can help or pray for them. Share your story when asked.

Respond to people in the ministry when they encourage you. Send a card or note to say, "Thank you!" or "Well done!" When someone completes or carries out a ministry assignment or is granted a new role or position, be the first to offer congratulations.

Your top desk drawer should be filled with cards for all occasions — sympathy, thank-you, congratulations, anniversary, and birthday. No one will be unhappy with communication from you.

Be honest.

Keep your promises.

Work hard.

Ask the Right Questions

When you begin to meet with people in your assigned area of ministry, talk. It is important that you ask questions. You have probably already shared your goals and dreams during the candidating process. However, now that you are a staff member, your opinions can wait. Your personal dreams can be postponed. As delighted as the people are to have you on the staff team, they did not ask you to come and undo everything they have done, or insult their efforts by being the "answer associate." Some questions you may learn to ask in the early days are:

- What are your greatest memories in this ministry?
- What identifies our reputation in and outside this ministry?
- What would you like to see accomplished over the next few months? (Not everyone thinks in an annual or long-term perspective.)
- What do you hope that I will do to help you?
- What are you concerned that I might do or not do that would hinder your desires for this ministry?

As you listen, be sure to affirm and encourage as much as possible. Reinforce and support the hard work of the people. Be a cheerleader right away.

Let Everyone Know That You Love Your New Role

Anyone who loves someone is willing to make sacrifices. Isn't that built into our biblical definition of love? If you love God, and God's people, you will demonstrate that love with selfless acts of service. In addition, when people love doing something, they always want others to share the joy. Don't be afraid to:

- Take on or volunteer for the "extra assignment."
- Go the extra mile for people who cannot do it themselves.
- Strive for excellence by sweating the details.
- Ask others to join you in your new adventures.

Press on, like a good soldier, a disciplined athlete, or a hardworking farmer. Winston Churchill said it well, "Never give in—never, never, never, never." Keep on keeping on!

Do What You Can to Build Trust

It can take months or years to build another's trust, and only one phrase or ill-conceived act to destroy it. Trust is established by making good promises and keeping them.

There are no quick routes to trust; earning it is the result of lifelong investments. In the Old Testament, Job was willing to die to maintain his worth of honest and earnest living. Nothing, including his spouse, closest friends, or

20 Trust Builders

1. Keep appointments (write them down).
2. Keep promises (write them down too).
3. Always be on time, better to be early.
4. Don't take sick days unless you are sick.
5. Don't whine and complain … you are perceived as a leader.
6. Know your limitations and be willing to share them.
7. Do not overextend yourself or you will let people down.
8. Treat confidence as a precious jewel or a tender child.
9. Resist exaggeration and putting a positive spin on modest results.
10. Ask others to point out your blind spots and respond with gratitude.
11. Forget counting hours so that people can count on you.
12. Know the difference between dreams and reality.
13. Don't look for excuses, blame, or shortcuts.
14. Learn to initiate the words "I am sorry" and "Will you forgive me?"
15. Show up for the Christmas party and stay toward the end, even if you hate parties.
16. Read, read, and read … then contribute when you know that what you are talking about has substance and meaning (charm only lasts for seconds).
17. When being vulnerable is appropriate, be vulnerable.
18. Make sure you have someone in your life to "dump on."
19. "Don't put off until tomorrow …" (you know the rest).
20. You know when you are not honest; confess and repent when you have not been honest or truthful.

the attacks of the Evil One, could destroy the reputation of a man known for his integrity. Being honest meant everything.

In the beginning days of your ministry, be a person of your word. Be careful of the promises you make. Don't promise to impress. "Say what you mean and mean what you say" (see James 5:12).

Someone said, "You only have one chance to make a first impression." Often, an impression is the mold to which others will conform. Paul encouraged believers to "follow my example, as I follow the example of Christ" (1 Corinthians 11:1). The impression you create in front of others may be indelible. People will follow your example. Will it be a godly impression? Will they be godly because of you?

So, how will you start? It may determine how you finish. Start carefully, faithfully, and deliberately. No one can start for you. No one else can run your race.

Jumping into the Project Pond

Often your new job will demand that you initiate or coordinate a new ministry or program. The following are healthy steps to start and finish well.

1. Gather people who are the "target audience" of the new ministry and listen to what they need or desire.

2. Resist talking only to individuals at this time, but encourage people to share and listen in community through open forums. Try not to start projects and ministries from behind your own desk. (It is seldom a good practice to do only what you think is a great idea. Remember you are new and don't know what others know.)

3. Gather *potential* leaders and have them listen to the needs of select members from the target audience.

4. Define a mission statement with the *potential* leaders.

5. Define a list of objectives and methods (strategy) to reach those objectives with the *potential* leaders.

6. *Now,* ask the *potential* leaders to "sign up" for the adventure.

7. Provide permission and resources for your leaders to lead.

8. Share the lead with them (don't stand on the sidelines) until they ask you to be the coach.

9. Pray and talk through all the details.

10. Have the leadership launch when they are ready ... and not before.

Are you now reading this, realizing you did not get off to a good start? If so, step back. Reevaluate. Start again. God may grant you a fresh start. God's grace provides new beginnings. It is amazing how many of God's people want to give you that chance to start over again.

Additional Reading

Coyner, Michael J. *Making a Good Move.* Nashville: Abingdon, 2000.

Radcliffe, Robert J. *Effective Ministry as an Associate Pastor.* Grand Rapids, Mich.: Kregel, 1998.

Defining and Communicating Biblical Values and Vision

To do what is right and just is more acceptable
to the Lord than sacrifice.

Proverbs 21:3

A primary purpose of values is to guide our actions
and our decisions, not just our words.

Adapted from Walk the Talk ...
And Get the Results You Want
by Eric Harvey and Al Lucia

B en is a charismatic leader loved by all. A college graduate with several years of youth ministry experience, he's always one to try something different. In addition, his church just sent him to the international youth pastors' forum and he now has three more notebooks, five new CDs, and six recently published books with more ideas than Ben could ever use in a lifetime as a youth pastor.

Actually, all of the ideas and programs that Ben wants to import to the First Avenue Church are very good. They have been tried and tested by well-respected youth pastors around the globe and have impacted many teenagers for Christ. With great enthusiasm, Ben boards the airplane, barely able to wait to share his discoveries.

Within a week, Ben is standing in front of his leadership team sharing one idea after another with all of the gusto and PowerPoint he can muster. When at last he opens the floor for questions, Chuck Anderson, volunteer leader of nearly fourteen years, asks: "Ben, when are you going to find a partner to help me with my Thursday night senior high Bible study group?" Ben is about to explode. Miraculously he keeps his cool.

Tom and soon the others reveal little or no appreciation for either Ben's new energy or great ideas. Ben goes home discouraged, wondering if three years have been long enough at First Avenue Church.

Unfortunately, Ben is not driven by the values and vision of the ministry to reach teenagers in the community surrounding First Avenue Church. Sure, Ben loves teens and Ben loves God. No doubt, he is committed. However, Ben is enamored by his goals, desires, and dream to build the "best" youth program in the county.

What Ben does not realize is that the newfound values and vision of others might not automatically translate to the younger people and leaders in his community. Even if the ideas were Ben's very own, he is still misguided with a purpose that is rather nearsighted and short on value. His vision has come from inspiring speakers and a few seasoned veterans he had lunch with at the youth pastors' forum. Ben has been listening to good voices, but not to the voices in the ministry at First Avenue Church.

Ben needs to think through and define his own biblical values. He will do well to discover what God says about making disciples and to listen to the teenagers, parents, and leaders in his own community.

He must ask what he and the others on his team would be willing to do at great sacrifice, and not be so hasty to change course when the next great idea comes along. At that point, Ben will be able to see his way more clearly as an effective ministry leader. With effective communication tools, Ben will then be able to lead his leaders toward shared values and a common commitment to ministry vision and goals. New motivation will emerge. Results will be significant and worth "dying for."

How to Define and Determine Core Values
The Importance of Values

In recent years, the older, traditional authoritarian style of leadership has given way to a new participative, permission-granting management style. In the former, the charismatic leader was the authority and glue that held the organization together. Today, a set of core values is the bonding agent.

As a ministry staff leader, you are expected to provide direction to your area of ministry. At some point, you will need to support the direction for the ministry. You will also be expected to connect with people. I cannot think of anything that provides support, direction, and connection better than identifying a set of biblical core values.

If leadership does not intentionally set biblical core values for the ministry, "other" core values will be established by default, such as:

- The next event must be bigger and better.
- Our success is first determined by increasing attendance.
- Presentation and performance are emphasized more than people and purpose.
- Only leadership has the good ideas.
- One hour a week is enough.
- We need to keep comparing ourselves with other ministries.

Establishing biblical core values is the beginning of a healthy ministry strategy. A ministry vision created by the passion and desire to reach a particular people group follows the core values. Out of biblical values and a passionate vision for people flow a mission statement. Finally, objectives with clear goals (see chapter 3) provide the means to reach and accomplish the mission.

In my home church, there is one essential core value: "Preach the Word." The next value is "Loving People." The third is "Serving Jesus." Those three core values provide our leadership with direction and connection. They also are what best connects the hundreds of congregants together in community. Every church ministry is driven by teaching, creating loving community groups, and serving one another as Christ is served.

For years, management guru Peter Drucker has made it clear that the mission is what drives nonprofit organizations. A strong mission has clearly stated and well-founded core values. In ministry, those are biblical core values.

With a host of volunteers making the wheels spin and forming the nucleus of energy and sustaining strength, one will find certain core values that keep the not-for-profit organization (in this case a church or parachurch ministry) thriving and vital to its cause. Volunteers will most often ask, "What is my time *worth*? Why am I willing to give above and beyond to make this ministry move forward?" The answer is usually found in a simple mission statement, which reflects the ministry's core values.

A Definition of Value

So what is value? By simple definition it is *worth, significance,* and *importance.* Value is tested by our level of care and attention to what is most important to us. Value has a price tag. For example, I value my wife, daughter, and son-in-law; I will gladly give my life for theirs. I greatly value my faith in God; it has already cost me my future choices and the life I now live.

When we refer to biblical values we can only think of something or someone of great worth. The New Testament talks about the "pearl of great price," the "lost son," the "birds of the air," and of course our own great value to God (see Matthew 6:25 – 32). The value placed on our lives by God cost him his Son. Now *that* is value.

So, what is valuable to you? What should your area of ministry pursue at all costs? Where should you place the majority of your time, resources, and energy? What are you willing to pursue and seek without hesitation or distraction? What will cause you not to give up easily?

Two Significant Steps to Determining Your Values

As an associate or ministry staff member, you will be given one or two major areas of responsibility. First, embrace the values of the larger ministry, whether church or parachurch. Embrace their core values (e.g., evangelism, discipleship, prayer, small group ministry). Then, begin to consider the core values for the specific area of assigned ministry. The values may be the same. They may complement each other. However, they cannot be in opposition.

1. Listen to God and the People Around You

To determine your biblical core values, spend time with your ministry leaders and participants doing the following (this could happen on a retreat weekend, or two or three consecutive Saturday mornings or Sunday afternoons):

- Read God's Word.
- Devote yourself to prayer, listening to God's Spirit, and asking questions.
- Create open forums to listen to your leadership team and participants in ministry.
- Listen to your target audience, especially those not already part of your ministry.
- Collect, collate, and coordinate all of the above "voices" and start to determine what is of great worth, significance, and importance. Ask the following questions:
  What do I hear repeatedly?
  What are the Bible and people saying that is the same?
  Which values will result in changed lives?
  Which values most convict me to give over and above?
  Which values do our people seem to have in common?
  Which values cause me to unashamedly invite anyone to join me?

Which values are constantly on my heart and mind?

What recurring values begin to emerge? Begin by listing several.

2. Write Your Desired Mission Outcome

Begin with a simple missional focus. A short statement expressing your desired outcome will serve you best. Former General Electric CEO Jack Welch's popular blueprint for success was, "Keep it simple!" The statement does not need to be a stroke of genius. An example in your ministry may be, "Make teenage disciples in our city." Even this brief statement reflects three core values: make disciples, teenagers, our city. All three elements have great value.

How to Determine a Biblical Vision

Just because we are good people and have good motives does not mean that our vision is God's vision. We cannot demand or expect God to meet our visionary dream. *God's ways are not our ways*, and we do well to keep reminding ourselves of that biblical principle.

Once you have determined a set of core values (I would suggest three to seven, never become confined to one or two), you can now begin to envision how these values will be realized in your ministry context.

I remember traveling with author and speaker Josh McDowell one evening after sharing a day of ministry in Minneapolis. Josh leaned over in the car and said with tired eyes, "Our ministry tried twelve different things this year. Ten miserably failed." Then Josh's eyes brightened. "But the two that succeeded ... WOW!" Josh is value-driven. His vision is broad and expansive. But Josh knows how to bring the two together and when they do, WOW!

Vision means seeing. Good vision sees as God sees. It also sees as others see. It is nothing more than that. Clear vision gives others clarity to the direction of your ministry. Good leadership provides clear direction. To help your people develop their ministry eyesight, consider the following steps:

> **Examples of Biblical Core Values for Ministry**
>
> • Prayer
> • Making disciples
> • Transformational worship
> • Biblical teaching
> • Training young leaders
> • Loving and caring for the poor
> • Intergenerational community

- As a leadership team, memorize your five- to ten-word mission statement.
- Communicate your core values to your present and future leaders.

- Allow time to discuss your core values and mission openly.
- Encourage leaders to think through what could be done. Ask, "What do our mission statement and core values demand that we do?"
- Take all of your leaders on a "vision trip" (see sidebar on page 35).
- Create an open forum for everyone in your ministry area to engage in a visionary discussion. What others "see" needs to be seen by everyone.
- Ask the following questions:
  Are we excited about the vision before us?
  Will this vision stretch our faith and ministry?
  What is each of us willing to expend to achieve the vision?
  Can we recruit and gather other people to accomplish our vision?
  Can we develop the necessary resources to accomplish our vision?
  Is our vision short enough to grab us?
  Is our vision long enough to keep us?
  Is our vision realistic and does it give us clear direction?
  Is our vision still fixed to our mission and values?
  Will our vision result in changed lives?
- Determine two or three visionary ventures to pursue over the course of a year or more. (Again, never become confined to just one.)
- Make sure your ruling or governing body (board or committee) understands, embraces, and supports your vision.

How to Join Values and Vision

David Schmidt offers sound advice on closing the value gap, suggesting six simple steps to bring values and vision together.* Your leadership team is a good place to begin this process. Take them through David's six points, then do the same with your entire ministry.

1. Start on your knees. Ask God if there is one particular value that you need to develop to the next level.
2. Create renewed awareness. Have your senior minister or a guest come to your ministry area in order to inspire and address visionary ideas for this identified core value.
3. Talk about it. Create open forums, Bible studies, discussion groups; print new literature; and create other venues to get people to talk about the value and how it can be lived out in your area of ministry.

---

*Adapted from David Schmidt, "Steps for Closing the Value Gap," *Christian Management Report*, April 2002: 21–22.

4. Do something together. Go out and test the vision by creating a "test run" or "ministry experiment." Create a "taste and see" event. Keep it simple, but value-driven and focused on the new vision.
5. Put it on the ministry calendar. Someone said, "Fail to plan, plan to fail." Make a commitment so that everyone can see that the vision will be realized and the value lived out.
6. Repeat steps one through four until everyone is talking about the vision, the value, and asking permission to do more!

How to Communicate Values and Vision to Your Leadership Team and Constituency

Abraham Lincoln delivered his famous 1863 Gettysburg Address in just 272 poignant words. Many young Americans have memorized this value-driven speech that motivated people to new commitment after a difficult Civil War battle.

Values and vision will carry you through tough times as well as to wonderful victories. What can we learn from Abraham Lincoln, Jack Welch, and others? Keep it simple; write out your values-and-vision statement; and then rewrite it again shorter and shorter until not an extraneous word remains. Then mold those words into your story and tell that story over and over again.

Keeping it short and simple is not an easy task. It requires discipline, listening, and hard work, but the effort will pay enormous dividends in the end.

However, most vision-and-value statements are not spoken. They are lived. They come up everywhere, all

Take a Vision Trip

The following are a few ideas to help your leaders "see" what they do not "see." Your objective is to expand their vision and begin to apply your core values to ministry. When they "see it" they will not only understand but will be willing to give above and beyond. It is often best to do the following as a leadership team, rather than with just a few select leaders.

- Drive to the highest point of your city at night and pray over the lights, which represent the people in your community.

- Visit with your volunteers a model "teaching church."

- Visit a parachurch ministry, such as a city rescue mission, youth center, halfway house, or Salvation Army center.

- Drive through a needy section of your city, then drive through the most affluent part of town. Afterward, discuss your core values.

- Go to a mall on Sunday morning. Ask, "Who did you see there?"

- Ask your leaders to go alone to a different church some Sunday, then bring everyone together to discuss each person's experience.

the time. Every story in your ministry should reflect and carry the values and vision of the ministry. You will know the values and vision have been "caught" (rather than taught) when volunteers and participants begin talking about your ministry core values and vision when telling their stories.

How Values and Vision Can Really Work for You

Biblical values, united with a bold vision, guide you when to say yes and when to say no. A ministry staff person can easily be persuaded or seduced by all kinds of choices. A strong set of values and a clear, concise vision will allow you to sort through all of your options.

When I was a single-adult minister, it was always important to remember that our values were focused on single adults who were both broken people and growing people. One vision was to reach the single adults in our community with the life-changing message of Jesus Christ. So, we said yes to divorce recovery workshops, even when that was not a popular decision among some of the church leadership. We also said yes to presenting the gospel of Jesus at the workshops where broken lives were changed. We said yes to mission teams and discipleship groups to help people grow. However, we said no to many general community events where single adults would only come as spectators and not participants. We said no to the purchase of a camp. Our values and vision taught us how to answer.

Ed Dobson at Calvary Church in Grand Rapids, Michigan, has often simply stated, "We are a church." Being a church is a core value. A biblical *ecclesia* is at the core of many ministry decisions. Knowing what is most valuable has caused Calvary Church to say no to building schools, retirement apartments, radio stations, and more.

A value-and-vision driven ministry will answer the tough questions of *why you exist* and *what you believe.* Well-crafted and defined vision-and-value statements will help people understand *where you are going* and even *how you are organized.* And

Examples of Vision Statements

- To create small groups for every person in our ministry
- To present the gospel once to everyone within a five-mile radius
- To provide warm clothes and a warm place to sleep for every homeless person in our community
- To give every member a cross-cultural opportunity in the next five years
- To train godly mentors for every teenager in our church
- To create prayer teams in every area of our ministry
- To provide excellence in leadership training for future leaders

from a personal perspective, you will have a better idea of *what you will do* today and determine tomorrow *how you are doing.* Values and vision will reflect your culture and help shape your culture.

A ministry driven by biblical values and a vision for building up people really works. I call it V^2. Try it. You will like it. Continually communicate your ministry's values and vision. When people begin to repeat them, communicate the values and vision again, and again, and again.

Additional Reading

Collins, Jim. *Good to Great.* New York: HarperCollins, 2001.

Covey, Stephen. *First Things First.* New York: Simon and Schuster, 1994.

Malphurs, Aubrey. *Values-Driven Leadership.* Grand Rapids, Mich.: Baker, 1996.

Tichy, Noel M. *The Leadership Engine.* New York: HarperCollins, 1997.

Creating Personal and Ministry Objectives

When a man's ways are pleasing to the LORD, he makes
even his enemies live at peace with him.

When a country is rebellious, it has many rulers, but a man of
understanding and knowledge maintains order.

Proverbs 16:7; 28:2

There is no wisdom, no insight, no plan that can
succeed against the LORD.

Proverbs 21:30

Fail to plan; plan to fail.

It hit Anne like a tidal wave. The number of participants and leaders in small groups is in decline and as the new director for small group ministries, hired four months ago, she's responsible for the eight-year-old program.

Margaret, the "super volunteer" with little to no knowledge or training in small group ministries, is the most popular and most energetic nonpaid member on the team. Two years ago she was considered for Anne's job. Now, Margaret only points out the problems to Anne. Several other volunteer leaders "need a break" and want a year off. Three group leaders were recruited by the new youth pastor to work in the middle school department. Four former leaders, some of the best, are attending the church down the street that just hired a new pastor. The remaining volunteers have little direction and lots of history. Anne picks up the ringing phone. One more volunteer begs off.

Anne's vision and core values are clear and well articulated. In fact, they hang on the wall in her office area for everyone to see. The church board gives her continual support and affirmation. The pastor preaches a series each year on small group communities and why everyone in Central Church needs to become involved. Anne ponders, *So, why is the small group ministry declining when church attendance is increasing?*

Don, one of Anne's successful small group leaders, stops by Anne's office and asks three revealing questions throughout their conversation: "Anne, after meeting for three years, what is the next step you would like me to take with my small group? Since the group has doubled in size, do you want me to divide my group or keep doing what we have been doing? Is there something new our group could do or study this next year?"

Anne is embarrassed, but remains in charge. She doesn't want to end the day with one fewer volunteer. Intuitively, she blurts out a few good ideas and thoughts. Don did not know that these were as new to Anne as they were to him. Seemingly content, he leaves the office with a smile and commitment for one more year.

As Anne drives home, she knows she has not served Don well. Actually, she knows she has not been serving the other leaders well either. The second tidal wave hit. She realizes she needs to develop a strategic plan with some clear objectives, both short and long term — a personal plan for herself, Margaret, and all of the Dons leading small groups — to bring everyone's ideas, resources, and energy together to achieve the core values-and-vision statement nicely framed on her office wall.

Defining Objectives and Goals

Often the terms *objectives* and *goals* are used synonymously. I prefer to define objectives as the bigger picture of what we are trying to accomplish, and goals as the specific targets used collectively to meet the greater objective. For example, my objective is to write this book. My goal is to complete the writing of this chapter today.

Or think of the concepts this way: If we were taking a vacation trip together, *vision* will tell you in general the kind of trip we are going to take (say, a fishing trip). *Objectives* begin to tell everyone exactly where we are destined to go (Lake Geneva) and how we are going to get there (by car). *Goals* tell everyone what time we will all arrive and who is doing the driving.

Objectives and goals for the ministry staff person will fall into three arenas. Let's look at each.

1. *Corporate Objectives:* Most likely, there are certain objectives and specific goals that your church needs to accomplish this year or within the next five years. It is your role and responsibility to own those objectives. You will do well to embrace those in your opportunities to share with people in your ministry area and beyond.

2. *Area Ministry Objectives:* The next set of objectives and goals will be found within your area of ministry. If you are Anne in this chapter's story, you will develop a number of objectives and goals for small group ministries.

3. *Personal Objectives:* You will do well to design and develop some personal objectives and goals related to the ministry and your personal life. People in your area of ministry need to see you as a person who is growing and maturing. Personal objectives and goals may be in the area of education, health, relationships, or personal adventures and hobbies.

I remember Darrell who resisted educational and personal growth objectives and goals. Darrell was the best in his field at the time, but time caught up with him and he is no longer in ministry. I believe Darrell would still be leading in ministry today if he had established some personal growth objectives.

Developing Objectives and Goals

One of the subthemes running through this handbook is *listening.* In order to develop healthy and realistic goals you will need to use your ears before your creative genius and ability to sell people on your great ideas.

Many of the leaders in your area would love to contribute to the ministry's objectives to accomplish the united values and vision. Seldom are they given a chance to speak. Too

---

Identifying the Need for Personal Goals and Objectives

Ask yourself the following questions:

- What am I reading?
- Where have I become stale and repetitive?
- Where have I lost my zeal and energy?
- What do I get most excited about?
- What are people asking me the most?
- What situations and questions are becoming more difficult to handle?
- What do I avoid or resist the most?
- How is my health?
- Do I have any new close friends or are there fewer?
- What are other leaders and ministry participants trying to tell me?

---

often, they come to a meeting only to listen to the leader. Reverse that reality. Be the leader who listens to the people.

Collectively, your people have great ideas. Together, their collaborative idea will often be stronger, more significant, and just plain better than your one idea. Believe that. Ask them to share and give them time to respond. Ask them again and give them more time to think, pray, and respond. Encourage them to think deeper. You will be amazed at the results. I know what some of you are thinking, *That takes too long.* However, it takes no longer than when you are trying to sell, persuade, and influence people to go with your idea.

Jill was recently placed in charge

> ### Developing SPIRO Goals
>
> Ask the following questions of your written goals:
>
> Are our goals …
>
> - **S**pecific? Is it clear what we are going to do?
>
> - **P**ersonal? Can people personally identify with the goal?
>
> - **I**nvolvement oriented? Is it obvious how people can get involved?
>
> - **R**ealistic? Is this "pie-in-the-sky" or down-to-earth and attainable?
>
> - **O**bservable? Will there be results the people (not just leadership) can all see and that will lead them to agree that what we did may be worth doing again?

of a ministry committee. It was crystal clear to Jill what the values and vision were for the committee's mission and assignment. However, Jill was clueless how to get from point A to point B.

As Jill chaired her first committee meeting, she began by sharing the values and vision with the committee. Then she declared, "I have no idea how we are going to accomplish our mission. I hope some of you have an idea, because I don't. So, what do you think?" For the next three hours, one idea led to another and another, and before long three power-packed objectives were placed on the whiteboard. Each member assigned themselves to one of the objectives.

Jill asked the right question, she listened, she found results—all because she believed in a fundamental principle that many people will most often have a better idea than any one person (see chapter 7). Jill is a good leader.

Communicating Objectives and Goals

People want to know *where* you are going, *when* you are going, *how* you are getting there, *who* is going to be there, *what* you are going to do when you get there (and *what* it will cost), and *why* you need to go now. The italicized words in the previous sentence are considered the basic questions of a good journalist. What they boil down to is this: "I want to know what is going on." When you start hearing people ask these questions, then you know that you have not communicated in a timely or thorough manner. Answer the questions *before* they are asked.

One of the biggest omissions in ministry communication seems to be the real reason for the event or program. Potential participants are often told when and where and sometimes who, but seldom what the reason is for this program, what it will lead to, and what they can take home from the gathering. Today, more than ever, people want to attach purpose to their time and resources. No wonder the concept of a purpose-driven life and Rick Warren's book by that title became so popular.

When Tony was hired as men's ministry director, one of his first events was to bring all of the fathers and sons together for a Saturday breakfast, an idea he saw used successfully at another church. So he and his volunteer assistant began to plan the event, in the process producing one of the sharpest, eye-catching invitational brochures ever. The attendance and final results were abysmal. Tony was clueless.

Finally, a wise senior adult put his arm around Tony and explained that if Tony had shared this idea with a few of the men before he sent out his brochure, he would have learned that his program was doomed. Tony learned by listening too late that the event date was in the middle of hunting season. Tony also learned that

---

Indicators of Personal Progress in Ministry

Draw your conclusions after answering the following questions:

- Are people talking about values or programs?
- Are people referring to the vision in their own words?
- Are people asking permission to create new ministry models?
- Are you developing better forethought on ministry projects?
- Are you developing a better sense of afterthought on ministry results?
- Are you reviewing the real results or just counting heads?
- Are you asking more questions or giving more answers?
- Are the ministry models you are using meeting your core values and objectives?
- Are people offering to contribute more than you need or are you constantly trying to get people to do what you need done?
- Are people starting to complain about being too tired or of lacking sufficient time or resources to support the goals?
- Are you excited about doing again what you just did?
- Are others trying to sabotage this ministry?

Setting Strategic Objectives through SWOT Analysis

A growing number of organizations use the following process to establish objectives and goals. It's easy to do. Gather your leaders and committed participants together and lead them through each topic. Write everything down for all to see.

- **Strengths.** Ask everyone to list the ministry's strengths.
- **Weaknesses.** Ask for a list of the ministry's weak points.
- **Opportunities.** Ask, "What should we do to accomplish our mission?"
- **Threats.** Ask, "What are the outside or inside factors that may prevent us from doing what we need to do?"

    Final Question: In light of what we've learned from this analysis, what is (are) our next strategic objective(s) to accomplish our mission?

---

the speaker was an unknown (at least in these parts) and that the men in the community could care less about the subject matter. Today, Tony asks good questions and takes time to listen.

Additional Reading

Anderson, Leith. *Dying for Change*. Minneapolis: Bethany House, 1990.

Collins, James C. and Jerry I. Porras. *Built to Last*. New York: HarperCollins, 1994.

Hershey, Paul, Kenneth H. Blanchard, and Dewey E. Johnson. *Management of Organizational Behavior*. 7th ed. Upper Saddle River, N.J.: Prentice Hall, 1996.

Martoia, Ron. *Morph! The Texture of Leadership for Tomorrow's Church*. Loveland, Colo.: Group, 2003.

Growing through Evaluation

Whoever gives heed to instruction prospers and blessed is he
who trusts in the LORD.

Proverbs 16:20

Can I handle negative comments calmly, fairly, and objectively?
If not, then don't ask!

Kevin was doing well in ministry. Liked and appreciated by his peers, subordinates, and supervisor, the board continually praised Kevin for his good work. From outward appearances, Kevin was the ideal staff member.

Then Kevin did a gutsy thing. Some called it reckless, vocational suicide. Indeed he was asked, "Are you nuts?"

Interest piqued? What did Kevin do to cause colleagues and peers to question his sanity and common sense? Kevin asked his leadership team to evaluate him. Why? Was something wrong? Was he feeling insecure? Was this just his way to get kudos? Was it expected by his superior, board, or committee? No! None of the above. Kevin simply wanted honest feedback to better serve his team and his Lord. He acknowledged that nobody could evaluate him better than those who work with him every day.

So, you are now asking, "How did it go?" If you ask Kevin, it went well … with a few bumps and bruises. At the end of a thorough written and oral evaluation, Kevin was affirmed by the men and women who report to him. He also learned about a couple of blind spots.

Today, Kevin is confident and comfortable in his role. He knows exactly what his team thinks of him, both positive and negative. He can handle the negative as he grows and attempts to avoid the blind spots. He is renewed in his role. And his team has more respect for him than can be imagined. They know they can go to Kevin anytime about anything and he will listen.

Now consider Gerry. She has not had a formal evaluation with her supervisor in four years. When she asks about her performance she gets a rather brief, cliché-laden response, "Fine, you are doing a great job; keep up the good work." However, Gerry wonders about some of the changes in the organization and does not understand some of the shifts in her job responsibilities. She is beginning to feel rather insecure.

Gerry would never do what Kevin did. It would have too many unknowns, especially because her supervisor has not been there to adequately support her role. She just keeps doing her job, hoping a sudden decision by someone above her in the ministry doesn't land her among the unemployed. That happened a few months ago to one of her colleagues.

Gerry has pulled back more and more from her supervisor, fearing the worst. She does not really believe the few nice things that were said; other actions speak far louder. She is now looking through the Christian Ministry classifieds.

Evaluation Is Most Often Feared

Evaluation is one of the most dreaded and avoided areas of our lives. We have heard, "The truth hurts." Indeed it does. That is why we avoid it. Maybe it goes back to a school exam we failed or reminds us of the dentist's probe of our sensitive teeth and gums. Perhaps it brings back memories of when we were "busted" with the truth about a character weakness, which was far too painful to hear.

However, evaluation is imperative for effective and long-lasting ministry. If we never took a test in school or went to the doctor or dentist, our minds and bodies would not make it for the long haul. So it is with ministry evaluation; as painful as it is, we need it.

Evaluation Upward, Downward, and Level

Upward Evaluation

Upward evaluation is when your supervisor gives you the opportunity to share your goals, performance record, joys, and frustrations. This type of evaluation is often more structured and can tend to be a bit formal (see chapter 33). Formats can be objective or subjective. Both formats can work. So use both.

If your supervisor does not give you a format for dialogue, create your own (see sidebar on page 46). Before meeting with your supervisor, write down a number of comments, answering some of your own questions that pertain to your role and performance. Then, talk it through. But be sure to let your leader know what you are feeling and experiencing in your job. Be honest. Be vulnerable. If your supervisor is not happy with your performance, your vulnerability will not be the deciding factor on your future.

Downward Evaluation

Downward evaluation is when you to listen to the people you serve, when you grant permission to certain ministry participants and volunteer leaders to evaluate you. If you think of it in medical terms, it's a sort of "elective surgery." But do it intentionally and with careful selection of who can best evaluate you and your ministry performance.

Create a safe, open, and warm environment that allows your requested "critics" to embrace this time as valuable and helpful to all involved. Ask them for open, honest, and even brutal input on your ministry effectiveness. Give them permission to enter your life and ministry. Ask tough questions. Then listen and listen well. Be sure to make notes of their suggestions and ways you can improve. People will only respect you for that.

Personal Peer Evaluation

Personal peer evaluation is when you grant a peer member the opportunity to provide kind, honest feedback. Typically done one-on-one, it is best shared with someone you trust and who knows your performance firsthand. But be careful, it is a very sensitive process.

I remember when a fellow ministry staff member once asked if I would point out a weakness to help

Performance Evaluation Questions

The following are simple questions to ask yourself as an outline for dialogue with your supervisor or others to whom you may grant permission to have honest feedback through personal dialogue.

1. What do I like most about my job?
2. What do I find most difficult in my job?
3. Where would I like to learn more and grow?
4. What one thing would I like to change in my job description?
5. What would I like to accomplish in ministry over the next year?
6. What personal goals would I like to consider?
7. Where do you think I can best improve my performance?
8. What could I have done differently this past year?
9. Are there any blind spots I may be missing or avoiding?
10. How can we serve each other better this year?

another colleague. I simply said, "I don't have permission." It was rather obvious that this particular colleague did not want to be evaluated. Any constructive comments would have fallen on deaf ears; defensiveness would have been immediate. A built-in defensive guard will prevent some of your best feedback from being heard. We could all grow so much more if we gave one another permission to enter our lives and ministry.

Personal Peer Evaluation Feedback

Grant one or two of your trusted peers permission to circle no more than three of the following items they would like to see you pay more attention to. Then arrange an informal time to share an open discussion.

Relax more.	**Talk more.**	**Don't be so formal in your work.**
Listen better.	**Talk less.**	**Be more personal with me.**
Smile more.	**Ask me questions.**	**Show more interest in my work.**
Slow down.	**Include me more.**	**Tell me when I do a good job.**

Team Peer Evaluation

Some leaders may attempt a more formal evaluation among peers, say the youth ministry team, worship team, or entire staff. This type of evaluation requires a skilled leader, able to regulate and control a very personal and confidential setting. All of the team members' personalities and potential responses to criticism must be fairly evaluated and considered before doing a peer evaluation. Helpful tools to create open and honest dialogue are the Myers-Briggs Type Indicator, the DiSC instrument, or the Team Inventory by Patrick Hanley. (See Additional Reading at the end of chapter 7 for more information on ordering these instruments.)

The purpose of this groupwide evaluation should be to point out the positive, constructive contribution of each staff member involved. As such, team building can occur; of course, so can the opposite if the session becomes overly negative or a free-for-all. Properly monitored, however, it can safeguard against or counter the following staff issues:

- A critical, negative, and high-stress work environment
- Artificial (political) relationships
- Personal devaluation, pain, or embarrassment
- Dangerous and insensitive comments about one another
- Unhealthy alliances

Self Evaluation

Every now and then, it is good to come down off the mountain or step away from the speeding train of life and take a personal inventory. Ask yourself the following questions.

- Where am I going?
- How am I treating people?
- Where am I leading people?
- Am I equipping and training other people, or focusing too narrowly on my own performance?
- Have I compromised my personal core values and this mission?
- What did I accomplish this year, for which I can give God praise?
- Have I grown and matured since the last time I asked this question?
- What am I doing that I should not be doing?
- [Ask God] In what new areas do I need to grow?

Ministry Evaluation

The major focus of your ministry is people. The ministry happens because of volunteers. You don't want to lose them. However, sometimes they leave because they are not being heard. Sometimes they may speak loudly, because you did not give them an opportunity to speak quietly.

> **Peter Drucker's Five Essential Questions***
>
> 1. What is our mission?
> 2. Who is our customer?
> 3. What does the customer value?
> 4. What are our results?
> 5. What is our plan?

Create open forums and personal one-on-one evaluations. The open forum is not your platform to do all of the talking. The forum and one-on-one meetings are times for the people to speak. Ask two main questions:

- How are you doing?
- How do you think our ministry is doing?

Often you will not need to ask more than that. Ask the same two questions in different ways. Be sure to let everyone know that you are listening and paying attention to their feedback.

---

*Peter F. Drucker, *Self-Assessment: The First Action Requirement of Leadership*. Leader to Leader Institute, www.drucker.org.

Read Between the Lines

No one likes to get an unkind letter or negative feedback. In fact, most ministry leaders do not read anonymous letters. However, there are times when someone may attempt to give you advice or an unrequested opinion. It may be delivered with kindness or not; the comments may be well articulated or rather fuzzy and unwarranted. Regardless, learn to read between the lines.

When you hear your critics, ask yourself these questions: What are you really trying to say? Is there truth between the sour and destructive comments? Should I listen more and defend less? Do I have blind spots and is this person trying to save me from imminent disaster? What can I learn? How can these comments encourage my personal growth and professional maturity?

After you have realized the truth … set yourself free. Don't beat yourself up. Thank your critic. You may win a new friend. Thank God for this opportunity to grow.

Feedback takes time and can be easily avoided. But, whatever your role, you need feedback. Sometimes it is all too tempting to just move on to the next program, project, event, performance, or meeting. Take the time to learn from your encouragers and critics. You have both, so give them permission and safety to speak. When they do, you may find a new freedom, as Kevin did at the beginning of this chapter.

> **Ten Ways to Let People Know That You Heard Their Evaluation**
>
> 1. Write down some of the things that were said.
> 2. Ask for clarification on one or two main points.
> 3. Ask people to expand on their ideas and concerns.
> 4. Ask for a follow-up time and actually have it in order to listen more.
> 5. If you make a promise, keep it.
> 6. Look for ways to connect and not distance yourself during the dialogue.
> 7. Don't try to "fix things" that are perceived by others as broken, or deny the perceptions of people, or talk down to them.
> 8. Keep your door open to all of your critics … invite them back.
> 9. Affirm the commentator whether they have been positive or negative. Say thank you!
> 10. Ask permission to pray together.

A man of knowledge uses words with restraint,
and a man of understanding is even-tempered.
Even a fool is thought wise if he keeps silent,
and discerning if he holds his tongue.

Proverbs 17:27–28

Additional Reading

McIntosh, Gary L. *One Size Doesn't Fit All.* Grand Rapids, Mich.: Fleming H. Revell, 1999.

Mittelberg, Mark. *Building a Contagious Church.* Grand Rapids, Mich.: Zondervan, 2002.

Schwartz, Christian A. *Natural Church Development.* Carol Stream, Ill.: ChurchSmart Resources, 1998.

Schwartz, Christian A. and Christoph Schalk. *Implementation Guide to Natural Church Development.* Carol Stream, Ill.: ChurchSmart Resources, 1998.

Redefining the Role of the Nonpaid Staff Member

A gift opens the way for the giver and ushers him
into the presence of the great.

Proverbs 18:16

Spiritual leadership is doing what God wants,
as long as God wants me to do it.

Ed Dobson,
"Famous Last Words" sermon at Calvary Church,
January 21, 1996

Peter and Henry, both Christians and longtime members in local churches, have just received notice of their early retirement options from the Fortune 500 company they have served for the last thirty-one and thirty-three years, respectively. There is no pretending, these are early "buyouts." The company is downsizing due to a drop in market share and can't afford their higher paid directors.

Henry is not happy. He did not plan on this adjustment in his income and lifestyle and is not ready to redefine his identity from being a company executive. He is having a hard time giving up his company car keys and membership at the corporate health club. He sees the one-year severance package as a kick in the stomach.

However, Peter is elated. He can't wait for his last day; his company keys, credit card, health club card, and laptop computer are already in the box marked, "business office." In fact, he is trying to make the release date as early as possible.

So, why the difference?

Peter has a plan, and it's all about ministry. Peter is ready and willing to use his thirty-one years of corporate experience to serve his local church. He has been talking to the administrative pastor, the staff, and board members, and details are almost set.

Peter will be using his spiritual gifts to make a difference in people's lives, and is more excited about the future than he has ever been before. He sees his severance package as a gift from God and an opportunity to trust God for the future. Peter is joining the church staff as a nonpaid staff member.

Equipping the Saints

Dallas Willard has said, "Our role as Christian leaders is to equip saints to do what saints are supposed to do." I like that simple paraphrase of Ephesians 4:12. I heard one pastor refer to this text as a "mandate from God," a biblical imperative for ministry leaders to equip ministry volunteers at the highest level of quality, excellence, and empowerment.

Today, more than ever in church history, the laity is educated and gifted—ready, willing, and capable of rising far above the traditional roles of teaching a Sunday school class or casting an opinion and vote at the next committee or board meeting. Many can do more than serve an hour or two each week or write a check from the pew. It is the ministry staff leader's role to identify, recruit, and train laity who are eager to serve, even in a staff position.

The verb *equip* in Ephesians 4:12 (TNIV) is from the Greek word *katartizo*, from the two root words *kata* (to join) and *adios* (complete, fresh). Its full meaning is to "complete thoroughly." It is not just about giving someone a single tool to help them become better or stronger in just one area of their lives, even if it means doing it with excellence.

God has so much more in mind when he asks us to "equip the saints." He wants us to help "perfect" or to bring to a sense of completion that which already exists. Question: what already exists? Answer: a believer with resources of time and energy, spiritual gifts, and a passion for people and ministry, who desires to personally grow in Christ and make a difference for his kingdom. Our responsibility as ministry staff is to thoroughly bring together all of the pieces, those marvelous God-given resources, to a sense of completion.

Marlene Wilson said it well: "We have been created with unique and valuable gifts meant to be discovered, developed, and used on behalf of others. As Oscar Feuchet declares, 'The individual Christian has a mission in the world no one else can perform for him [her]. It is untransferrable.' We each have something valuable to give."*

The Difference between *Kleros* and *Laos*

The Greek word for clergy is *kleros* and the Greek word for laity is *laos*. When we think of these two role designations for people in the church, immediate differences come to our mind. So, we do well to ask the question, "What are the real differences?" Is it just paid staff versus volunteer leaders? Is it having an office or not? Is it determined by one's amount of Bible college or seminary training? (I know many laypeople in our church who work in industry and have an earned seminary degree.) In lamenting the downsizing of the word *laity*, Macon Crowles provides a historical perspective as we consider the role of the people in our churches and parachurch ministries. He wrote in 1937:

> [*Laity*] refers to an amateur who does not know much about a particular field and so is not qualified to speak about it. We should understand that this is a perversion of the original meaning of the word. The category of an unauthorized amateur was not recognized in the beginnings of the Christian church. The fact that this unfortunate change of meanings occurred has affected the whole course of the church's history.[†]

Martin Luther indicated that the church of his day suffered terribly because of the great gulf which existed between the clergy and the laity. However, it does not take us long to come to some obvious points of similarity. Clergy and laity share the same spiritual gifts. We are members of the same body, called by God "a chosen people, royal priesthood, a holy nation, a people belonging to God" (1 Peter 2:9). A general reading of the text carries thoughts of unity, oneness, and shared ministry. It is also understood that the trained are to train the untrained. Those with theological and ministry tools should impart that knowledge and skill to those who also are equally called by God to serve, whether paid or not paid.

The biblical order to prepare "all of the saints to do what the saints are supposed to do" is the call of the day. While we can all agree that ordained staff members carry certain ecclesiastical responsibility, laity can be trained and brought alongside the clergy in the work of the ministry.

Indeed, there are many ready-to-be-trained people in the church just sitting in your pews, waiting to be asked. They are on your membership role

---

*Marlene Wilson, *How to Mobilize Volunteers* (Minneapolis: Augsburg, 1983), 15.
[†]S. Macon Cowles Jr., *Ministers All* (Boston: United Church Press, 1967), 12–13.

with time and talent available. They want to be invited and included in what you are doing. Several share your passion. Some want to share your burden. And a few want to give more than one or two hours a week.

A Paradigm Shift: The Harmony of Paid and Nonpaid Staff

According to businessman and author Bob Buford, whose book *Halftime* struck a chord a number of years ago, scores of Christian men and women are entering the "second half" of their lives having achieved success and financial stability. They are now ready to give their lives to ministry and achieve significance by using their spiritual gifts and personal resources (time being the greatest) to finish well.

I recently talked to a fifty-three-year-old schoolteacher who is planning to retire within the next two years. When I asked him what he was going to do next, he replied, "I want to pastor a small country church that cannot afford a full-time pastor. But I need someone to train me." I am making that a personal challenge.

Several years ago, as an executive pastor in my church, I challenged an early retired career executive to consider joining me on staff at the church. I said, "I cannot give you a salary, insurance, or other benefits, but I will give you a ministry director's title, a significant role of leadership as a staff person, your name on the door of your office, a phone, a set of office keys, and a small operating budget. And," I added, "I will expect you to be at the weekly staff meeting, staff luncheon, annual staff retreat, holiday parties, and write a monthly report." He still said yes. And a new adventure in ministry began.

You're Never Too Old

- Actor George Burns won his first Oscar at age eighty.
- Grandma Moses started painting at age eighty.
- Golda Meir became prime minister of Israel at age seventy-one.
- Michelangelo painted the Sistine Chapel at age seventy-one.
- Chuck Reed started seminary at age seventy-seven.
- Fred Fischel began his first church plant at age sixty-one.
- Noe Palacios joined a seminary staff at age sixty-one, creating a lifelong learning center, after twenty-three years as a director in a large corporation.
- Don Vogel started a full-time ministry at the age of fifty-seven.

Grant Responsibility with Equal Authority

No one likes responsibility without the authority that goes with it.

That statement is not just for the egomaniacs and control freaks. It is a fundamental principle for any leader to get the job done. For his or her respective area of ministry, the nonpaid staff member should have the same level of authority as a peer paid staff member.

First of all, whether paid or nonpaid, all staff should be committed to a structure of accountability. Everyone reports to someone. There are no lone rangers. Secondly, each staff person (paid or not) has a job title with a job description, clearly identifying specific responsibilities. Each staff member should be given the resources and the ability to make approved budget and procedural decisions. Nonpaid staff are full staff members, not junior staff members, not second string. They are called and gifted by God. They are doing ministry. They simply do not receive a paycheck from the ministry.

> **Resources for the Nonpaid Staff Member**
>
> Provide the following "basics" for your nonpaid staff person:
>
> - Ministry staff title, e.g., *Director of ...*, or *Minister of ...* included among the various listing(s) of other staff
> - Name on the door and appropriate name tags
> - Office supplies (the basics found at your local office supply store)
> - A few "perks" such as a cell phone, book allowance, entertainment allowance for car and lunches, or reimbursement for continuing education
> - Personal access to the senior minister, board chair, and other staff
> - Opportunity for public presentation of ministry
> - Keys to the building
> - Office hours

The Nonpaid Staff Member's Job Description

Every staff member should have a written job description, available to the board, committees of the church, and other staff members. In fact, it is good for the volunteers in any given area of ministry to have a copy of their staff person's job description.

The nonpaid staff person's job description should look no different than a paid staff person's job description and should include the following:

1. A title
2. Qualifications
3. Responsibilities (both general and specific)
4. Reporting relationships (who the staff person reports to, who the staff person is required to work with, and who reports to the staff person)

These four simple items can be carefully and thoughtfully written on one page. There should be no question on what the nonpaid staff person is responsible to do and to whom he or she reports. Other working relationships should be included.

NOTE: Obviously, the nonpaid staff person may not fit into an ordained role, depending on your ministerial tradition. However, if the person meets the ministry's ordination qualifications, the absence of a paycheck should not preclude those privileges or responsibilities.

Communicate the Role of the Nonpaid Staff Member to the Paid Staff Member(s)

"Hiring nonpaid staff" sounds like an oxymoron. "Hiring nonpaid staff" to some paid staff members sounds like a threat to their job security. I remember when we "hired" our first nonpaid staff person. One staff member had a lot of questions; insecurities rose to the surface. It took time for all the staff to realize that the nonpaid staff member was not the beginning of their end.

The key was communicating to paid staff exactly why the new position/person was being added. It wasn't about saving money or sending a message. It was all about ministry and equipping the saints; about God calling a few of our laity to now do the work of the ministry as staff members with more responsibility and authority, in order that we might more effectively fulfill our mission. That was it, nothing more. Before long, the paid staff were welcoming and embracing the nonpaid staff.

What Does a Nonpaid Staff Member Really Cost?

It's a common truth: nothing is free! Everything costs something. So, what are the real costs to bring on nonpaid staff?

A few have already been suggested: office equipment, office space, a few itemized "perks."

However, the real cost is time invested in relationship. When I brought on board our first nonpaid staff persons, I spent significant time training and mentoring them. They were unusually gifted and talented; they knew how to do some things better than I. What they did not know were the culture and traditions of working on the church staff. I quickly realized how much I took for granted. All of that had to be taught and modeled—both by me and other paid staff—and it took valuable time. However, the dividends were enormous.

How Does a Nonpaid Staff Member Really Get Paid?

This is an easy question to answer. The nonpaid staff person is paid in personal fulfillment, the joy of ministry, and deeper relationships with people in ministry. Significance takes on a new definition when people invest their lives in other people, for the kingdom of God and not personal material gain.

Nonpaid staff are paid by the time you spend with them. They receive remuneration when they go home fulfilled, knowing God used the spiritual gift he gave them. They receive a "bonus check" when they hear the results of the ministry, changed lives.

It is a rather new paradigm, but it's happening in more and more churches and nonprofit organizations: volunteers are starting to lead! They could be in the office next to yours.

Additional Reading

De Pree, Max. *Called to Serve.* Grand Rapids, Mich.: Eerdmans, 2001.

Fields, Doug. *Help, I'm a Volunteer Youth Worker.* Grand Rapids, Mich.: Zondervan, 1993.

Hybels, Bill. *The Volunteer Revolution.* Grand Rapids, Mich.: Zondervan, 2004.

Johnston, Kurt. *Go Team.* Loveland, Colo.: Group, 2004.

Logan, Robert E. *Beyond Church Growth.* Grand Rapids, Mich.: Revell, 1989.

PART 2

Becoming a Servant

Becoming an Intentional Servant Leader

Love and faithfulness keep a king safe;
through love his throne is made secure.

Proverbs 20:28

"I am Jesus.... I have appeared to you [Paul] to appoint you
as a servant and as a witness of what you have seen of me
and what I will show you."

Acts 26:15–16

Though I am free and belong to no man, I [Paul] make myself a
slave to everyone, to win as many as possible.

1 Corinthians 9:19

For the past seven months, Kip has been an associate director of *Teens For Jesus*, the national evangelistic youth organization with a chapter in his Colorado community. As a teenager, Kip attended TFJ Bible studies and traveled on two mission trips. At the recommendation of his TFJ director, he went away to Bible college, where he met Susan. They just celebrated their second wedding anniversary.

A powerful communicator and charismatic leader, Kip was able, in record time, to raise all of the couple's required financial support among family, friends, several churches, and a few community businesspeople. Susan's part-time job in the local high school is just perfect to help make ends meet and provides him easy access to all of the school functions. Kip is having the time of his life!

Kip's boss, Barry, the area director for TFJ, stopped by this afternoon and Kip immediately noticed the troubled expression on Barry's face. "What's up?" Kip asked. Barry cut right to the chase. "Kip, I got off the phone an hour ago with one of our staff interns and she is ready to quit. In the last week two of our volunteer campus leaders told me they feel like you talk down to them. Apparently, you give them the impression that you're the only one who knows anything about putting the TFJ programs together. While everyone appreciates your 'teen talks' and the kids seem to follow you like the Pied Piper, your leadership team is ready to bail. I have to say, I've observed similar behavior as I've watched you work with some of our adult volunteers and a few of the parents. I should have had this conversation with you earlier. I hope I'm not too late."

Kip hung his head in shame and embarrassment. His first thought was, *How dare those people say that about me.* His second thought: *I have really blown it.*

After an hour of honest discussion with Barry, Kip went home with the humble realization that his top-down leadership style needed to change. Leadership does not automatically happen when he puts on his name tag, sits behind his desk to detail another program, or stands up in front of people with an exciting new idea that he dreamed up while driving through the mountains.

Kip realized through Barry's kindness and example that Christian leadership begins by "washing people's feet." It starts by serving. Kip was learning that Christ-centered leadership looks for ways to make others successful, even the newest and youngest teenager. Kip now understood he had some choices to make. They were choices now focused on others, not himself.

Servant Leadership

With five shelves of leadership books in my office (from the likes of Drucker, Tichey, Collins, Blanchard, Peters, Maxwell, Anderson, and De Pree), I admit that I wonder what nuggets of value I can add in this chapter on leadership.

There are so many ways to define leadership, the art of human organization and development. I have almost given up on a single definition of leadership. Yet Leighton Ford's book *Transforming Leadership* stands out in my mind as a leadership classic. While the book doesn't say everything about leadership, it reminds me of the basics from the Master, the Lord of all, our Leader and Head of the church. Often, it comes back to what Jesus said to an aggressive mother wanting her sons to be at the top: be a servant!

Instead, whoever wants to become great among you must be your servant, and whoever wants to be first must be your slave—just as the Son of Man did not come to be served, but to serve, and to give his life as a ransom for many.

Matthew 20:26–28

While Jesus and later the apostle Paul talk about believers being slaves and servants, that kind of language is decidedly abnormal in our twenty-first-century North American context. We can only go back to our history books, oral traditions, and stories from other nations to catch a glimpse of what this kind of leadership is all about. It is neither natural nor comfortable for us. Even the idea of washing people's feet has become more of a ritualistic act and worshipful moment rather than a deep truth which affects individual leadership style and lifestyle.

Maybe it all comes down to the songwriter's words: "It is not about me, but it's all about you, Jesus" ... and others. Servant leadership is about you. Servant leadership is not about me.

Seven Practical Ways to Be a Servant Leader

1. Call three people you have never talked to and ask them questions to begin a dialogue about the ministry.

2. Write five "well done" notes to people in your ministry.

3. Ask someone else to do your favorite "upfront" job.

4. Apologize to someone for not being totally honest with them.

5. Perform an anonymous act of giving ... maybe sacrificially.

6. Spend time more than once with a "least of these."

7. Bring your leaders together in a circle and take the time to have them share what is happening in their lives, then have a time of prayer ... and nothing more.

What Servant Leadership Is Not

Being in control is not being a servant leader. The director of the Association of Theological Schools said this to a group of seminary presidents he was addressing: "You have been given a charge. You are not in charge." What you *can* be in charge of is your own spiritual growth, personal conduct, schedule, tongue, checkbook, and calendar. You *can* be in charge of a proper focus on the people to whom God has called you to serve. As Christian ministry staff leaders, we are not in control of the lives of other people. That is God's job.

Being the answer person is not being a servant leader. Others have good answers too. Collectively, everyone has a great answer. Servant leaders listen well.

Becoming a Servant

Always being up front is not being a servant leader. I am not saying, don't ever be up front. But servant leaders put other people up front, even with *their* script. (People know who the leader is … give them credit for that.)

Rah-rah cheerleading is not synonymous with being a servant leader; it is only one aspect of serving others. Servant leadership does not need extra props. Servant leaders don't need "pom-poms" to do the job. NOTE: I'm not suggesting that you ignore people and act indifferent about the ministry. Servant leaders will naturally exude enthusiasm and joy from the inside out.

Being the loudest and first in line is not being a servant-leader. Enough said.

How to Recognize Servant Leadership

My human radar naturally tunes in to the overt, charismatic leadership styles of the successful. Famous large-church pastors and well-known international ministry leaders are some of the images that first come to mind. Then I think about the leadership of a Mother Teresa or Roger Greeley. Roger who? That is my point. Very few people in the world know Roger Greeley. I do. And he is a great servant leader. Why? He serves others with a selfless, Christlike spirit; so much so that only a few who will ever read this book know Roger.

How can we recognize servant leadership in others or in ourselves? Consider the following:

Other people talk about the servant leader. Servant leaders do not need to self-promote and seldom talk about themselves.

People who don't have to, follow servant leaders. Servant leaders do not need to demand, require, or insist that others follow them.

On the other end of the phone, servant leaders initiate relationships that are deep and meaningful. Servant leaders know when and how to make the first call. You will most likely get a note of encouragement from a servant leader … hand-written and signed.

Ten Servant Leader Killers

1. Don't listen, keep talking.
2. Give everyone all of the reasons why they should follow you.
3. Don't respond; just sit there, maintaining perfect composure.
4. Believe that exaggeration is better than bad news.
5. Keep everything close to your chest.
6. Don't let others step up to the plate.
7. Business sense is nonsense in ministry.
8. Make sure you always win.
9. When you are losing, get real loud or real quiet, your choice.
10. Hide and make people find you.

A can-do spirit is always at the forefront of their heart and mind. Their first thought is, *What can we do to reach these people and help them through this time in their lives?* With respect for resources, methods, policies, and people's time, servant leaders look for every possible way to serve the needs of the "least of these."

Turns a little red every time you give them a compliment. They were not expecting it.

Talks to the lonely people who others rush past.

Give, give, and give some more is what they do best. They are not takers. They look for people to give to and try to find more "things" to give away.

Seldom looking in the mirror, servant leaders are not concerned how they look to others. Their first concern is, "How are you doing?" And when they see that someone else does not look well, they often take the lead, carefully and quietly, and make a difference.

Face-to-face, their service is up-front and personal. It is important that servant leaders see your expression and response. You are not always looking at their back.

Without question there are loud leaders, self-promoting leaders, negative leaders, overly confident leaders, self-indulging leaders. Some of them will get the job done. Many will be used of God and be blessed in their ministry staff role. A few will figure out the system and culture of their ministry and last a long time in a leadership role. Nonetheless, you have a choice of the kind of leader you want to be. Maybe this would be a good time to pause and talk to God about this matter.

Four Characteristics of Servant Leaders

1. **They are honest.** They cannot think of sharing anything but the truth.

2. **They are present.** They are not hard to find. They are always just there.

3. **They are flexible.** They can adjust and adapt to the needs of others.

4. **They are engaging.** They are always seeking to draw out of others their feelings, thoughts, ideas, and dreams.

Where Ministry Staff Can Find Servant Leaders

As a ministry staff person, you will often be looking for leaders. Many reading this handbook will have the word *recruit* written in their job description. Godly, faithful, and gifted leaders often are hard to find. Why? Because they are not out promoting themselves. So, you may find some of your best leaders in these unlikely places:

Becoming a Servant

Out of the back row are some of the finest servant leaders who, because their of spiritual maturity, are not always vying for attention and the spotlight.

From every level and background God grooms and matures servant leaders. Servant leadership is not a respecter of race, age, gender, education, or personality.

Your blind spots may reveal some incredible godly men and women in leadership. Don't look for the obvious, like Israel did when they wanted a king and looked for the tallest, strongest, and most handsome man in town (who was hiding in the baggage department, see 1 Samuel 10:20–22).

Listening to you are some servant leaders who are eager to learn and grow. Don't let the quiet ones get away without listening to them.

Somewhere in the circle are servant leaders. They are not at the head of the table or always sitting behind their desk. They are not standing up front all the time. Often, they bring people into a casual community of conversation. The others are talking, yet the servant leader made it happen.

When you find them, get to know them. Establish a spiritual and ministry relationship. Train, resource, and support them in their God-given role and responsibility to serve others.

Scripture summarizes this topic best:

> Be shepherds of God's flock that is under your care, serving as overseers – not because you must, but because you are willing, as God wants you to be; not greedy for money, but eager to serve; not lording it over those entrusted to you, but being examples to the flock.
>
> *1 Peter 5:2–3*

Additional Reading

De Pree, Max. *Leadership Jazz.* New York: Dell, 1993.

Dibbert, Michael T. *Spiritual Leadership, Responsible Management.* Grand Rapids, Mich.: Zondervan, 1989.

Ford, Leighton. *Transforming Leadership.* Downers Grove, Ill.: InterVarsity Press, 1991.

Sanders, Oswald. *Spiritual Leadership.* Chicago: Moody Press, 1967.

Stowell, Joseph M. *Shepherding the Church.* Chicago: Moody Press, 1994.

Defining Your Style of Leadership

My son, preserve sound judgment and discernment,
do not let them out of your sight; they will be life for you.... Then you
will go on your way in safety.

Proverbs 3:21–23

Leaders get best results by not restricting themselves
to one leadership style.

Daniel Goleman, Harvard Business Review

Nancy Williams needed results. She was hired as an associate minister in her church with the responsibility to organize and develop the single adult ministry. The task was enormous: new programs needed to be created, an army of volunteer workers needed to be recruited, quality leaders needed to be trained.

For months, Nancy recruited relentlessly to enlist that small army of volunteers. It was in her decisive design that recruits would promote, administrate the details, raise and manage the budget, set up rooms, lead discussion groups, organize and execute a monthly outreach event, and host social events. That was only the beginning of a long, exhausting list of ideas and opportunities. The ministry was clear in Nancy's mind. She could see it happening in her church and community. She had a vision.

Nancy modeled great wisdom in realizing the necessity to train volunteers. She worked diligently to develop a high-powered, six-week training program. With a strong educational background and four years in corporate sales before graduate school, Nancy was confidently equipped to train willing recruits.

Becoming a Servant

The first training night arrived. As volunteers walked into the church fellowship lounge, they were greeted with engraved plastic nametags, bite-sized desserts, punch, and the warm aroma of decaf hazelnut coffee. Soft music was playing in the background. Nancy had not missed one detail. At each decorated round table, future workers were greeted with an impressive, well-organized training manual, every section carefully tabbed with four-color entries. Dressed in a well-tailored business suit and a smile beaming on her face, Nancy enthusiastically greeted everyone by their first name. She was ready to lead.

Nancy's carefully created computer-generated visual presentation was excellent. Several single adults from the community were invited for an on-stage interview, their stories helping convince the volunteer audience of the need for a single adult ministry. Nancy persuaded the people with powerful emotion. Her commitment was undeniable.

At the second session, attendance had increased by nearly 20 percent. The training session went much like the first, some said better. But Nancy could not help noticing that everyone left looking tired.

In the third session, Nancy realized she needed to "spice things up." She used more visuals and reduced the session from ninety to seventy-five minutes. Attendance was down. But almost everyone signed up for one of the many tasks, so that was at least encouraging.

By the last session, Nancy felt defeated. Her "army" had reduced to about 50 percent of the first evening's numbers, six weeks prior—despite the fact that she had worked harder and smarter. *It must be people's busy lives, or they are afraid to commit,* she thought, half in anger, half in frustration.

As the diminished group filed out, Kate, who had not missed any of the training, held back. Respectfully approaching Nancy, she said with a soft voice, "Ms. Williams, this has been great. But when are we going to have input and get to discuss all of the things you've talked about?" Nancy was helpless without her notes and prepared presentation, yet suddenly she got it.

One Leadership Style Won't Cut It

Competent, savvy leaders know that leading cannot be confined to one particular style. Their first thought is not, *What am I going to say or do?* but *What do the people need to experience and how will they most effectively engage in the process or our mission?* Simply put, "How do they want to be treated?" Knowledgeable leaders know how to connect and unite their people with the vision and values being shared, and are able to adapt their methods to be most effective in their goal.

Personalize your leadership style. When you discover where your audience is, you can adjust how to approach and engage them in the mission.

For example, if your paid or volunteer leaders are:

- *Clueless*, they need information.
- *Knowledgeable*, they desire opportunity to exercise thoughts and ideas.
- *Experienced*, they need to be brought together.
- *United*, they need a new challenge to renew their confidence.
- *Confident*, they want to be sent out to do the work of the ministry.

To bring people through these stages of development, you must flex according to their needs and ministry maturity. If they are without information, you cannot send them out to do the work on pure hype and emotion. They will be killed in battle. If they are knowledgeable, united, and ready to go, you will create apathy if you hold them back to give more information.

You will need a variety of leadership styles in your personal portfolio. It will require godly wisdom and careful understanding to discern which style to use at any give time. Occasionally, you may need to combine two styles.

Four Leadership Styles for Ministry Staff

Literature on leadership styles is voluminous. You may have seen the four leadership style quadrants: *Telling, Selling, Participating*, and *Entrusting*, which seem to accurately visualize the four arenas of the leader. Another common corporate adaptation of leadership styles comes from the Hay/McBer consulting firm. They delineate six different approaches: *Coercive, Authoritative, Affiliative, Democratic, Pacesetting*, and *Coaching*.

In his Role Preference Inventory, Bobb Biehl of Masterplanning Group International brilliantly defines three styles: *Designer, Developer*, and *Manager/Maximizer*. I have often presented those three styles in my own training. (See the Additional Reading section at the end of this chapter for contact information.)

However, for the ministry staff member and within a ministry context I would like to suggest the following four adaptable leadership styles:

1. Imparting (telling) toward Discovering
2. Sharing (selling) toward Participating
3. Involving (participating) toward Committing
4. Delegating (entrusting) toward Doing

Just remember, the style should never be perceived as an end in itself. Each has an observable objective, motivating the participant to the next level of growth and maturity.

Imparting toward Discovering

This style is one of the most common for the ministry leader. It begins by presenting information and knowledge to the people, because sometimes they don't know what they don't know.

Here, the leader usually teaches, or perhaps preaches. The leader may use a host of techniques to facilitate effective learning (some call this pedagogy). However, be sure not to confuse *learning* styles with *leadership* styles. Presenting information is the leadership style. Choosing a proper presentation method involves employing a learning style (see sidebar adapted from Marlene LeFever).

> **Four Learning Styles***
>
> 1. **Imaginative Learner.** Why do I need to know this? (Meaning)
> 2. **Analytic Learner.** What do I need to know? (Content)
> 3. **Common Sense Learner.** How does this work? (Experiment)
> 4. **Dynamic Learner.** What can this become? (Application)

Imparting information should be objective, to encourage the learner to know how to discover more information, or make direct application to validate the newfound knowledge. In other words, motivate people to ask, "Is there more to know and does it work? At this teachable moment, the leader does well to give a pragmatic assignment to further explore or experience the body of information. That assignment leads to the next style in the process: sharing toward participating.

Using this style you can begin to impart vision, direction, and information necessary to the vision. You have given helpful information. The people now know what they need to know.

Sharing toward Participating

This style brings people together to interact with the information the leader has just imparted. The leader is now a facilitator. He or she gathers everyone in an open forum and motivates them to share. That means *they* talk. A variety of techniques—from audio visual to large-group dynamic "games"—may be used to foster discussion. The people are sharing what *they* know.

When using this facilitating style of leadership you begin to help the people become personally identified with your ministry and mission, and draw them toward one another in the process. They have become more than spectators; they are participants. You have asked the right questions.

---

*Adapted from Marlene LeFever, *Learning Styles* (Colorado Springs: David C. Cook, 1995).

They are now beginning to share the ministry's values and vision.

Involving toward Committing

If the vision has been well cast and the mission is defined with clear values, many people will want to get involved. In fact, several are ready to test their leadership skills. They have learned and participated. They are ready to move forward.

At this stage the leader initiates forming a small group of participants into a leadership team. Everyone on this team is knowledgeable, having participated in the process and discussion. The leader is an important resource to the group, but wisely waits to see if others will begin to demonstrate leadership as well.

The objective here is to move the people toward a united commitment to the mission. It is at this stage and with this style that they will best volunteer their gifts and resources, not merely their presence. With knowledge and unified participation, they are ready to give so much more. They now feel like they own the ministry in which they are about to become fully engaged. They are committed.

Delegating toward Doing

This style may best describe the leader as a coach. A coach manages from the sidelines; he or she observes, cheers, and remains available to the team to answer questions, consult, and bind up their wounds. Occasionally, a coach will give an order, but many coaches reserve this seldom-used action for strategic moments.

Discussion on Leadership Styles

Reread the story at the beginning of this chapter, then personally consider or gather a small group to discuss the following:

- What did Nancy do well?
- What styles did Nancy most likely employ in her training program?
- What other leadership styles could Nancy use?
- If you were given Nancy's charge, what would you do differently?

Respect the Natural Sequence of Leadership Styles

It is important to not move to style three (Involving toward Committing) if the people have not experienced styles one and two. I remember watching a leader stand in front of a large group for the very first time and ask them if they had any ideas for the growth and development of that particular ministry. The silence was deafening. After several attempts to get the people to respond, a few side comments were shared and unrelated questions were asked. The leader had not informed or encouraged the people to participate in the basic knowledge, vision, or values of the mission. They were clueless. They had never been participants. They were not united.

Becoming a Servant

Delegating means letting go. It comes as the final stage of the maturation process of the people of God in ministry. It goes beyond the adolescent stage to a stage of independence, or better yet, interdependence with God (see John 15:5) and godly coaches. The people are fully engaged, doing what God wants them to do. As some churches say, they are "fully devoted followers of Jesus Christ."

Back to the football analogy for a moment. During most games, the coach's time is spent carefully watching his team and observing the opposition. Occasionally, a coach will send a player to the huddle with some new information. Sometimes, a bewildered quarterback will run to the sidelines and ask the coach to tell him something he needs to know or request a helpful reminder. Other times, the coach calls a timeout and moves back to another leadership style and asks (rather than tells) the team what needs to be done next. In the locker room during halftime, the coach carefully decides which of the four styles to use. It all depends on how the players are doing and if they are accomplishing the mission.

Styles to Avoid with Volunteer-Based Leadership

- **Coercive:** Demanding compliance. Problem: Whose directives?

- **Dictatorship:** Following only one leader. Problem: Who?

- **Hands off:** Searching for leadership. Problem: The weakest lead.

- **Micromanagement:** Strangling growth. Problem: Unnecessary rules.

- **Like it or leave:** Granting one choice. Problem: Who decides?

- **Consensus:** Striving for 100 percent agreement. Problem: Not realistic.

- **Competitive:** Creating unrealistic standards. Problem: Many losers.

- **Anger:** Creating fear by losing control. Problem: It too often works.

Tailor Your Leadership Style to Meet Needs

My brother is ambidextrous, meaning he can do the same task right-handed or lefthanded with equal precision. I remember when he broke his right arm he quickly learned to use his left hand to write. No problem. He just did it. He adapted.

As you discover the importance and validity to each leadership style, you will learn which is needed at which time. Be wise. Be adaptable. Be ambidextrous. Also, be willing to supplement your leadership weakness by engaging someone from your ministry staff or leadership team to do what you are not ready to do, or do not feel capable of doing. That shows healthy leadership.

Choosing a leadership style is not without its tensions. The tension exists between controlling the decision-making process and letting go. That can often translate to authoritarian versus democratic styles of leadership and management. The choice requires a great deal of wisdom and understanding of the volunteers you are serving as well the mission you are trying to accomplish.

In tailoring one's style, there are a few basic principles to respect and observe. The following steps reflect the four leadership styles described in this chapter. They also respect the importance, input, and interaction of volunteers who are very much invested in the ministry.

Step one: Talk with your participants and volunteer leaders about the issues at hand. Make sure everyone understands the problem and need for a solution. Make it very clear in the beginning who has the responsibility and authority to make a decision and how the decision-making process will work. Everyone will perform better when the outcomes are clear.

Step two: Be a facilitator to affirm what people are saying. Create an atmosphere where people feel free to express both thoughts and feelings. Encourage everyone to articulate ideas, ask questions, and exhaust their agenda and concerns. Be willing to make adjustments to the original assumptions in step one.

Step three: As soon as the issue, desired outcomes, and plan of direction are clear, empower and grant permission to the decision-maker—whether that is you, your team, or another committee or leader. Once that is understood, those who need to lead must lead. The inverse is equally obvious: those who need to let go and step aside must do so.

Step four: Pay attention to the progress of completing the task. Know your ministry staff role as a leader, participant, or resource provider. Fulfill that role and don't change your style in the midst of the agreed upon process. In other words, if you have declared you are going to step aside and only be a resource to the team, resist stepping back in as an authoritative leader.

Additional Reading

Biehl, Bobb, *Masterplanning: A Complete Guide for Building a Strategic Plan for Your Business, Church, or Organization.* Nashville: Broadman and Holman, 1997. (See Bobb's leadership style self-study instruments at www.Masterplanning Group.com; PO Box 952499, Lake Mary, FL 32795; phone 800-443-1976.)

Buckingham, Marcus and Donald O. Clifton. *Now, Discover Your Strengths.* New York: Free Press, 2001.

Ellis, Lee. *Leading Talents, Leading Teams.* Chicago: Northfield, 2003.

Handley, Patrick. *Inventory Insight.* Kansas City, Mo.: Insight Institute, 1988. (See Patrick's self-study leadership style inventory at Insight Institute, 100 Westport Square #166, Kansas City, MO 64111.)

Keirsey, David and Marilyn Bates. *Please Understand Me.* Del Mar, Calif.: Prometheus Nemesis, 1978.

Also:

DiSC Type Indicator available from Success Performance Solutions, 2137 Embassy Drive, Suite 218, Lancaster, PA 17603; phone 717-291-4640 or 800-803-4303; fax 717-427-2020; email: www.super-solutions.com.

Establishing Healthy Motives and Agendas

There is a way that seems right to a man,
but in the end it leads to death.

Proverbs 14:12

Desire to treat others the same way you desire to be treated.

Adapted from the Golden Rule

Grant has been the children's director at Northville Community Church for nearly eleven years and has been involved in children's ministries twice that long. He is known in Christian education circles as a children's curriculum genius. The first eight years at Northville were great. New teachers were recruited and trained, and programs grew to the point that the church had to build an educational wing.

But the last three years have been difficult. Grant has struggled staying fresh and excited about his role. Children's ministry does not get a lot of press and Grant is not an especially gifted communicator in front of the congregation. Numbers are very flat and he has often had to validate the existence of a few declining ministry programs to the children's ministry committee. There are days when he feels he should leave and go to another church, although he seriously wonders who would have him.

A couple months ago though, Grant had a long-distance call from his friend Tim, who outlined a program that has increased their children's ministry by nearly 20 percent in the last year. Energized, Grant made an appointment to visit Tim's church to evaluate the new program.

Now, three months later and feeling ten years younger, Grant has a new proposal ready for his committee. He's sure it's the answer to the declining numbers and stale programs at Northville. This is what Grant needs.

After Grant spends forty-five minutes laying out every detail, one committee member asks a question—a good question. Grant perspires as he gives his best answer with an apparent air of self-confidence. He squirms, hoping there are no more follow-up questions. The issue appears to go away.

But a few minutes later one of the more influential committee members reminds the rest of the committee that the new program does not fit the budget. Grant loses it. He raises his voice and defends that they cannot afford *not* to purchase the new program. The committee is divided. The proposal is tabled. Grant never got to sleep that night. He called in sick the next three days. He's sure his ministry career is finished.

Unhealthy Motives and Agendas in Ministry

Staff members and volunteers often encounter a degree of tension between personal desires and what is best for the ministry. Personal tastes, priorities, and preferences sometimes get in the way of good motives and wise decisions. Consider just three pitfalls:

Envy. It is so easy to fall off-course by simply becoming jealous of another person in ministry, perhaps even someone in your current ministry context. You know, the "other staff member" who is popular, can do no wrong, and is highly favored by everyone, including the senior pastor.

Doubt. Doubt and displeasure connected to your own role and calling also may result when you dialogue with another colleague at a ministry conference or convention. You begin to compare notes. You hear about their budget, staff, and program that is twice the size of yours, and you fall into sinful thoughts that create guilt and spiritual defeat. You hear a "perfect" story, one that's clearly not yours. All of a sudden your story doesn't seem to matter. Your motivation to try harder or give up goes off the charts. You find yourself walking in circles at the carnal corral.

Pride. Weeks later you are sitting in a committee meeting with the people who have been designated by the church to "be there for you." You want everyone in the room to celebrate and become excited about your new idea. Someone on your committee challenges only one point of several you have just made. A part of you wants to run out of the room. Another part of you makes one or two defensive comments and reattempts to "sell" your concept, hoping that everyone will keep further questions to themselves.

These are normal tendencies—we all feel them. But each one creates expectations of others that may or not be met. We want to feel good and get an overdue pat on the back; to be perceived as the one and only person who had this idea; to recruit more workers even if they come from other areas of ministry; to get the first of budgeted funds because what we're doing is most important; to win support for our area and perhaps move up the organizational chart.

Unhealthy motives may be as natural as walking. But just because that's true does not mean they are healthy for you or the people around you. As a ministry staff leader, you need to set a healthy example in your designated area of ministry.

> ### Four Common Ministry Temptations
>
> **Wantonness:** Craving, coveting, and yearning for the ministry of another.
>
> **Restlessness:** Always discontent, wanting bigger numbers and a better program.
>
> **Rapidness:** To bypass all of the systems and make things happen now. Some often quote this unhealthy mantra, "It is better to ask forgiveness than permission." Not true!
>
> **Laziness:** To look for the quickest way to get ministry results and go home.

Healthy Motives and Agendas

Enough of the negative stuff. It is time to be positive and move forward. I believe most ministry staff members desire a healthy ministry with healthy relationships. I believe they earnestly and sincerely desire to do what they believe God has called them to do, the work of the ministry. Healthy motives and agendas will lead a staff person in the right direction. Here are a few thoughts to help develop a healthy framework:

- Think through the overall mission of your church or parachurch ministry.
- Share your ministry goals and ideas with other staff *before* you place them into formal proposals.
- Develop the rhythm of developing forethought and afterthought ... thinking through all of the implications and results of your agenda.
- Pray through the entire process.
- Never present a ministry agenda under undue pressure or when you know the timing is not right.
- Check your personal agenda at the door ... the ego stuff.

- Prepare someone else to present your idea, step into the backdrop of ministry, and share the joy.
- Offer that your agendas be tabled or considered at a later date. Try not to rush the process, creating unnecessary tension.

Creating and Maintaining a Healthy Environment

When do temptation and unhealthy motives most often invade? To answer that question, I list my own experiences, knowing you may likely relate to such situations in your life and ministry:

- When I am tired and exhausted
- When I am discouraged and fail to hear "well done"
- When I am unwilling to confront a disappointment or problem
- When I am moving too fast and have lost perspective
- When I have not moved at all
- When my list of friends has become shorter
- When I have erred and genuinely failed others
- When I have missed my quiet time with God

To work through these difficult situations, and perhaps avoid a "next time," we would do well to reread 1 Kings 19 — Elijah's encounter with God at Mount Horeb — and remember this basic advice the Lord gave his prophet: *Take care of yourself and let God take care of the rest.*

I am often reminded of the flight attendants' words in the case of a crisis: "Be sure to place the oxygen mask on yourself first before you attempt to assist others." So, here are a few helpful suggestions for good health in ministry. Some are for today. Some are for the long haul. They begin with taking care of you.

- Slow everything down, even if for only a couple of hours. Then ask a trusted friend or colleague to pray for you.
- Take care of your body (sleep, eat right, exercise). Ask someone to tell you when you appear tired and unhealthy.
- Make your family and close friends a high priority. Make sure your spouse has access to your calendar. Schedule vacations and days off.
- Have a trusted friend periodically monitor your expenses, debt, and savings account.
- Maintain spiritual disciplines (including confession of unhealthy motives and agendas) with someone to hold you accountable.
- Create regular reading habits and develop a hobby you can afford.

- Initiate a close friendship to help you maintain emotional stability.
- Begin the habit of praying *for* all of your fellow staff and leadership team and pray *with* them often.
- Create time in your schedule for other staff, ministry leaders, and new people. (Try not to get in the rut of always going to lunch or coffee with the same people.)
- Identify a ministry growth goal, including a course of study, vision trip, visit to other ministries, or contacts with other ministry leaders.
- Ask a seasoned ministry leader from another ministry to meet with you once or twice a year for feedback on your ministry.
- Take a day or a half day once a month and do nothing but plan the following month and consider your annual ministry objectives, goals, and calendar.
- Keep your values, vision, mission statement, objectives, and goals on one piece of paper on your desk or in a visible place in your office.
- Have ministry and personal prayer requests written in your calendar. Be willing to share those with others.
- Memorize Psalm 84:10: "Better is one day in your courts than a thousand elsewhere; I would rather be a doorkeeper in the house of my God than dwell in the tents of the wicked."

Additional Reading

Crabb, Larry. *Soul Talk*. Brentwood, Tenn.: Integrity, 2003.

McNeal, Reggie. *A Work of Heart: Understanding How God Shapes Spiritual Leaders*. San Francisco: Jossey-Bass, 2000.

Powlison, David. *Seeing with New Eyes*. Phillipsburg, N.J.: Presbyterian and Reformed, 2003.

9

Establishing Healthy Boundaries of Responsibility and Accountability

All a man's ways seem right to him, but the Lord weighs the heart.

Haughty eyes and a proud heart, the lamp of the wicked, are sin!

Proverbs 21:2, 4

What we ask of you is to accept responsibility for being the very best at your job so we can be the best at our jobs.

David Cottrell,
Listen Up, Leader!

Bob loves his job. He has never been more fulfilled personally than he is now as the business manager for the large city rescue mission. A college graduate who for years has worked as the chief financial officer and comptroller of a very successful manufacturing company in a neighboring town, he was able to take an enormous salary cut to work at the mission. Without question, he brings great value to the ministry because he sees the big picture and knows the mission's key supporters and board members very well, having previously served on the board.

Bob is a hard worker, a supervisor's dream. He can do his job in record time but often finds that he is rather bored with the continual review of the budget and accounts payable. He is also very conscientious and would never leave early. Many times Bob looks for something to do. This is where Bob steps into Cindy's story.

Cindy, a seventeen-year employee, is responsible for all of the housekeeping duties for the 125 beds at the mission. Despite her conscientous work habits, she never has time at the end of the day or week to sit back and take inventory of her role and many detailed responsibilities.

In the beginning it was Bob's role to help Cindy cut a few corners and save money. She really appreciated his input. But now he's making more and more suggestions on how Cindy might improve her time management skills and leadership style. Last week he questioned her several times why she had to take a vacation day just before a holiday. He's even been hanging out with a number of her volunteers, asking them questions which had nothing to do with her budget. She has noticed during the last two months some of her best volunteers becoming more critical of the housekeeping program. One volunteer recently quit because she felt that Cindy was not a good steward of her time and the mission's resources.

"Bob is interfering with my job," Cindy at last told her supervisor. "Cindy, Bob is just trying to help and feels that you could learn and develop a few new time management skills," responded Cindy's supervisor. "So, now he is talking to you about my job!" Cindy said. The supervisor wished he could have retracted his last comment. It was too late. Cindy stormed out of the office, the sound of the slamming door echoing down the hall.

Responsibilty

You are responsible only for your job description. In other words, "Do YOUR job." That truth and guideline cannot be clearer or simpler. No one else has the responsibility that you have. Other staff members, volunteers, board members, and your supervisor expect you to do your job, not theirs. When you fail to fulfill your job duties, it is not healthy for you or others around you. In our story, Bob was wrong.

When you fail to do your job, others will either criticize or step in to do your job. When they criticize, they fall into the sin of unkind judgment toward you or those who work alongside you. The blame game begins.

If they step in to do your job, soon they begin to become critical as well. They wonder why you could not do what they are now doing. They either say or think, "You are being paid to do this job, not me."

In either case, you are disadvantaged in your leadership role. First of all, you have unknowingly created a critical climate where others see you as incompetent, incapable, or both. Their temptation is to become critical of not just you but of the ministry. And should the situation become significant, your supervisor or board may realize they don't need you. If it was not your

Seven Responsibility Pitfalls to Avoid

1. Avoid talking about another associate's lack of performance.
2. Avoid comparing others' resources, performance, and popularity.
3. Avoid becoming a part of an unhealthy alliance with other staff.
4. Avoid complaining, especially in the middle of a project or ministry before God reveals his results.
5. Avoid dreaming unrealistic dreams with disgruntled associates or volunteers.
6. Avoid running and hiding when you don't feel good about your role.
7. Avoid targeting certain people, board members, or the system as the enemy.

original plan to work yourself out of a job, you may still find yourself out of a job or miserable in your job.

There is only one good response to these unhealthy scenarios. Do your job ... with all your heart, soul, mind, and strength. Feel good about going home tired at the end of the day. Do your work as to the Lord. Does that sound biblical? It should, because it is.

If you are responsible to supervise another person(s), do just that: *supervise*. Again, don't do their job. Your role is to be their source of encouragement, to provide resources, direction, and vision. For some talented and gifted leaders, knowing they can do another's job better can become an enormous liability.

Conversely, there is a difference in managing up and doing your supervisor's job. Managing up is working *with* your supervisor, through your resources and ideas, to move together toward the same objective. But actually doing your supervisor's job is unwise and unhealthy. You may foster a very unstable work environment. Do your job!

Accountability

Accountability Begins with Respect

Healthy limits and boundaries are often established under a sound system of accountability. In most cases a ministry staff person reports to another person. Your supervisor begins your personal "chain of command." It is important to remember, your supervisor is responsible for you.

Often your supervisor will give account to other people on the board or a committee for your ministry and actions. Many times, you will not be aware of his or her support for you. Sometimes a supervisor will "stick their neck out for you." Sometimes they don't. But a ministry staff member will always do well to intentionally enhance the reputation of those responsible for their ministry role.

God reminds all of us to respect, honor, and give tribute to those in authority (see Romans 13:1–5; Titus 3:1–2; 1 Peter 2:13ff; more about this subject in chapter 16). I have often said, "When a staff member cannot respect the significant person(s) or team in authority, it may be time to consider a significant change." In his "Love and Respect" seminars Emerson Eggerich talks about "unconditional respect"

> **Insecure Leaders Produce ...**
>
> • Too much control
> • Too much arrogance
> • Too much fear of failure
> • Too much avoidance of risk
> • Too much time behind their desk
> • Too much "yes" and not enough "truth"

between a husband and a wife. I think he has keen insight to an important concept. Staff members will only do well to grow in their unconditional (not blind) respect of other staff and those who partner in ministry.

Accountability Begins with You

A staff member also does well to initiate building a proper relationship with his or her supervisor. Over the years, I have informally surveyed ministry staff members who say that particular responsibility should rest solely with the supervisor, but I think it works best as a two-way street.

Certainly, the supervisor should initiate and protect the vision, values, and objectives of the ministry and mission with each staff member, but consider the following five actions a staff member can take to initiate a growing relationship with a supervisor:

1. Ask your supervisor for a regular meeting if one is not already scheduled.
2. Make a high priority of the above meeting. Let your supervisor know that you value and respect his or her time with you.
3. Invite your supervisor into your ministry as a participant and a resource.
4. Invite your supervisor into your personal life and family, more than once.
5. Ask your supervisor to pray with you after sharing personal and ministry prayer requests.

A staff member also must remember that a supervisor (1) has this same responsibility to initiate with the board or their own supervisor, (2) may be required to provide care and supervision of many staff members, not just you, and (3) may or may not be capable of building as deep a working relationship as you desire.

Healthy Boundaries Bring Great Joy

Healthy Boundaries Are an Asset

Your job possesses certain assets and privileges. Your assets are your giftedness, experience, and personality. Your privileges include your job description and your ministry context. When you work within the scope of your (1) giftedness, (2) experience, (3) personality, (4) job description, and (5) the vision of the overall ministry, you will often find a sense of joy and fulfillment.

> **Three Levels of Accountability**
>
> 1. You report TO one other person (hopefully, not a committee).
> 2. You work WITH other staff members on the ministry team.
> 3. You may be responsible FOR other staff members and/or volunteers.

Keep these five boundary lines in balance. Stepping outside of them may create new and unnecessary stress. Don't go there. Stay within the scope of what God has called you to be and do. Grow within that context. Make your job as big as you can and allow God to grow and bless the ministry. At the end of the day, celebrate. Don't give away your joy and don't let others steal it.

Even with Healthy Boundaries There Are Certain Liabilities

Every job has some downsides. You may have already discovered that everything in ministry is not perfect. I am guessing that your ministry role today is not what you thought it would be when you first started in ministry or even your current position. Somehow, things changed. The ministry looks different. Consider these liabilities:

Change. Often I have counseled young ministry leaders, "In one year, your ministry will not look anything like you think it will." I have tested that statement with many who have discovered it to be true. Ministry has a way of changing. For some, change is difficult, while others love it. But change can often make ministry a hard place to navigate, not knowing what is around the corner.

Lonely days. Some days you will find yourself rather lonely, a cold reminder that no one really understands or shares your role in life and ministry. Even in the midst of a healthy team context, you are the only one doing what you do. That is when you need an accountability partner, someone to talk to and pray with. It is only right to have someone who will just "be there" when others have gone.

No answers. Your job requires that you give answers to the problems in your area of responsibility. You will work hard to provide those answers. Some days you will have them. Other days you will fall short. Give yourself permission to *not* know it all.

Unrealistic expectations. Expectations can be the greatest gift or the greatest malady. Expectations are a gift when we see the exciting results of being stretched to new arenas of personal or ministry growth. Expectations are not a gift when others expect the associate to do what he or she cannot do.

If you are *not* doing your job, the expectation of others is a constant reminder of certain weaknesses. If you *are* doing your job, people's unrealistically high expectations can drive you to distraction with overwork as you try to satisfy them. That is not where you want to live.

Failure. What you planned may not work. There are things you thought you could control. You found out otherwise. Failure happens. How you deal with it is important. May you develop the spirit of pastor Erwin Lutzer who titled one of his books, *Failure: The Backdoor to Success.*

You. The worst unrealistic expectations may come from you. Your own unrealistic expectations and personal insecurities may only result in the continual pursuit of the "carrot" you may never catch. Be realistic. Be accountable.

You need boundaries to protect you and your ministry. Seldom will any one else build them for you. No one else experiences what you experience. The volunteers and people around you do not take home what you take

---

Ten Healthy Habits You Can Establish

1. Always communicate what you are doing. Resist turning your job into a guessing game among other associates and volunteers.

2. Consider ways to enhance your job description by going one step above and beyond what is expected. Place your energies there.

3. Build evaluation tools into every area of your ministry.

4. Know when to say no and when to say yes.

5. Be sure your supervisor will support your yes or your no.

6. Continually ask others to pray about your area of ministry.

7. Be available, especially when you don't have all of the answers.

8. Look for creative ways to compliment and encourage other staff.

9. Often ask your supervisor and others, "How could I do this better?"

10. Keep asking yourself, "Am I stuck in any kind of a rut?"

---

home. Without careful thought, they will expect you to do more. Healthy boundaries will guide you in your response to these three common comments: good job; you can do better; do more.

Your job is your job. It belongs at this time to you and you alone. Do it the best you can. Be a model to others of integrity without mediocrity. Invite Jesus into your ministry role each and every day. It is Jesus who said, "I am the vine; you are the branches.... Apart from me you can do nothing" (John 15:5).

Additional Reading

Cloud, Henry and John Townsend. *Boundaries*. Grand Rapids, Mich.: Zondervan, 1992.

Doehring, Carrie. *Taking Care: Monitoring Power Dynamics and Relationship Boundaries in Pastoral Care and Counseling*. Nashville: Abingdon, 1995.

Grenz, Stanley J. and Roy D. Bell, *Betrayal of Trust: Sexual Misconduct in the Pastorate*. Downers Grove, Ill.: InterVarsity Press, 1995.

Hunt, Richard, John Hinkle Jr., and H. Newton Malony, eds., *Clergy Assessment and Career Development*. Nashville: Abingdon, 1990.

Trull, Joe E. and James E. Carter, *Ministerial Ethics: Being a Good Minister in a Not-So-Good World*. Nashville: Broadman and Holman, 1993.

Triangulation: A Dangerous Move

The man of integrity walks securely, but he who takes
crooked paths will be found out.

Proverbs 10:9

Kings take pleasure in honest lips; they value a man
who speaks the truth.

Proverbs 16:13

To make matters worse, there will always be a third party who
sees to it that calm is impossible.

H. B. London

Beverly became a member of the Urban Community Outreach Ministry (UCOM) with the highest of credentials and the most celebrated work experience. She had completed master's degrees in sociology from the state university and a theology degree from an accredited seminary. Her work experience included a director's position at a large urban ministry in a metropolitan area. Beverly's supervisor, Eli, the executive director of UCOM, was thrilled to have her on staff.

Beverly quickly acclimated to her job and new surroundings. It did not take her long to know the people and the apparent needs of the ministry's constituency. Within short order, she developed a carefully written strategy for UCOM, one that had worked well in her former ministry context. After thorough preparations, she approached her supervisor with the idea, absolutely convinced that her idea would be welcomed, embraced, and implemented within the current budget year.

Eli listened thoughtfully to Beverly's proposal and asked a few questions. Beverly provided the answers. But afterward, he explained UCOM had unsuccessfully attempted her "new" ministry model a few years ago in a slightly different format. Because that failed attempt had understandably left a negative impression in some board members' minds, he indicated that it would be best to put this idea on hold for a while.

Displeased with Eli's response, Beverly began to question his ability to lead. She believed that she was brought to UCOM to bring growth and fresh new ideas to the ministry. She was not going to give up that easily.

Within a month, Beverly had shared her ideas with several other staff members and two of the seven board members. Everyone seemed to agree with Beverly. They liked her enthusiasm, her vivacious spirit. Not one person questioned her ideas.

At the next staff meeting one of the staff members asked Beverly to share her new model for ministry at UCOM. At the moment the request was made, she looked at Eli. He returned the glance and said nothing. When another staff member affirmed the idea to hear what Beverly had already shared with him, Eli granted permission for Beverly to share her new concept.

Three months later, the board adopted Beverly's new idea and appropriated budget dollars to proceed as soon as possible. Eli and Beverly continued on staff together, but with a strained relationship.

What Is Triangulation?

Triangulation is getting your way by using a secondary authority to undermine a primary authority. It is doing a so-called "end run" around others, bypassing the corporate structure to achieve fast and sometimes risky results. Certainly, triangulation has often been used to promote a good agenda but at the expense of undermining others and possibly demonstrating disrespect to a supervisor or leadership team.

Triangulation happens. In most ministry contexts it may not be avoided. In her article titled "Codependency in the Church," Margie Cash writes, "In my observations as a staff member, I saw rampant triangulation, particularly in the area of personnel matters. If a staff member became a problem or a threat in some way to the status quo, this was rarely dealt with directly by the senior pastor, but was more often handled by way of other staff members applying pressure to conform or by involving the ministry elders in a similar, witch-hunt fashion."* What starts as innocent and personal rears its giant head and causes enormous devastation.

*www.margiecash.com/codependency.htm.

There are two common arenas in which triangulation takes place. One is when an employee exerts influence or promotes a particular agenda over the head of another employee. The staff member has a great idea. The supervisor is not keen on it, for whatever reason. Still intent, the staff member goes over the supervisor's head to another authority, whether another supervisor, committee, or board. If they find an agreeable audience, the staff member will work in that arena to get what they want.

The second common form of triangulation, sometimes known as creating alliances, is when an employee combines strengths and resources with another employee to work an agenda apart from or against a supervisor. The end result is the same as the first arena—the staff member gets what they want.

> **Where a Staff Member May Tend to Triangulate**
>
> To whom might a staff member go when their supervisor does not buy in to their agenda?
>
> - The senior pastor
> - Another team leader
> - A "trusted" fellow staff member
> - A volunteer with strong influence
> - A committee or board member (usually, one member at a time)
> - A group of listening volunteers, who together create strength

Why Triangulation Often Happens

Lack of a complete system for problem solving. Triangulation may emerge when a staff member is frustrated with the system, unable to solve a problem or develop a dream through conventional methods. Sometimes the system may break down at the point of direct supervision and an impatient, inexperienced staff member chooses to go around the supervisor to another "authority." At other times the structure exhibits inconsistencies and maladies which indirectly teach the staff member that triangulation is a natural form of problem solving.

Lack of leadership skills. Some staff members in leadership roles have not received leadership training. They have learned to promote their agendas through triangulation and other unhealthy methods, such as demand or anger. People who exhibit good leadership skills tend to not triangulate. Triangulation is not natural or necessary to a respected leader.

Lack of healthy self-esteem. When people don't get what they want, they might take it personally. Many have learned that getting a personal agenda accomplished will boost self-esteem, move them up the leadership ladder, or both. Using unconventional methods (such as triangulation) to get their way can be a sign of a greater personal dysfunction.

Lack of seeing the big picture or having enough information. It is easy to not see the big picture. A limited view of the organization may create dangerous movements among its personnel. A sense of history, clear understanding of the culture, and protection of the values and vision of the ministry are important factors in establishing constructive objectives and pursuing legitimate, admirable agendas.

Sometimes personal agendas may have only been tested with a few others or with one who is a charismatic leader. A knowledgeable view of the entire ministry should be carefully shared and owned by the entire leadership team, both paid and volunteer. That complete view will open the door for effective communication among leaders and participants. The result is always lesser triangulation.

The Results of Triangulation

Broken trust. Broken trust is the most obvious result of triangulation. Very few people trust another who goes around the agreed systems of authority to accomplish their agendas.

Eight Healthy Ways to Work with Your Supervisor

1. Learn and accept the process of time and structure in your ministry.
2. Be willing to accept "no" or "not now."
3. Be a good worker with a good attitude and a gentle spirit.
4. Always speak with openness and honesty.
5. Keep your promises and commitments.
6. Make sure your idea is thoroughly researched and matches the core values of the overall ministry.
7. Involve your supervisor to help you develop your ideas and agenda.
8. Ask your supervisor's permission to pursue your agenda with others and respect his or her counsel.

Loss of effective communication. Once a staff member has compromised the leadership structure and attempted triangulation, it will be more difficult to establish healthy communication with one's supervisor or other authoritative structures.

Unhealthy alliances. Those who encourage triangulation are not a healthy source of future leadership effectiveness. Unhealthy alliances are just that, unhealthy. These temporary self-created alliances become unstable, injurious, and detrimental to others. Often the allies themselves become enemies.

False system of problem solving. Using triangulation may provide immediate gratification or quicker results. However, the long-term success of triangulation is virtually nonexistent. The triangulating system is unstructured, based on personal agendas, and operates in cloistered secrecy, generally defying open, clear, and respected dialogue. Because it is based on selfish or self-serving agendas, triangulation can become a breeding ground for untruths.

High risk. The ministry may find itself at high risk if you have followed unconventional procedures in gaining your personal agendas. The final result may be a failed program or ministry. Or, the program may require harder effort than usual to keep it going without full support of your peers, committee, or supervisor.

Three Ways to Develop a Healthy Leadership Triangle

1. Develop Open Communication with Your Supervisor

This does not require cloning. It does not demand that you always agree with or even like the direction established by the authority over you. You don't even need to be best friends with your leader. However, avoiding unhealthy triangulation requires open, honest communication. Talk. Listen. Ask questions. Share where you are right now.

Don't be fearful of sharing your insights, even if perceived as negative. Learn to qualify your own thoughts and ideas as not fully matured or complete. Leave room for growth, yours and your supervisor's. Accept the fact that your personal processing is going to be different than others. Where your processing is faster or slower than those around you, be open and honest about that. Try not to shut off the natural and needed flow of communication with your leader. In your communications, strive for:

- A joy-filled spirit of optimism and enthusiasm
- A realistic spirit of objectivity and sensitivity
- A nonjudgmental and forgiving nature
- Openness to change your agenda and patience to wait on others
- Honesty, integrity, and humility

2. Maintain Ongoing Respect for the Ministry and Its Core Values

It is imperative that you not see your personal values, mission, vision, and agenda as superior to the ministry. It is possible that your values and vision were not clearly matched with the ministry when you were a candidate. Or, the match of values and vision is now different as you grow or the ministry changes. Indeed, maybe the ministry values or vision have changed since you began your employment. If so, pray, then consider how to bring your personal vision into alignment with the ministry.

Strive to work hard to be unified in your approach. Celebrate the strengths of where God has placed you. Consider how your personal strengths (gifts and experience) can best support the growth and development of the ministry. That alignment can best be achieved if you:

- Talk about the history and current culture with many in the ministry.
- Verbally reinforce your belief in the ministry's values and vision.
- Align your speech and objectives with the mission of the ministry.
- Provide ongoing honest feedback about the ministry in open meetings.
- Avoid discussions that tend to create ministry division or diversion.

3. Develop Spiritual Disciplines within the Context of Your Role

As a staff member on a ministry team, you are perceived by others as a spiritual leader. Others will look to you for advice and feedback. Even if you are at the bottom of the organizational chart, a "key" leader may look to you for input and insight. You can prevent unwanted triangulation by being the person God desires. You can:

- Pray for the organization every day.
- Learn to pray before or after or in the middle of any meeting.
- Study the Bible to discern wisdom from above.

Six Creative Steps to Solve Problems and Avoid Triangulation

1. Get all the facts. (Resist listening to one point of view.)
2. Accurately define the issue. (Reduce the issue to one statement. Repeat it often. Test it on others. Be confident of your definition.)
3. Bring the issue to your supervisor and leadership team until you begin hearing it repeated with clarity. Work toward a spirit of unity. (If clarity is achieved and your supervisor or lead team indicates dropping or delaying the issue as their preference, do just that. Move on to a more opportune time.)
4. Initiate dialogue from many within the organization's leadership to openly discuss solutions and options for change. Creativity is problem solving.
5. Conceptualize every possible solution with adequate forethought and afterthought. Visualize the entire scope of the issue before, during, and after execution.
6. Agree with others on an execution of the plan with a system for accountability. (Failure to engage others is where the "lone ranger" gets in trouble.)

- Exhibit the fruit of the Spirit in the context of a unified Christlike fellowship, both in how you treat others and how you share the organization's values and vision with others.
- Ask God to make you a good steward of the ministry's financial and human resources.

So, how will you react when the malice of others knocks you off your bearings? How do you regain your course? Read Psalm 141 for powerful abiding insights.

Additional Reading

Friel, J. C. and L. D. Friel, *Adult Children: The Secrets of Dysfunctional Families.* Deerfield Beach, Fla.: Health Communications, 1988.

Graves, Stephen R. and Thomas G. Addington. *The Fourth Frontier: Exploring the World of Work.* Nashville: Word, 2000.

Hall, Jerry D. *A Multi-Case Study of Clergy Termination.* Virginia Beach, Va.: Regent University Dissertation Publications, 2004.

Hopkins, Nancy Myer and Mark Laasar, eds. *Restoring the Soul of a Church.* Herndon, Va.: Alban Institute, 1998.

PART 3

Working Hard

Getting the Job Done

A little sleep, a little slumber, a little folding of the hands to rest – and poverty will come on you like a bandit and scarcity like an armed man.

The sluggard's craving will be the death of him,
because his hands refuse to work.

He who works his land will have abundant food, but the one
who chases fantasies will have his fill of poverty.

Proverbs 24:33 – 34; 21:25; 28:19

Genius is 1 percent inspiration and 99 percent perspiration.

Thomas Edison

A good leader starts by asking, "Where are we going and what needs
to be done to get there?" instead of "What do I need?"

Darren joined the staff of a fast-growing church, a leadership team known for being highly organized, with clearly defined objectives for the team as well as for each member top to bottom. The staff worked hard, admittedly too hard at times.

If the staff had a model of how to build relationships, Darren was it. He was a "people magnet." As a shepherd to those placed under his care and in his area of ministry, he sensed that his job was nothing more than taking care of the sheep.

Darren's schedule was dotted with breakfasts, coffee meetings, and luncheons with various adults in his ministry area. He could spend hours listening, sharing, and offering spiritual encouragement. Darren's cell phone minutes were off the charts.

With all of this flurry of people activity, it was common for him to miss or double-book appointments each week. He also had a habit of not returning phone calls or emails, and was often seen coming in late and scurrying around the office trying to catch up with his work assignments. The details began to fall through the cracks.

Darren's assistant became more and more frustrated, especially when people called looking for him and she could not give good answers. His calendar was a mess. Other staff began to comment on Darren's incomplete projects and lack of attendance at staff meetings. Tensions mounted in the office; feelings of disappointment and neglect were common among parishioners whose meetings with Darren had to be rescheduled or never happened.

Darren had planned to be in his role for a long time. However, he began to hear and realize he was not getting the job done for which he was hired. After his first year of ministry, he began looking for another position elsewhere. He was gone before his second anniversary.

"Get the Job Done!"

Of the many definitions of leadership, one of the best is, "Leadership gets the job done." That phrase sounds so simple, so easy. But those who have been in leadership know how difficult it is.

While no leadership definition is complete in itself, this particular one begs two questions. The first is, "What is the job that needs to be done?" The second is, "How do we know when the job is done?"

What is the job? The job must be clear to everyone involved. Ministry staff leaders will do well to ask the following questions: What is our leadership team attempting to accomplish? What is the desired outcome? In other words, people want to know, "Where are we going?" And then, "How are we going to get there?" The ministry staff leader is responsible to make the direction clear and to guide the process to that destination.

How do we know the job is done? I suppose the easy answer is, "When we get there." When taking a trip, if the destination, the time of arrival, and the expected travel plans are obvious, then everyone will automatically celebrate on arrival. At a sporting event, when the game or match is over and the favored team wins, celebration is spontaneous. Every fan has an expected outcome. Similarly, effective leadership can confidently say, "This is our expected outcome, so you will know when we get there."

The desired outcomes should be obvious, the path to victory clear, the celebration automatic. The leader and team should be able to look back, give glory to God, and conclude, "We got the job done; completed the course; finished the task."

Again, it sounds so simple and easy. But it demands hard work. The job does not get done by itself. As God's workmen, we are required to do good work.

Get to Work

I have become convinced that some of the most sincere and dedicated leaders in ministry earnestly believe a job can get done "by itself." I have heard leaders say, "Just pray about it," or "Just trust God to take care of it."

And sometimes, leaders observe with great wonder and amazement, God does just that. Indeed, God knows how to get the job done without us, a powerful reminder that we ultimately follow a sovereign God. Likewise, prayer does get results. However, even prayer, especially leading others to pray, can be hard work. Waiting on God and praying requires dedicated, intentional effort. James 2:17 – 22 – the "faith without deeds" passage – is worth reading.

> **Making Directions Clear**
>
> - Know your destination.
> - Speak the follower's language.
> - Make the directions clear and simple.
> - Write, speak, or illustrate and repeat directions over and over again.
> - Get moving.

God has given us spiritual gifts and amazing resources to do his work, to complete the work Jesus left for us to do. Spiritual gifts are jobs from God. And God's Spirit assigns a work order to each and every believer. God does not expect us to stand around and just watch him do what he has gifted us to do.

I have not met a follower who does not expect the leader to lead. If leading is hard work, then the leader needs to get to work. Followers expect their leaders to work hard. Followers do not want to hear from their boss, "Go." They want to hear from their leader, "Let's go!"

While leadership styles, temperaments, backgrounds, and methods to get the job done are varied, characteristics of hard-working staff persons boil down to a common few:

- Conscientious (sweating the details and creating a detailed plan)
- Collaborative (training leaders and volunteers)
- Committed (people see the staff person present, not just knowledgeable)
- Caring (continually focused on what really matters)

- Contributory (working and involved alongside others)
- Consistent (constantly engaged and involved in the entire process to get the job done)

Pick the Right People

You just recognized you can't do it all by yourself. You can't finish the task. There is too much to do and not enough time to do it.

As a ministry staff member, it will be necessary to recruit and train volunteers to get the job done. Recruiting the right people is imperative. While much more is said about working with volunteers in chapter 18, here are a few principles for bringing the right people onto your team.

One key to effective "followership" is setting the bar high but not too high. If you expect too much, people will become discouraged and give up. However, if you set the bar so low that everyone can jump it, people become bored and you've created another lose-lose situation. Stretch your volunteers with tough challenges that can be accomplished by using their spiritual gifts and following their passions.

The following characteristics are worth consideration if you are going to get the job done. Find people who are:

- *Servants* ... already serving and participating without being asked.
- *Unified* ... sharing core values and clarity of the mission.
- *Faithful* ... regularly attending without being coerced or bribed.
- *Accountable* ... willing to submit to and respect other workers and those in leadership.
- *Respected* ... drawing others to themselves without consciously trying.
- *Committed* ... having demonstrated other commitments in life.

- *Open* ... willing to learn and desire additional training and direction.
- *Confident* ... filling in the blanks and compensating for the lack of others.
- *Spirit led* ... having a peaceable spirit rather than a critical or self-centered spirit.

Stick to the Obvious

The main thing is the main thing. That phrase has emerged as one of the mantras in our current culture. One of the chapters in Peters and Waterman's book *In Search of Excellence* is titled, "Stick to the Knitting." The authors recite story after story of how success was achieved by "getting back to the basics." How many times have we heard that? Especially in ministry!

There are multiple truths buried in this idea: define and remain dedicated to the core values; stay focused; persevere; exhibit the courage to say no; say yes to the things that matter (ultimately, to give glory to God).

> **Ask People Questions Before Engaging Them in Ministry**
>
> Don't overlook people who are:
> - **Past failures.** Ask them why things did not work out.
> - **First-time volunteers.** Ask them about their gifts and passion.
> - **Not well known.** Ask them to share their story.
> - **Young and inexperienced.** Ask them to follow you around.
> - **Insecure and lack confidence.** Ask them to start with simple tasks.

It is easy to get sidetracked in ministry. It's an understandable liability among ministry staff with the temptation to meet so many needs and requests from volunteers. When "chasing the new rabbit" happens, objectives can go on hold and may risk becoming extinct. Before long, volunteers lose confidence in the now-current direction and, if the pattern continues, the organization becomes a breeding ground for insecurity. Everyone begins to do what they think they ought to do. Yes, *jobs* are getting done; it's just likely the *right job* is not getting done. Chaos and division build.

Here are a few suggestions to stay on ministry target:

- Keep reminding participants of the purpose and objective, not just the task.
- Encourage volunteers to participate in sharing ongoing results.
- Celebrate benchmarks along the way and continue to pray through the process.

- Applaud people throughout the entire process, not only at completion.
- Don't value change just to make a change.
- Remind people how they are connected to the big picture and final results.
- Resist majoring on setbacks, bloopers, or foul-ups that may enter into the process. However, try not to ignore the problems, cast blame, or hide embarrassing mistakes. Learn from them.
- Let everyone know of the ministry's ongoing progress. Don't hold back stories and statistics that let people know where you are, even if the "numbers" don't look good to you. People want to know the truth.

Respect the Issues of Change

How often have we heard, "Change is obvious"? Some people love change, thrive on it. Others cannot handle change and avoid or resist it at all costs.

Change can be a great gift. Newness and freshness can revive a struggling ministry. Change can also get in the way of completing the task in front of you. Another direction may discourage those who have committed to the current course. Resources could be perceived as wasted or misappropriated.

Change can keep you from completing the right task. Your challenge is to not be seduced by a latest trend or idea that prevents the goal from being accomplished. I have observed bored and frustrated ministry staff attempting to accomplish good, healthy objectives only to become enamored and distracted by something more exciting, new and improved, bigger and better. They accomplished a great victory. It just had nothing to do with the ministry's purpose, values, or vision.

> **Six Characteristics of a Leader Who Gets the Job Done**
>
> Leith Anderson offers the following six points in his book *Leadership That Works:*
>
> 1. Do what needs to be done.
> 2. Live Christianly.
> 3. Choose multiple mentors.
> 4. Learn the leadership context (where you are called to lead).
> 5. Beware of the cutting edge.
> 6. Trust God for the long term.

Right change can encourage you to complete the right task. Sometimes ministry staff can make rapid change, especially if your arena of ministry is simple and uncomplicated. However, impulsive change limited to a few staff members can create a narrow and limited response among the people.

Remain focused on moving toward the right changes. Slow down the process and carefully consider what needs to be done. Set out on the new course without dismantling everything that has been accomplished. Take your time. You are simply attempting to get the job done. Today, you are not changing the world. Besides, God will do that!

Consider these worthy principles to make change work for you to complete the task:

- Wisely consider the timing of the change as being as important as the change itself.
- Continual, methodical, deliberate change is often healthier than abrupt, sudden changes.
- Let people know what is happening. A new sense of urgency requires people to know facts and figures (empirical data) which support the change.
- Make sure leadership has completely participated and had adequate time and energy to weigh in on the change.
- Maintain a new level of constancy and commitment to the change, realizing that another change directly following this one may not be wise. In other words, make change stick.
- Give late adapters space and time to grieve their losses.
- Consider the option of adding a new ministry and letting the old ministry die a natural death rather than simply replacing the old with something new.
- Be sure to retrain and reempower your people for the change.

> *Jesus Christ did not send you to your church to start the ministry, he sent you there to finish it.*
>
> **Leith Anderson**

Additional Reading

Anderson, Leith. *Leadership That Works*. Minneapolis: Bethany House, 2001.

Collins, James C. and Jerry I. Porras. *Built to Last*. New York: HarperBusiness, 1994.

Hybels, Bill. *Courageous Leadership*. Grand Rapids, Mich.: Zondervan, 2002.

Peters, Thomas J. and Robert H. Waterman Jr. *In Search of Excellence*. New York: Warner Books, 1982.

Schaller, Lyle E. *Getting Things Done*. Nashville: Abingdon, 1986.

Making Wise Decisions in the Midst of Change

For the LORD gives wisdom, and from his mouth come
knowledge and understanding.

Proverbs 2:6

The imperative need for social change today has made almost
everyone an agent of change, in one capacity or another.

Lyle E. Schaller

One of the skills needed by leaders in the twenty-first century
is the ability to initiate and lead change.

William Bridges

Sandi loves change. When ministry programs are fresh, new, and different than before, Sandi is in her element.

As the women's ministry director at her church, Sandi was frustrated by the program's lack of growth. And her discontent only multiplied as she read the latest ministry magazines, visited other churches, attended conferences, and constantly talked to her network of women's ministry directors. She was restless and in search of a new program.

One Wednesday morning, as Sandi finished her quiet time and coffee, "it" came: the concept to bring growth to the ministry. The vision was crystal-clear—everything but the chorus of angels singing "hallelujah"—and she carefully outlined it on a note card. Sandi could not wait to tell her leaders at that evening's women's leadership team meeting.

At the end of her presentation that night, she asked for questions. There were none. Her final comment was, "That should help us grow and reach more people." And who could argue with that? With renewed confidence and boldness, Sandi left the building believing her new idea would bring blockbusting change. Surely, she felt, everyone was on board.

Sandi was right; her idea was going to bring blockbusting change. She was also wrong; her leadership team was not on board. They were in shock. They could not frame questions within the context of Sandi's apparent passion. Danielle wanted to ask a question, but feared she would be perceived as a "naysayer." Unfortunately, by their silence, the women gave Sandi the signal they were behind her, especially when Martha thanked Sandi in front of the group and offered to close the meeting in thanksgiving and prayer.

The leadership team was not at all prepared for Sandi's new program. The new schedule, format, content, and need for more leaders was overwhelming. They too were concerned about the ministry, but believed their current program reflected their core values. Removing outdated elements and improving weak areas where they had become sloppy and inconsistent, they felt, would produce better results. They wanted Sandi to lead them, not revamp the entire program. The phone lines and coffee shops were busy the next few days.

The following Monday morning when Sandi walked into her office, things looked different. Her desk and chair were gone, a card table was in place. On the table sat a small cardboard box. Inside were a cordless phone, a phone book, a street map, and a pair of tennis shoes. Attached was a small note, "This should help us grow and reach more people." Sandi got the point. She used the phone to call her leaders.

On Tuesday night the leadership team had a special meeting. Sandi listened. She led well. Many new ideas emerged, including some of Sandi's. Together, they planned a schedule to develop the ideas further. One year later, women are inviting their neighbors to the women's ministry. They are reaching more people for Christ.

Wisdom and Understanding

Wisdom is seeing as God's sees. Understanding is the ability to discern the truth while considering closely all the facts and surrounding realities. Understanding takes into account what others think and how they see. All of this is foundational to making good decisions, wise choices.

It is important that the spiritual leader knows what God says. The Bible is a guide and lamp to decision-making. It is also important to know what

<table>
<tr><td>

The Ministry Staff Leader's Resistance toward Change

Even leaders don't always welcome and embrace change. For some it means more work and a loss of some of their security. Let the following be a sort of "attitude check" before you consider resisting a needed change:

- Is this change going to be a personal nuisance, creating a lot of extra hard work?

- Are you thinking more about your personal losses and adjustments than what is best for the mission or ministry?

- Are you resisting this change because it is someone else's idea, not yours?

- Will this change get in the way of your own agenda and ministry goals?

- Is this a change which spotlights others, not you?

- Are you thinking, *This change is too risky and I am 0–3 right now on new ideas … so let's just play it safe and say no?*

</td></tr>
</table>

people are thinking. What input do they have on the subject or issue at hand? What affect will the decision have on their lives? A wise leader listens to God *and* to people.

Recently some major changes were made in a local church. Things did not go well. A board member asked me if I could discern what went wrong. I assured him I did not know. But I asked the question, "Did anyone ask the people if they wanted this change?" His nonverbal response answered the now rhetorical question.

Wait on Change

The best advice I can give any associate minister or ministry staff leader is to not make any changes within the first three to six months of a new assignment. Depending on your ministry context, it may even be wise to wait a year before initiating any significant, life-altering, ministry-adjusting decisions.

Initially, a ministry staff person will do well to spend time developing trusting relationships. Beyond that, give everything you have to your job (including building relationships, for it is from these new collegial supporters that future change will come); and only "fix" the really broken things that are detrimental to the ministry (and which have been clearly identified before or soon after your arrival).

Other reasons to wait or slow down the process include: you need more facts; you need to gain confidence of the system that will help create your change; you may discover a greater need for change while you are in the midst of making a premature change. Some changes you make will affect people's lives. If poorly done, some changes may cost more to reverse than they did to implement.

Change Gets Way Too Much Press

Change is not all it is cracked up to be. Change can bring great joy, while at the same time generate additional problems. Needed resources, volunteer labor, staff energy, facility demands, and budget pressures can all come with change.

Before making any changes, ask: will the positives outweigh the negatives? But at the same time, do not neglect considering the needs and issues of the negatives. Confused? Take these items one at a time. You should find a balance on the scale once you discern all of the possible outcomes.

Gather all the information you can before making a change. It is not good to answer the tough questions with, "I am sorry, I have no idea." Change requires plenty of behind-the-scenes investigation. Do your homework. One of the toughest courses in graduate school is called Statistics and Analysis. It is tough for a reason. Remember too, people want the facts, not your "spin" of the facts.

A good leader or manager realizes that changes do not come next-day delivery. The most effective changes take time and require long-term, ongoing, trusted relationships. Trust leads to respect; leads to understanding; leads to buy-in; brings lasting and meaningful change. However, 100 percent buy-in, or total consensus is not always realistic, depending on the size of the group or ministry. Keep doing everything necessary to gain people's respect. If they respect your leadership, they will at least accept the changes, whether they agree or not.

People and Change

The following four categories of people depict a typical organization going through change. You will need to work with each group. While it is easy to ignore the last group, remind yourself that this is ministry to the people.

1. **Visionary leaders and followers (10 – 20 percent):** They see the need for change and can embrace your new story with clarity and excitement. They will lead others toward the changes. Let them lead.

2. **Early adapters (30 – 40 percent):** They have been blessed and are excited about the ministry. They are ready to sign on to the new ideas. Go after them.

3. **Skeptics (30 – 40 percent):** This group perceives themselves as the hardworking backbone of the ministry that created the current structure. They do not quite understand why you want them to change. Communicate and listen to them. Demonstrate the fruit of patience.

4. **Resisters (10 – 20 percent):** These people love the status quo. They really do. You will most likely not change their mind. Earn their respect with love and personal care. Bless them if they leave your area of ministry.

Steps toward Change

The following are a series of eight steps to consider in making effective changes in your ministry. Each step requires wisdom and maturity on your part to navigate through the process. It is easy to jump over and around, or run quickly through the following bold headings. If you do, be careful, especially if you are responsible. Affecting change can be an exciting or a dangerous ride.

1. Recognize the Need for Change

Has nothing changed over the last several years? Has complacency set in as a major malady holding the ministry back from further growth and maturity? Have recent attempts to generate excitement or change miserably failed? Has a major crisis just taken place or do you sense one is brewing and about to explode? Is there a significant God-given ministry opportunity staring your leadership nose-to-nose and if you don't seize the hour it may be lost for a long time or forever? Are some people asking for a change? Does your gut tell you that it is time for a change? (Don't be afraid of *intuition*. This Latin-based word means "to look within" to find insight and understanding. If you know that inner language, use it.)

If the answer to any of the preceding questions is yes, then a change may be needed. When you come to that conclusion, survey the landscape of your personnel resources and ask a few additional questions. Who are the volunteers available to help with the change? Who among the ministry leadership will be supportive of the change? Do you have the time to see the ministry into and through the change? Is this a community of people who will best bring about change?

2. Form a Team to Guide the Change

Do not allow the new change(s) to rely solely on you or your office. While you could be the hero in the end, you could also become a martyr. Besides, God has called us to work as a body — together. Therefore, it is wise to form a short-term task force to implement change. (In this case, *short-term* spans the time from the initial dream to the first evaluations after actual implementation.) Here are several reasons to create a small change-agent group:

- It will not overburden people already too busy in the ongoing ministry.
- You can be selective of people with the necessary skills and talents needed for your area of change.

- A special group can be highly focused to venture into new territory without carrying additional baggage from other areas.
- A focused team can bring fresh new direction to the current issues and needs.

When you form your "change task force," make sure they are endorsed or blessed by a governing body of leaders (whether entire staff, board, or committee) so that their activities or recommendations are not suspect. So blessed, they will have a sense of freedom to discuss change ideas with the majority of the people in your area of ministry, gaining input and insight, which results in healthy buy-in.

Discern if this short-term team needs any special training or input. You may need to take a vision trip to another ministry that is already doing what you hope to accomplish. It may be wise to spend time with an outside consultant, or read some of the same books or articles. As much as possible, make sure everyone is speaking the same language. This will speed the process and increase efficiency.

3. Review Your Core Values and Vision Statement

With your new task force in place, start with the basics. Make sure that the group clearly understands the overall mission and core values of the ministry. Then bring everyone up to speed on the task at hand. Encourage questions and answer each one. Make sure there are no "elephants" hiding in the room. If issues appear at all fuzzy to your team, review them again.

Next, give the task force all of the specifics, time lines, and so on. Make sure they understand the budget and what funds will be available to tackle this new adventure. Give them a clear avenue of how decisions will be made and things will get done in the ministry structure. Talk strategy and supply them with details, details, and more details.

4. Tell the Old Stories Creating a Sense of Need Rather Than Urgency

Everyone loves a good story. Frame your ministry's sense of need from real stories. If the need is for a new facility arrangement for the youth ministry, share stories of overcrowding.

Make the stories as personal as possible. The best stories will include the names of people in your ministry. Tell how a ministry was restricted from growing by limited space. Report how a family was inconvenienced by the hassles created in the current program. You will know you have communicated

> ## Rolf Smith's Levels of Change
>
> 1. **Effectiveness:** Doing the right things.
> 2. **Efficiency:** Doing things right.
> 3. **Improving:** Doing things better.
> 4. **Deleting:** Doing away with.
> 5. **Copying:** Doing what others have done.
> 6. **Different:** Doing what others have not done.
> 7. **Impossible:** Actually doing what can't be done.

the need for change well when other people contribute additional stories or you hear them repeating your stories to others.

It is through these stories that you begin to share the core values of your ministry. It also directs people's thoughts toward your mission and the real needs of those in your ministry.

At the end, people should have a clear sense of need with a conviction to respond well, rather than a sense of panic or urgency. Ministry participants and other leaders will have time to think through what their role can be in the new venture. The Spirit of God will be able to impress on each participant the level of urgency needed to affect change. It is now time to move to create a new story.

5. Create a New Story with Meaning and Purpose

As you begin to tell your new story of change and expanding ministry, bear three things in mind. First, keep the story simple. Long, complicated, detailed stories will bore or confuse people. Second, make sure people understand what will actually be different. Leave very little to a person's imagination. At this point you may fight the tension of too much or not enough of the details. Third, tell what will *not* be the same as before. Let people know that things will be different before they become disappointed by false expectations and narrow assumptions. Prepare them for some losses before the new wins.

The new story is the *future*. It is the story of *what can be*. It emerges out of the old stories, a painting of the change you hope to bring.

I had lunch with a medical doctor not long ago who shared a powerful story of his need for theological training. I told that story to our seminary dean and to everyone I met. Out of that story, a new theological training program (new story) for professional people emerged. We kept telling Dr. Jim's story (old story) along with our new program story. A marvelous new ministry was born. Several of us told both stories over and over again. The stories are still being told.

Imagine yourself as an architect who has just drawn a picture of a new building. Everyone can now see it. They in turn can tell others how the new building is going to look. When people see the rendering, they get excited. In the world of creating new buildings, that happens all the time.

In ministry, you will be asked to paint a picture of how you envision the new ministry and changes will look. You become a ministry architect. What will the new changes include? Who will be in the picture? What will happen when we get there? How much will this change cost? These questions and more can often be painted into your new story.

Keep telling the story over and over. Soon, others will be telling the new story and reproduce your vision. Often they will infuse additional meaning and purpose. The new story can remove clogged channels of skepticism and doubt, even answer questions before they are ever asked.

At this point, people can "see" a future. Now they are eager to do something. That leads to the next step.

6. Test the Winds of Change

It is time to stop talking and do something. In fact, if you tell the new story too long and don't do anything, people will begin to call it a myth or fable. People want to see results. They want to visualize or experience some progress.

Try a few short experiments along the way. "Taste and see" events can whet people's appetite for greater changes. Besides, typically it is much safer and wiser to introduce change in short programmatic bites rather than launching a major change all at once. Consider such stressors very carefully.

Short-term wins will create a sense of security and safety for both volunteers and participants, send positive signals to your governing body that you are on the right track, and help cynics or naysayers realize the change as viable.

During this time it is also good to allow some failures. If you are just testing the soil, a small failure need not destroy the entire ministry change. Be honest and let people know your experiment failed. Keep trying new things. (If there are too many failures, however, maybe it is time to go back to step one.)

7. Communicate a Clear Plan for Change

Change agents don't let up. Keep communication alive. Place details in front of people as early, often, and consistently as possible (remember: who, what, when, where, why, and how/how much). Avoid secret and surprise tactics, sudden announcements, or rumors that could sabotage the plan.

Try to place yourself in the opposition's seat. Imagine a good reason that you do not want to see the change. By performing that exercise you are thinking through the final issues and details. Address each one. Bring meaning and clarity to your new story.

Keep moving the change forward. Don't stop the process. Sometimes spontaneous-style leaders get bogged down with the details of change and tend to give up too early. This only discourages volunteers, who then are more reluctant to try the next change idea.

8. Keep Your Promises to Make the Change Stick

How many politicians make ludicrous promises to get elected or reelected, only to be privately or openly criticized when they do not keep their promises? Ministry is no different. Keep your promises. Be consistent over the long haul. You may delegate all the details or things you do not do well. But keep telling the story!

As mentioned earlier, be careful how many changes you introduce early in your ministry. People can handle just so much change at a time. Every change creates a degree of loss. Even if the loss is good, it is still a loss and some people need time to grieve the loss and grow beyond it.

Too many changes, even exciting ones, can potentially create a depressing atmosphere. Why? People are mourning their losses on the inside while trying hard to celebrate change on the outside.

So, make change a joy. Deliver changes one at a time. Get others on board. Do your homework. Communicate old and new stories. Keep your commitments and celebrate the changes.

Five Basic Tips for Communicating Change

1. Before announcing change, make sure everyone has shared their agenda and ideas and that you have responded with a positive spirit, giving hope to all involved.
2. Keep your supervisor (and governing board) and other staff well informed of your intentions and progress.
3. After announcing a change, allow time for facts and feelings to be shared, even if it is a free-for-all of ideas and emotions. (Give people an incubation period.)
4. Incorporate people's comments, both positive and negative, in your plan's adjustments and alterations. Prove to them that you were listening.
5. With a solid and mature burst of energy, let everyone know when and where you are going and how they can join you.

Additional Reading

Bridges, William. *Managing Transitions*. Reading, Mass.: Addison-Wesley, 1991.

Herrington, Jim with Mike Bonem and James H. Furr. *Leading Congregational Change*. San Francisco: Jossey-Bass, 2000.

Johnson, Barry. *Polarity Management: Identifying and Managing Unsolvable Problems*. Amherst, Mass.: HRD Press, 1992.

Robinson, Haddon. *Decision-Making By the Book*. Wheaton, Ill.: Victor Books, 1991.

Schaller, Lyle E. *The Change Agent*. Nashville: Abingdon, 1972.

Scherrer, David. *Celebrating Changes*. Colorado Springs: Cook Communications, 2004.

13

Dealing with Conflict

A hot-tempered man stirs up dissension,
but a patient man calms a quarrel.

Proverbs 15:18

Why do you make me look at injustice? Why do you tolerate wrong?
Destruction and violence are before me; there is strife,
and conflict abounds.

Habakkuk 1:3

We cannot solve problems with the same thinking that created them.

Attributed to Albert Einstein
by Carnegie S. Calian

Keith had barely settled into his new office on his second day as the new music minister at Winston Memorial Church when Sarah, his associate, walked in with several questions about Sunday's worship service. Her questions were brief, to the point, and within minutes she was on her way.

When Keith candidated for this position, he learned that Sarah, the interim music minister, also had applied for the job but after numerous interviews, reference checks, and much deliberation, the search committee had eliminated her as a viable candidate. Though deeply hurt by the rejection, she agreed to continue in her associate role and vowed to support the new minister.

Keith shared this information with a few trusted colleagues before taking the position. Without fail, each confidant encouraged him to help Sarah find another position in another church. In other words, let her go. But because of his amicable, gracious personality and "I can work with anyone" attitude, he ruled out that option. Unfortunately, Sarah was not so gracious.

In her bitterness, she conspired against him, always quick to quietly and carefully let leadership know of any errors or poor judgment calls on his part. Keith had no idea that Sarah was creating a groundswell of skepticism, doubt, and division among the music department, church leadership, and other staff including the senior pastor.

Within less than a year, Sarah felt empowered enough by some of these negative vibes regarding Keith's decisions and leadership style that she decided to bring a minor situation to the leadership. She carefully lobbied and stated her case against Keith, dividing the music committee.

Keith was shocked. In fact, he was so taken back by the surprise attack that he could not defend his cause well enough to overturn the loss of confidence in his ability to lead. Within the next eight months, he was gone. Sarah became the interim music minister for the second time. Keith remembered his close friends' advice.

No One Is Exempt from Conflicts

Disputes happen, sometimes daily. Ever since the fall in the garden, man has been in conflict with God, other people, and the earth itself. Problems are natural, all too natural. Conflicts do not go unnoticed as much as we wish they would just go away.

Be the first to notice and admit there is a conflict. Begin by acknowledging, "This conflict is real, but does not need to be the end." Remind yourself that God is in control. Remain confident that you worship a supernatural God who can receive glory in the midst of conflict (see Genesis 50; John 9).

Conflicts between people often fall into at least four different categories.

- Perceived conflicts
- Potential conflicts
- Real conflicts which can be resolved
- Real conflicts which cannot be resolved

Perceived conflicts are just that, perceived. While perception can indeed be reality, an individual's perception also may be based on false information. What one person considers a conflict may only be another's limited or personal negative viewpoint. Simply talk through the various perceptions.

Potential conflicts usually begin with misperceptions, differences of opinion, or disagreements between individuals. Minor, petty, personal priorities, left undiscussed, can become a breeding ground for future conflicts which may become major issues, detracting from the mission and ministry objectives. Recognize and attempt to resolve these potential conflicts rather quickly with honest, open communication. Don't ignore the "little" issues, which may be huge to others.

> ### Areas of Potential Conflict for Ministry Staff
>
> - A group of ministry participants who no longer support your direction
> - A personal shift of values and vision from the overall ministry
> - Internal conflict at home
> - Broken relationship with another staff member
> - Loss of respect by or for the senior staff leader

Real conflicts which can be solved are usually the result of individuals who have drifted in two opposing directions through poor communication. Personal agendas, misconceptions, and movement away from biblical core values can fuel major conflicts.

Such differences can be resolved with the commitment of believers to work through them toward a common mission and goal to honor God and others. When things are difficult, don't make them more difficult by making promises that you cannot keep, or projections that are not true. Don't say, "It is going to be alright" when it may not end that way.

Real conflicts which cannot be resolved break the heart of God and stain the reputation of Christ's church and mission. Unfortunately, ministry staff members need to realize that they cannot resolve every ministry conflict. Sometimes God will expect you to simply let go and move forward. That requires wisdom from above, spiritual insight, and godly counsel.

Identifying the Real Conflict

To determine the real conflict, begin by taking *personal inventory.* Consider the following:

1. Examine what you have contributed to the conflict. Be honest. Confess to God any wrongdoing on your part. Ask for courage to ask forgiveness of others. Spend time in prayer and personal examination (see Psalm 139).
2. Don't be afraid to ask, "How have I made this existing conflict worse?"
3. Also ask, "Have I set a predetermined solution to the conflict?" Be willing to admit that solution may be wrong.
4. As a leader, consider how others might contribute to conflict resolution. Don't believe that you are the only one to solve the

problem. God can use others to offer healthy counsel and bring unity of heart and mind.

After you have taken a *personal inventory*, take a step back and take an *objective inventory*. It is important to see the big picture, forming an intentional, reasonable view of the circumstances and situation. Here are several viewpoints that will help you see more clearly.

1. Investigate all the facts in your ministry context. Check out everyone's story. Ask plenty of questions.
2. Try to step outside of your own ministry context by collecting data from a ministry situation similar to yours. Learn from their experience.
3. Respect everyone involved in the conflict. Let others know that you are listening and have not formed an early preconceived opinion or judgment.
4. Bring everyone together who is involved in the conflict and ask each person to share their entire viewpoint. Ask again. Then ask if there is anything else they would like to share.

Ten Don'ts When Conflict Comes

1. Don't run to another staff person or other ministry leader.
2. Don't run to your senior pastor.
3. Don't create alliances to protect yourself. (Align with God in prayer.)
4. Don't assume everything is true, affixing blame and making unfair assumptions.
5. Don't let negative perceptions fester and foster an unrealistic scenario.
6. Don't focus on who is telling the truth, but on what is the truth.
7. Don't consider revenge, punitive plans, or designs on developing justice.
8. Don't treat a conflict with a cavalier or lighthearted approach.
9. Don't believe that compromise is always a weak or lesser position.
10. Don't offer quick solutions or ultimatums even if you believe them to be the best. (In a conflict situation, people need time to process and work through a variety of feelings, thoughts, history, and personalities.)

Finally, develop a complete assessment of the situation and people involved. Be sure that you have thoroughly thought through every aspect of the conflict. Again, diagnostic questions will be your best tools to move forward through the conflict situation. In this final stage of identification, ask the following:

1. Have we considered God's Word and have we prayed together?
2. What have others suggested as reasonable solutions to the conflict?
3. Has there been enough time for everyone to adequately process their feelings, thoughts, and recommendations?

4. [In the event of an impasse] Is there an outside individual or group who should participate in resolving the conflict? Let the people involved in the conflict participate in that decision.

Two Choices When Facing Conflict: Run or Resolve

The easiest and least painful immediate response to any conflict is avoidance. In ministry situations we are more prone to "flight" than "fight," likely due to the idea that we think conflict is un-Christian or because we have not been taught conflict resolution skills. However, as appealing as quitting or running away from a difficult situation seems, it is usually far more detrimental in the long run.

So, rather than avoidance, consider the following practical steps:

- Pray. Ask God for insight, wisdom, and courage to uphold truth.
- Write down the specific conflict issues. Often it is important to keep good records and written documentation of events and circumstances for future reference. These documents must be confidentially filed under strict privacy.
- Write down a desired outcome. Write down the conflict and everyone's suggestions, including the current results, desired results, and the future potential results if this conflict is not resolved.

Four Ways to Hide and Postpone the Conflict

Obviously, the following are not the best choices, but they are sometimes the easiest, even though they can be expensive and require hard work:

- **Bigger and better:** Conflict may go away when we focus on other more exciting projects and programs. (Unresolved conflict only remains dormant.)
- **New and improved:** Conflict can be minimized when we create excitement over something new or different. (Unresolved conflict will return.)
- **It is all in your head:** Tell everyone the problem is imaginary and they will believe that for awhile. (Unresolved conflict is real conflict.)
- **You will get over it:** Tell others that the problem is no big deal. Sometimes that is true. Other times, it can be defeating to marginalize or minimize a problem and pretend that real conflict will just totally disappear and go away by itself. (Real unresolved problems may be bigger than they appear.)

- Develop a resolution process which goes deeper than the surface conflict issues.
  1. Let everyone know that you are taking this conflict seriously.

Handling a Personal Conflict with Another Leader or Ministry Participant

1. Spend time alone in personal reflection and prayer for the other. Confess any known sin. Ask God to give you the fruit of his Spirit and remove any unhealthy feelings and wrong attitudes.
2. Refrain from talking with other staff or ministry participants before you talk to the one with whom you have a conflict.
3. Ask God for courage and good timing to meet with the person in conflict. Initiate the meeting. Try not to procrastinate.
4. During your resolution meeting:
   - Meet at their choice of place and time.
   - Attempt to remain calm.
   - Offer any necessary apologies and take responsibility you may have in the conflict.
   - Ask questions and grant permission for the other to share their viewpoint of the conflict. Don't be afraid to say, "I need your help to resolve this tension between us."
   - Ask permission to share your insights and observations. (Try to not have a written list in front of you, reading your concerns.)
   - Ask the other what he or she would suggest you could each do to resolve the conflict.
   - If there is an apparent impasse, ask for a follow-up meeting to continue the dialogue toward resolution (sooner is better).
   - Take the initiative to pray together.
5. Meet again: Agree to meet under casual circumstances in order to take steps to build or rebuild a healthy ministry relationship.

2. Maintain an open door, an open spirit, and an open mind to everyone involved. The unusual may just be the truth.
3. Determine truth in this conflict according to the Bible.
4. Develop a plan of communication. In the best possible way, communicate the suggestions and insights of others. If plausible, offer flexible insights, creative options and ideas, not inflexible demanding solutions.
5. Know when to communicate to and involve your senior supervisor or the necessary committee or board. And after the conflict is resolved, ask permission to share this conflict resolution with your senior leader to learn additional insights about process and resolution skills.

Resolving Conflict Without Avoidance and Without Intervention

Sometimes God calls us to live through a conflict situation. When a conflict falls into the "apparently irresolvable" category, rather than giving up,

> ## Timely Options
>
> Pray and ask God to show you the best timing in the resolution process. The following are all good and possible time frames for resolving conflict, but each one may not be the ideal or best for every situation all the time.
>
> - **Quickly and decisively:** Sometimes you cannot wait to resolve a conflict. If you are angry, don't delay (Ephesians 4:26–27).
> - **Prayerful contemplation:** Sometimes you need to wait on God. Let this time be a friend.
> - **Period of meditation:** Sometimes you will need to get alone with God to take some personal steps of maturity before stepping into a conflict resolution process.

the Scripture encourages us to persevere. Now, I realize that perseverance can become a passive avoidance approach, but it is not meant to be. You can become very active without confrontation. (This is not an excuse to avoid confrontation, especially if God's Spirit is encouraging you to take that first step to seek resolution.)

Actively give the conflict to God. Some considerations during this process include an active and persistent prayer life. Pray daily and often throughout the day over the conflict need.

Consider how you might personally grow through the situation. Ask God to reveal new insights and truths for personal growth and development. Study the issue in the Bible. Journal and reflect on your personal responses to this unique situation in your life.

Allow God to do the unusual. Instead of human intervention and confrontation, claim a position of strength, God's strength. Let go and let God do what only he can do in his time and in his way. Ask him to amaze you and he will reveal much about himself and how he works in the "impossible."

Allow others to come to grips with their own responsibility. Sometimes we impulsively attempt to fix people's problems and, so doing, prevent their own learning-through-pain process. Don't let others miss out on taking responsibility and experiencing firsthand what God can do.

One-Step Conflict Resolution

There are times when you will need to meet a conflict head-on. There is no good way to avoid or get around it. If so, be honest, humble, and willing to listen—and desire resolution, not just being right.

Additional Reading

Kale, David K. *Managing Conflict in the Church.* Kansas City, Mo.: Beacon Hill, 2003.

Osterhaus, James P., Joseph M. Jurkowski, and Todd A. Hahn, *Thriving through Ministry Conflict.* Grand Rapids, Mich.: Zondervan, 2005.

Prinzing, Fred W. *Handling Church Tensions Creatively.* Arlington Heights, Ill.: Harvest Publications, 1986.

Sande, Ken. Peacemakers Ministry. See resources from this ministry at www. HisPeace.org or by contacting 800-711-7118.

14

Responding After a Failure

Apply your heart to instruction and your ears to words of knowledge.
Proverbs 23:12

If you falter in times of trouble, how small is your strength!
Proverbs 24:10

O, God, I really messed up this time. How will you
get me out of this one?
Richard Kriegbaum, Leadership Prayers

The ministry office hallway at Eastside Church erupted in shouts and accusations. Ted was in Warren's face. Nose to nose, they battled their differences with no victory on either side. Those who passed by were embarrassed and ashamed that two staff members would behave so unprofessionally.

Both men had failed, though neither would admit it. Now the middle schoolers' summer camp trip was in jeopardy.

Warren, the youth ministry director, had been required to provide a signed contract and purchase order to the bus company that was transporting the kids. He handled the contract in a timely fashion. However, he had procrastinated for several weeks on getting the purchase order signed. In a moment of desperation, he handed the assignment to his administrative assistant to take care of. It was too late to get the job done.

As business manager, Ted was aware of Warren's shortcoming and decided to teach him a lesson about time management. While he had the signed contract on his desk, he would not notify the bus company until

Warren completed the final paperwork with the purchase order. Ted was well aware that the bus company was not confirmed.

The anticipated arrival of the bus was now forty minutes overdue, but no bus was on its way. Frustrated parents listened to Ted and Warren as they cast blame on one another. At last, several of them agreed to shuttle the bewildered kids to camp. But Ted and Warren lost the respect of many people that afternoon.

O

Gordy (not his real name) is my hero, one of the best role models I have seen in ministry. You see, Gordy *failed* ... in the church's eyes. He couldn't produce the numbers. His area of ministry did not grow and go as expected or hoped by others.

Gordy was asked to take a demotion as his replacement was hired. Gordy hung in there. He served the new leader as his associate and he served him well. The numbers still did not produce the expected results in his new subordinate position and he was asked to step down yet again. Yet, many years later, people still tell stories how Gordy impacted their lives like no one else.

Today Gordy is a volunteer, serving the Lord in the same ministry and still rejoicing and grateful to God for his goodness. He is a wonderful example of how to respond to *failure*. He did not become bitter nor did he blame others nor did he run and hide. Why is Gordy a role model to me? I could not have stayed, as Gordy did!

Is *Failure* Really Failure?

Throughout this chapter I have written the word *failure* in *italics* as a reminder that it is not always the negative, terrible thing we think it is. *Failure* may be a good thing, part of God's plan to help each of us develop and mature, to grow closer to him and others.

Failure is inevitable because we live in a fallen, broken world. Mistakes are everywhere and blunders are not a respecter of persons. For some ministry staff members, *failure* will arrive in their spirit if not in their reality.

Sam Walton, founder of Wal-Mart, believed that *failure* was the precursor to success. Sometimes our crash, breakdown, or catastrophe is exactly what God knew would help us (consider that your *failure* may have been designed by God) to best glorify himself in our lives and ministry. My friend Don Denyes preached, "Whatever humbles me, helps me!" You may need to consider that today's *failure* is:

- God's interruption to get your or others' attention
- God's pathway to do the supernatural in order to cause people to grow
- God's test of our humility, faith, and perseverance
- God's plan to abort our idea and do something greater than we could ever think or begin to imagine
- God's way of simply saying, "Do not go there!"

On the other hand, we do equally well to understand *success*. Without simply stating the opposites or creating antonyms from the above list, success for the believer is best defined and determined by God. Our achievement should only matter to him.

If success here and now is our goal and objective, then we are aiming in the wrong direction. Our self-esteem and value is already established by God; we don't need to do anything to merit his favor or blessing. We are already totally blessed by God (see Ephesians 1:3). If our need is to impress others, then we have fallen into a pattern that will never find fulfillment.

Immediately Following a Time of *Failure*

Failure can become a personal prison; it has a way of capturing our lives, redefining who we are, and destroying our sense of value and worth as a believer and servant of Christ. During the downtime that follows a crisis, consider these activities:

- Get away by yourself or with a few friends to pray, clear out the cobwebs, and talk.
- Begin right away to journal and read Scripture in order to exhaust negative and harmful thoughts.
- Eat, exercise, and sleep (but don't overdo any of these).
- Consider reading books or articles on recovering from *failure*.
- Take a mini-trip and experience something different and meaningful.
- Ask God to renew your spirit and give you the courage to move forward.

Take Inventory

Ask yourself the question, "What really just happened?" It is not less spiritual to ask, "What went wrong?" Not everything goes right. And there are often good reasons why things do not go as hoped or planned. Ask yourself, "What can I learn from this experience?" And then, give yourself some time for the answers. There may not always be quick answers to the tough questions; there may not be any answers at all. Nevertheless, use this time, after *failure*, to grow and move forward. Some additional tough questions to ask yourself may include:

- Did I fail to listen to the advice of others?
- Was I stubborn and bent on fulfilling my agenda?
- Was the timing off?
- Were my motives (and heart) in the wrong place?
- Did I fail to trust God?
- Did I fail to work with others?
- Was there sin "in the camp"?

Ask *others* the question, "What just happened?" It is often their insight that may be the best viewpoint. Remember the old adage that it is difficult to see the forest while standing in the trees. Others can help you see what you do not or cannot see. Let them magnify your own vision. Ask them:

- What could I have done differently?
- What would you have done differently?
- Were we in line with our mission?
- Did we stick to our core values?

> ## Five Personal Things to Consider Doing After a *Failure*
>
> 1. Remain in close contact (phone, email, mail, visits) with the people in your ministry. (Resist distancing yourself, believing everyone is ashamed of you.)
> 2. Be honest and open with your feelings with trusted friends and your supervisor. (Resist believing admission of *failure* is a sign of weakness.)
> 3. Celebrate the grace and goodness of God in your life.
> 4. Claim a song or verse of Scripture. Commit it to memory.
> 5. Determine today that you are going to discover a spiritual victory in the midst of *failure*.)

> ## Bible Characters Who Did Not Give Up After *Failure*
>
> **Job** ... after losing everything, he never gave up his integrity.
>
> **Joseph** ... several times betrayed, he was used of God to bring good to all.
>
> **Moses** ... self-exiled after murdering an Egyptian, he was chosen by God to lead the people of Israel.
>
> **Daniel** ... captured and thrown into the lions' den, he kept his faith and his wits.
>
> **Elijah** ... depressed and discouraged, he prepared Elisha to continue his prophetic mission.
>
> **Peter** ... denied the Lord, yet he had a significant ministry as an apostle.

- Should we attempt this project/program again or should we graciously allow it to die and move on?

Learn to Grow through *Failure*

The list is long of those who once *failed* and later became success stories. You can find them in business, ministry, and the Bible (see sidebar on page 125). Yet the first or natural reaction to *failure* is not to find the teachable, transferable, or transformation lesson within. That needs to become a point of discipline.

To grow through *failure* requires some new habits and intentional ingenuity. Some of those initiatives might be:

- Don't dwell on the bad news. Get the bad news, ask the tough questions, and make a new, positive goal to grow.
- Bring organizational closure to the *failure*, but don't forget the lessons learned.
- Ask others what they learned through this *failure*. The best learning takes place in community.
- Embrace the need for change as a friend of the second chance.
- Remind yourself that multiple *failures* are a classroom full of lessons learned.
- Don't let others rob you of your joy or love for God and ministry.
- Keep communicating, especially with people involved in your ministry and ministry veterans who are able to help you learn.
- Create a warm and open atmosphere (in other words, be genuine, transparent, vulnerable, and sincere) so that everyone involved can grow, rebuild trust, and restore confidence. Keep talking and praying with one another.

Seven Ways to Guarantee *Failure*

1. Dominate the people around you as the only real leader.
2. Abandon the core values of the larger ministry you serve under and create your own.
3. Make sure everyone comes to you for advice and permission.
4. Think "image" as much as you can.
5. Be sure to let people know that if they are not on board, you don't need them.
6. Don't listen to or believe the people who serve under you.
7. Keep doing the same thing in the same way and expect the same or even better results.

Additional Reading

Kesler, Jay. *Being Holy, Being Human.* Minneapolis: Bethany House, 1994.

Responding After a Failure

Lutzer, Erwin W. *Failure: The Back Door to Success.* Chicago: Moody Press, 1975.

Shelley, Marshall. *Well-Intentioned Dragons.* Minneapolis: Bethany House, 1994.

Yaconelli, Mike, "The Failure of Youth Ministry," *Youthworker Journal*, May/June, 2003.

Developing a Plan for Lifelong Learning

The discerning heart seeks knowledge.

The cheerful heart has a continual feast.

The way of the sluggard is blocked with thorns,
but the path of the upright is a highway.

Proverbs 15:14a, 15b, 19

Apply your heart to instruction and your ears to words of knowledge.

Proverbs 23:12

Learning ... is about giving up. It's about surrendering.
It's about unlearning!

Peter Senge

I do not think much of a man who is not wiser today
than he was yesterday.

Abraham Lincoln

Nelson served his church well for many years. No one wanted to see him take early retirement. Yet he realized a need to reinvent his life and mission. With a heart and passion for unchurched people, he began to pray and pursue new areas of ministry.

Within months, he set his goal to plant a church. Then, as if God wrote in the sky, he realized there was not a church serving the people in a neighboring community. That is where Nelson was convicted to start a church to share the good news of Christ's gospel.

Nelson read several books on church planting, which only served to strengthen his sense of call. Then he met Randy, who was planting a church in another nearby community. Shadowing this young church planter, half his age, Nelson's inspiration, hope, and excitement flowed more intensely through his spiritual veins. He could begin to see a new church in his mind and heart.

A regional church planting conference caught Nelson's attention. He attended and learned more about the how-tos of church planting. Now he couldn't wait to get started.

But he realized he needed still further preparation. Signing up for a formal church planting course at a seminary nearly five hundred miles away, he and his wife relocated for four months to complete the twelve credit hours of master's level training. Now they felt ready.

After several interviews and meetings with a denominational church planting lead team, Nelson began his work. Three years of learning and hard work later, the new church opened its doors with 127 attendees. The people in that community are hearing a new, life-changing message coming from a pastor who has grown and matured through personal choices and a deep personal desire to "reinvent" his life in ministry.

Plan to Grow

While Nelson's true story may be a bit extreme and radical for some, it serves as a benchmark for the principles of a lifelong learner. Nelson is still learning and growing.

Effective leaders keep their engines well tuned, operating at top RPMs. Running out of gas or oil is never an option to a growing leader. It requires a life of discipline. And discipline is not everyone's favorite word.

Being a disciplined person requires hard work, consistent planning, and deliberate choices. In time those good disciplines become automatic. Until then, for the young or new associate leader, intentional plans for growth are essential.

For every staff member, there seems to be four areas that need constant attention: *skill* (competency); *wisdom and knowledge* (learning and thinking); *spiritual formation* (godliness); and *personal development* (focus on the word *personal*).

Personal Evaluation for Lifelong Learning

Ask yourself the following questions to discover if you are on track or need to develop some long-range plans in these varied life domains:

Family

Does our family have future goals and travel plans?

Are we saving to develop a future project (home addition, cottage, boat)?

How are we connecting with our children?

As a couple, what hobbies, sport, travel plan, or educational experience are we really looking forward to sharing?

Ministry

What am I excited about that is not currently in place?

Am I confident of my gifts and future ministry goals?

Am I networking and growing in a desired area of ministry?

What are others saying to me about my role in ministry?

Education

Am I reading old, new, and challenging books and journals?

Am I traveling to places that will stimulate my thinking and emotions?

Am I networking with other ministry leaders?

Do I have a committed plan to train to the next level?

Personal Health

Do I see a doctor and dentist for regular checkups?

Am I exercising?

Are my weight and blood pressure under control?

How do I sleep at night?

Spiritual Vitality

When did I last read through the Bible?

How often do I get away to be alone with God?

When did I last fast?

Are my peers seeking me out with spiritual growth questions?

Develop a Plan for Skill Training

Coaches usually stand on the sidelines during the game. But during practice sessions, they are in each player's face, nose to nose, eye to eye. Coaches teach, demonstrate, and strategize how to perform a particular skill. Their desire is to win.

Ask yourself: Who is doing ministry with excellence at the level you hope to achieve in the future? Whose modeling of ministry skills and gifts is a good example for you? Who would you consider a "winner" in ministry? Who has God used to do the work of ministry? Who, by their spiritual gifts and natural talents, is getting the job done, a job that you aspire to do?

When I was in my most formative years in ministry, God placed Leith Anderson in my life. A man whose communication, organizational, and administrative skills were greatly admired by me and a host of others, Leith graciously allowed me entrance into his life and ministry. I watched him closely. I asked him questions. I listened to his counsel and observations. He taught me how to do many of the things I aspire to do today. Thank you, Leith.

> ## Characteristics of a Lifelong Learner
>
> The following may be a quick instrument to determine whether you are a short-term or lifelong learner:
>
> - **Constantly curious.** (Abounds with questions)
> - **Regular reader.** (Owns books galore)
> - **Open book.** (Remains open to new ideas and methods)
> - **Finds mentors.** (Develops relationships for growth)
> - **Intentional invention.** (Reinvents and attempts new things without fear)
> - **Leaves a legacy.** (Sought out by others for their growth)
> - **Healthy discontentment.** (Seeks to improve and do better next time)
> - **Lifelong relationships.** (Stays connected to people who have had positive input in life and ministry)
> - **Ministry passion.** "Does not work a job, but serves a mission!"

Develop a Plan for Growing in Wisdom and Knowledge

Wisdom and knowledge are attained through a variety of sources. Indeed, books, audio tapes, conferences, seminars, and more can provide many of the ministry insights needed for effective ministry. Yet, we can all agree, there is no replacement for a mentor who comes alongside and imparts lifelong insights and valuable lessons.

Ask yourself: Who demonstrates the ability to see the big picture and demonstrates wisdom from above by seeing as God sees? Who in your life has been there and done that? Who do you respect for their ability to lead and who has accomplished the level of ministry you aspire to personally experience?

Learning Styles

The following are the classic styles of how we learn. Create your lifelong learning plan around your best styles.

- **Visual learners** learn by seeing and make great discoveries through video, photos, art, maps, graphs, charts, vision trips, and watching others do their work.

- **Auditory learners** learn by listening and enjoy talking with other leaders as well as listening to lectures, tapes, and sermons. They make great discoveries in discussion groups.

- **Kinetic learners** learn by touching. They make their greatest discoveries on the job, doing, working with their hands, and being very active.

The answer to those questions may lie in your immediate supervisor or senior leader. Seek him or her out. Learn what they know by asking questions and observing their life and ministry choices. Burrow deep. Ask the tough questions, when you have earned that permission.

Develop a list of learning areas to pursue. Ask your "mentor" what books have most impacted his or her life. Ask who has had the greatest influence on their life choices. Seek to learn their ministry DNA, what makes them tick. This can be an exciting adventure in learning and personal growth.

Finally, take what you have discovered and forge out your own plan to read, learn, watch, and discover. It will take years. There is no quick fix or shortcut. Ask your leader to help you navigate your way.

Develop a Plan for Spiritual Formation

A variety of spiritual disciplines can help each of us grow in our relationship with God. Indeed, prayer, fasting, journaling, Bible reading, Bible memorization, and meditation all draw us closer to God and one another. They also draw us closer to our dreams and fulfillment of our life's mission.

Getting to that place is best done in spiritual community. A plan for spiritual formation begs for that one godly person to journey with us. A spiritual guide or director (or by whatever name we refer to such an individual) can keep us pointed and fixed on God.

Ask yourself: Who in my life imitates the person of Christ more than anyone else I know? Is that person available to respond to tough questions in order to help me grow in my spiritual life?

As a youth pastor in my early years of ministry, God placed two senior pastors, Bob Savage and Chuck Ver Straten, in my life to help me grow in my spiritual disciplines and walk with God. Pastor Bob taught me the importance of a quiet time and building a personal devotional life. He was

---

Venues for Lifelong Learning

Following are some suggestions of places and strategies for making your own lifelong discoveries. Don't hesitate to add other venues to the list of possibilities.

- *Get formal classroom training.* Consider a college, seminary, or graduate level course or program.
- *Attend a conference or seminar.* Ask for a budget or begin to save to attend an event that will stretch you. Invite a colleague or volunteer to join you.
- *Read books.* Commit to reading in new areas or an area that will stretch you. (Not a reader? Get a fresh supply of audio books.)
- *Visit a ministry.* Request and establish a visit to a seasoned veteran's ministry. Ask plenty of questions and use a tape recorder and camera, if permitted. Be accountable to a committee or colleague to give a detailed report of your discoveries.
- *Form a study group.* Find like-minded leaders or colleagues and develop a course of learning together. Who knows what will emerge.
- *Write.* Take on a writing project. Pick your hot topic of personal interest. With disciplined research and discovery of new ideas, you will grow.
- *Retreat.* Get away to think, pray, plan, and learn.
- *Teach.* Volunteer to teach in an area that may or may not be your expertise.
- *Travel.* Go someplace that will stimulate your learning experience. Try Israel or another foreign country, another church, even a Fortune 500 company.

---

consistent, but not pietistic. His genuine love for God, the Bible, and spiritual music was contagious. I learned the importance of reading God's Word as a primary discipline in my life and ministry.

Pastor Chuck modeled a life of prayer. I earnestly watched and admired how Chuck gave everything in ministry to God in prayer. Sometimes, as a young man, I would become frustrated with Chuck's lack of immediate decision-making skills, but that was my problem, not his. Now I look back with honor and respect for his ability to wait on God and trust the Holy Spirit to lead and guide. Today I pray like never before. I think of Pastor Chuck and his shepherd's prayers for God's work and God's people.

Time in God's Word and in God's throne room are very important in my ministry and life. Thank you, Bob and Chuck.

Develop a Plan for Personal Growth and Development

A personal growth plan requires accountability. Without someone to hold us accountable, the likelihood that we'll stall or get sidetracked increases significantly.

Characteristics of a Lifelong Coach

As you seek another leader to encourage you over the long haul in a coach/learner relationship, ask the following:

- Has this person been faithful to God, family, and ministry?
- Is this leader willing to be transparent and vulnerable?
- Will he or she ask me the really tough questions?
- Will this person not tell me what to do, but walk with me, even if it results in a *failure*?
- Is this person really interested in my life and personal growth?
- Is there enough chemistry for me to be honest and transparent with this mentor/coach?

Question: who knows you best? Answer: your family and closest friends. More than thirty years ago, I married Donna. That was, without question, one of my best decisions ever. She knows me better than anyone. She encouraged me to write my first book (and this one). She broke down every excuse I had to not earn a doctorate (she deserves my diploma). For other areas of personal growth and personal development, Donna has encouraged me to purchase power boats, take up snow skiing, and enjoy an annual weeklong kayak voyage (with the guys). Last year for my birthday, Donna gave me a gift certificate to become a certified scuba diver.

We all need someone in our life who is going to encourage us to grow and find a sense of balance in the busyness and pressure that ministry can bring. We need healthy interests to capture our body and mind, and to refresh our soul. That typically does not happen by itself. A close friend or family member can help us find those interests. Take their cues. Follow their advice. Accept their invitations or overtures to "get out of the office."

I have not only grown in ministry, but in life. I love life. I love my wife. Thank you, Donna.

> *We spend more time determining the kind of car we want to drive or where we'll take our next vacation than we do on our life work.*
>
> ***Anita Schamber***

Additional Reading

Buford, Bob. *Halftime*. Grand Rapids, Mich.: Zondervan, 1994.
Buford, Bob. *Stuck in Halftime*. Grand Rapids, Mich.: Zondervan, 2001.

Durey, David and Chuck Goldberg. *Steps Toward Balancing Life's Demands: One-to-One Mentoring for Effective Living.* Portland, Ore.: Intentional Discipleship Network Publishing, 1997.

Howard, J. Grant. *Balancing Life's Demands.* Portland, Ore.: Multnomah, 1983.

Jeff, Peter F. *Get a Grip on Your Dream.* Grand Rapids, Mich.: Possibility Press, 2002. (Also see www.possibilitypress.com.)

Paterson, Tom. *Living the Life You Were Meant to Live.* Nashville: Thomas Nelson, 1998.

PART 4

Serving Others

Working with My Leader

Like the coolness of snow at harvest time is a trustworthy messenger
to those who send him; he refreshes the spirit of his masters.

He who looks after his master will be honored.

Kings take pleasure in honest lips; they value a man who
speaks the truth.

Proverbs 25:13; 27:18b; 16:13

Paying attention to what is going on in my pastor's life makes me
feel more connected. As an associate I'm more aware of the hits
the senior pastor takes.

Kevin Finch

Joe was the most likeable pastor anyone could know. He was unusually friendly, kind, and outgoing. On most any given day he would rightfully earn "pastor or leader of the year" award. However, on this early Thursday morning, Jane, the minister of music, was not about to give Joe that award.

Joe and Jane had worked together for nearly four years. They could honestly say their working relationship was nearly impeccable. Seldom were there disagreements or unhealthy exchanges between these two leaders. Today was different.

Joe snapped at Jane about the order of service and some songs that were chosen for Sunday's worship hour. Jane argued and snapped back. Soon the two poured out laundry lists of pent-up disappointments and petty frustrations. The meeting did not end well. Jane refused to make certain changes.

Joe walked out of her office leaving a clear ultimatum that the changes would be made or Jane could consider a career change. Joe's style of leadership had shifted from a soft, sensitive shepherd to a bold, brash bureaucrat.

Jane stewed for the rest of the workday and at home that evening. After hours of careful thought and consideration of Joe's priorities and preferences, she knocked on the senior pastor's door Friday morning. Joe appeared delighted with Jane's presence.

The two reviewed the conversation from the day before. Then Jane admitted that she had not been communicating well with Joe over the past several months. Joe shared some of his stressors with the board and unkind attacks from several leaders in the church. Jane was aware of one situation, but not the others. Apologies went back and forth. Jane offered to pray. Joe prayed next.

Joe's requested changes were very simply achieved and God's people at Fourth Street Church were blessed that day.

Jane learned that she needed to keep Joe more informed from week to week and include him more in her worship thoughts and ideas. And she decided from that time forward to approach Joe as a friend and brother in Christ whenever she noticed him under pressure.

Learn, Respect, and Adapt to the Leadership of Your Leader

Leadership instruments, surveys, and literature describe a variety of leadership styles (see chapter 7). Your leader has a naturally distinctive and preferred style, as well as a secondary or backup style. A wise leader knows when to properly use any given style at any given time. The staff member does well to understand which leadership style is being employed throughout the course of a ministry season, specific task, or particular project.

For this discussion, four leadership styles will be identified for top ministry leaders. They are:

Authoritarian: There is primarily one person who makes the decisions, your leader, regardless of all of the team methods employed. Production matters most. Leadership clearly begins at the top and moves down. Most ideas come from behind the leader's desk. Staff members are hired to carry out the leader's ideas.

This leader's motto is clear: "Get the job done, no matter what!"

Danger: People leave sooner or later.

Controller: The leader needs to be aware and ultimately "in control" of every aspect of the ministry. Details matter. This can be a team approach, but there is no question who the team leader is. Associates may have the idea and strategy to achieve success, but the leader takes control of the project.

This leader's motto is often: "We need to be more efficient."

Danger: Effectiveness is sacrificed for efficiency.

Gentle shepherd: The leader is concerned about the personal and spiritual condition of everyone connected to his or her ministry. People matter more than programs. Job descriptions and organizational management are secondary, if valued at all.

This leader's motto is, "Everyone is valued and important to the team."

Danger: Organizational chaos may appear in due time.

Visionary: The leader jumps toward a new idea most every day. Dreams are very important. "New and improved" with "bigger and better" programs are constant mantras for this leader.

This leader's motto is simple: "We need to conquer that mountain."

Danger: The most recent "mountain" has not been cared for since the last victory.

Develop Respect and Understanding

The ministry staff member's goal is to respect, understand, accept, and support his or her leader's leadership style. Though occasionally difficult, it's a necessary task. One deterrent may be a charismatic leader who is also a strong extrovert. Such a leader appears very secure yet can be quite intimidating, sometimes subconsciously so.

The staff member ought to consider the following four questions as he or she seeks to move toward mutual understanding:

- What do I perceive as my leader's ultimate objective and desired outcome?
- Are my personal objectives in conflict with my leader's goals and objectives?
- Is my leader under unusual stress or demands from other ministry leaders or personal matters of concern?
- Is there missing information which may require a question for clarification or input to gain a better understanding?

The ultimate desired outcome in the relationship between you and your leader is mutual respect. As you work toward that outcome, always give your leader the benefit of the doubt and don't let your style preference get in the way.

Learn to Take Proper Initiatives

Most healthy leaders appreciate an associate who displays wise and helpful initiatives. I always appreciated staff members or volunteers who were open to pushing the limits toward excellence. However, some hold back out of personal fears or negative experiences from the past.

In order to show honest and healthy initiatives, consider the following:

- Seek to establish as much informal time with your leader as possible. Don't give up too early in this endeavor. Let your leader know that you appreciate his or her wisdom and insight and desire to learn more. This will grant opportunities to share your thoughts and ideas.
- Share your thoughts, dreams, goals, aspirations, and insights. Don't hold back when you have the opportunity with your leader. However, try not to dump all of those great ideas at once.

Showing Respect for Your Leader

- Speak well of your leader. Learn to enhance his/her reputation.
- Fulfill your leader's requests without complaining or grumbling.
- Seek to do more than what is asked or expected.
- Maintain your leader's confidence.
- Let your leader know that you are dependable.
- Run ideas by your leader first, to consider his or her insights and input, before running those ideas by others. (This will also protect you from unnecessary objections or oversights.)
- Remember: when you show respect for your leader, others will respect you and show you the same respect.

Understanding Your Leader

A wise associate will often do one of the following:

- Ask the leader questions for clarification or directions.
- Ask the leader's permission to share opinions, ideas, or general information.
- Repeat back to the leader what just happened.
- Ask the leader the desired outcome of a new decision or direction.
- Offer to gather more information or request more time before a decision is made.
- Offer to the leader, rather than others, your honest frustration or concern.
- Demonstrate a willingness to change your style or preferences rather than trying to change your leader.

- Read, read, and read. Talk to others. Gain unusual insight to your area of ministry, so you have something worthwhile to share. Ask what your leader is reading. Share the same new discoveries through literature.
- Ask your leader to share his or her dreams and goals. Ask the background, history, and turning points behind your leader's objectives.
- Be loyal, consistent, and full of integrity with your communication and commitments. Assure your leader that you are trustworthy with information and initiatives that are shared. Show confidentiality. That will lead to more sharing and greater depth of relationship.
- Share your story, dreams, and aspirations for the future. Let your leader know your depth of commitment and desire to share this ministry.
- Communicate in writing when you cannot communicate face to face. Keep your information clear, logical, and moving toward the big idea or main issue that is important for your leader to know.
- Serve your leader without patronizing or compromising your standards or the mission's core values.
- Offer to pray with your leader and/or ask how you can pray for your leader.
- Keep initiating time together. Just because "today" was a good day does not mean that will continue on an even keel. Nurture the relationship. Forget your frustration or unrealistic expectations of a busy or "distant" leader.

Seven Ways to Love Your Leader (or Bless Your Boss)

1. Anticipate important meetings and initiate getting together.
2. Submit periodic updates of your activities without being asked to do so.
3. Request personal or ministry prayer needs from your leader and initiate sharing your own personal and ministry prayer requests.
4. Let your leader know when he or she has taught you valuable insights along the way.
5. Look for an occasional opportunity to share something that has nothing to do with ministry, but everything to do with you or your leader.
6. When you see your leader under stress (often obvious), offer a specific way to help reduce the load.
7. Extend the invitation to include your leader in your ministry.

- Choose to love your leader (read 1 Corinthians 13).

Include Your Leader in Your Ministry

Everyone wants to be included and that includes your leader. It is your opportunity to create shared experiences with your leader. Invite, include, and involve your leader whenever you can. When a leader is not included, it is possible the following three thoughts may come to the leader's mind:

- My associate does not respect me.
- My staff member is not supporting our corporate mission and objectives.
- This staff person is out to establish his or her own kingdom and is not a team player.

It is not difficult to include your ministry leader. Keeping him or her informed of goings-on makes for a great "no surprise" policy. Ask your leader for advice. Invite the leader to your ministry events or programs (make it a personal invitation). Ask the leader to participate by speaking, praying, or even sharing a small part.

One time my youth pastor asked me, as his immediate supervisor, to work in the kitchen on a youth retreat. My wife joined me and we had the time of our lives. I sensed a greater respect and connection for the youth leader.

Remember your leaders, who spoke the word of God to you. Consider the outcome of their way of life and imitate their faith.

Hebrews 13:7

How Not to Offend Your Leader When You Disagree

Your leader will respect you for your honesty, if carried out in the following manner:

- Believe that it is okay to disagree over important issues.
- Share your disagreement privately.
- Leave your negative emotions at the door or at the altar of prayer.
- Do your homework to build your case and understand your leader's position.
- Be convinced that your input is not self-serving and may be a positive contribution to your leader or the ministry at large.

Additional Reading

Arterburn, Stephen. *Being God's Man by Pursuing Friendships*. New York: Random House, 2003.

Badowski, Rosanne and Roger Gittines. *Managing Up: How to Forge an Effective Relationship with Those Above You*. New York: Random House, 2004.

Hathaway, Patti and Susan D. Schubert. *Managing Upward: Strategies for Succeeding with Your Boss.* Mississauga, Ont.: Crisp Learning, 1992.

Peddy, Shirley. *The Art of Mentoring: Lead, Follow and Get Out of the Way.* Corpus Christi, Tex.: Bullion Books, 1999.

Rosenau, Jeff. *Building Bridges, Not Walls: Learning to Dialogue in the Spirit of Christ.* Colorado Springs: NavPress, 2003.

Working with Other Ministry Staff Leaders

Do not slander a servant to his master, or he will curse you,
and you will pay for it.

Proverbs 30:10

Two are better than one.

Ecclesiastes 4:9

Who ought to be the tenor in the quartet? Obviously,
the man who can sing tenor.

Henry Ford

Justin had been at Pine Mountain Community Church for about eleven months. As youth pastor, it was his responsibility to coordinate the annual high school mission trip. The only problem was that Justin had never participated in a mission trip, much less led one. This was all-new territory to the young, rather inexperienced staff member — and he was definitely struggling. Though he knew Linda, the missions coordinator, could be a resource, he wanted to prove to the volunteer leaders and parents that he could do this by himself.

Linda had served at Pine Mountain for the past nine years. She was well respected for her creativity and administrative gifts, a rare combination. Not only did Linda know how to cross every "t" and dot every "i" but she had an unlimited imagination. Sensing Justin's frustration at a recent staff meeting, she prayed that he would sense God's wisdom and direction. After the meeting, she offered him her help.

At first Justin struggled with Linda's offer. After all, *he* was the youth pastor, not Linda. This was a *youth* mission trip. He had read the mission training manuals and talked with other youth pastors who had led similar teams.

Finally, more out of desperation than a collegial spirit, Justin knocked on Linda's office door and stumbled through a request for assistance. Linda graciously agreed. Slowly Justin began to understand he had a partner in ministry and she was just two doors away. He recognized he could not and should not do everything. He also learned how the body of Christ can work.

Linda quietly worked in the background on Justin's behalf. (Later he admitted his pride and announced to others how she had bailed him out

> **Essential Questions for Healthy Staff Relationships**
>
> - Are you perceived as comfortable and friendly, with a sense of humor?
> - Do others include you in their plans and/or confide in you?
> - Do you patiently listen and sacrificially spend time with others?
> - Do others perceive that you value their input, to the point of action?
> - Do you have other staff members on your calendar without an agenda?
> - When you are with other staff members are you often behind your desk?
> - Are you perceived by others as spending time with all staff, or just a few?
> - Have you ever asked another staff person to forgive you, or initiated an apology for your wrong action or unkind words?

of a tough situation.) They became the best of friends. Parents and youth sponsors discovered how Justin utilized Linda's expertise and talents. Justin gained the volunteer leaders' respect for his collaboration with Linda. Everyone won. The trip was an enormous success. God was pleased.

"Teamship"

Good leadership is all about "teamship." *Teamship* first recognizes there are others providing ministry leadership besides you or your team leader. Second, *teamship* believes that "we" can do far better leading than "I."

If there are at least three people on your ministry staff, that means that you as a ministry staff member will work *with* a leader and work *alongside* another ministry staff person. With two or more, you have a team. In the previous chapter, we discussed the team of two. The team just expanded with that third staff member. The question is, How will you work together? Whose confidence will you build? To whom will you show loyalty and commitment? How will you cooperate with others?

Job Descriptions of One Another

Know the job description of other ministry staff. Become aware of their responsibilities and expectations, their day-to-day routines. Then, share your job description with other staff. It is not healthy for the community when staff members question the role or responsibilities of other staff.

In addition, some staff will be expected or required to offer services outside of their regular job description. Be especially sensitive and courteous to those who may be shouldering additional responsibilities. Extend your encouragement and help as you are able.

Giftedness of One Another

In ministry, a job description may minimally reflect an individual's overall contribution to the team. While staff members are responsible to fulfill the responsibilities of their job descriptions, they likely possess specific gifts, talents, and experiences that may also contribute to the ministry of other staff.

When the part-time drama director for our outreach ministry resigned during my time as a single-adult pastor, the senior pastor asked if I would step in. Limited as it was, I had the most drama experience of our eight-member staff. Though not what I was hired to do, by default I got the job, over and above my other responsibilities. God blessed the drama ministry throughout the next eleven years.

Some staff members will be able to contribute to other areas of ministry. That requires selflessness and a spirit of cooperation, but watch how it breaks down the silos and eliminates possible "turf wars." Contributing to another's ministry says, "I can let go of my agenda in order to help you succeed." Through it, God is glorified. Others see how the body of Christ can work together.

The ministry staff accountant may be an excellent communicator; if so, encourage her to speak or teach. The youth leader may be a gifted musician; ask him to sing in the praise band or play in the orchestra. The senior pastor may love the outdoors; invite him to go on a hike with the high school youth. As Eugene Peterson writes, "And the special gift of ministry you received ... keep that ablaze! God doesn't want us to be shy with his gifts, but bold and loving and sensible" (2 Timothy 1:6–7, MSG).

Partnership with the Office Next Door
Integration Can Be a Key to Successful Ministry

No more excuses! No more awkward rationales! Informal, intra-staff coalitions can be created in a spirit of unity and harmony, honoring one another, preferring one another above and beyond yourself (see Philippians 2:1 – 4).

Sadly, it is far more natural to integrate and share resources with a leader in another ministry down the street. Often youth leaders in two churches will work together. Occasionally music leaders will come together to create a community outreach. Senior pastors will coordinate a citywide Easter event. And each of those are wonderful. Now, how about collaborating with the person down the hall?

Other Ministry Staff May Not Be Like You

The following staff members may work alongside you. Learn to cooperate and create a growing healthy relationship with each of them:

- *Carl the Competitor* loves to whine, argue, quarrel, and is always right. Don't argue with Carl. Celebrate with Carl when he is right.

- *Tony Twiddles* loves to play and waste time; he failed Franklin-Covey. Simply model for Tony that being organized pays great dividends.

- *Sally Snail* is always late and doesn't realize it. Offer to take Sally with you to the next meeting. Don't let Sally upset you by her lateness.

- *Vic Visionary* announces "I have a dream ... make that two dreams, how about three?" Let Vic know you appreciate his dreams, but don't try to bless them all.

- *Hannah Hand-holder* needs constant supervision and encouragement. Occasionally give Hannah applause or send her a thank-you card.

- *Political Pete?* No one has a clue what he really does from day to day. Keep gently asking Pete to share his goals and objectives for the future.

- *Rene Retired* was done six months ago and can't wait to leave. Ask Rene what legacy she would like to leave before she is gone.

- *Wally Worker* is a high-achieving workaholic who sets an artificial standard for the rest of the team. Let Wally know you appreciate his friendship and talk about other things rather than discussing work all the time.

- *Alice Attitude* displays every emotion on any given day. Be patient and pray for Alice. Simply be her good friend.

- *Mike the Mystic* lives on a mountaintop, somewhere. Try to join him on the top of the mountain. The view can be wonderful. Then invite him into your valley for a light dose of reality.

Integration is not automatic. It requires initiative. Someone has to be the first to walk next door and ask for help. Destroy the myth of being a leader who can do it "all by themselves." Create an interactive environment, where you work alongside another staff member.

In addition, volunteers will emerge from every corner when they see a unified whole working toward a common goal. Far above independence, integration speaks volumes to the community of believers and perhaps beyond.

Be the First to Offer Help and Resources

We often hear quoted Ecclesiates 4:9: "Two are better than one." However, how often have we heard the next verse, "Pity the man who falls and has no one to help him up"? God calls us to help each other. That is his idea, not ours. Here are a few suggestions to serve together:

- Pray for another staff member's area of responsibility. Offer to pray together.
- Ask permission to share your ministry contribution or input with another staff member.
- Invite a staff member to participate in your area of ministry, without a sense of obligation or expectation for a return invitation.
- Offer resources from your area. That may include funding! Why not?
- Keep your door open to other staff. Build your personal relationship with them. Include them in your life, not just your ministry.
- Avoid negative or judgmental comments about another's area of ministry.
- Offer to be the initiator to bring together leaders, whether for lunch or a ministry opportunity.

- Ask for help from other staff. Pride and insecurity often say, do it yourself.

Be the First to Say, "Good Job"

Occasionally, a staff member may not hear "good job" or "well done." You have been there and so has your fellow staff member. Be the first to encourage and celebrate a job well done. Let others on staff know that you appreciate them.

Be aware and observant of the work of others. Stay connected. When appropriate, attend their ministry events and afterward give a word of encouragement. When you hear positive feedback about a staff member's ministry, tell them. That "secondhand compliment" will go a long way. They will be delighted you shared. So will you.

Additional Reading

Cordeiro, Wayne. *Doing Church as a Team.* Ventura, Calif.: Regal, 2005.

Hackman, J. Richard, ed. *Groups That Work (and Those That Don't): Creating Conditions for Effective Teamwork.* San Francisco: Jossey-Bass, 1990.

First Steps toward Resolving a Damaged Staff Relationship

- Identify the core issue and confess your contribution to the problem.
- Ask God to give you pure motives and a clean heart (confess pride and self-centeredness), with a right attitude for your colleague.
- Go to the staff person, sooner not later, and avoid talking to others in the meantime.
- "Bury the hatchet" and let go of (forgive) any unkind words or deeds.
- Strive for unity of spirit (prayer) and the ability to work together (create a common goal to achieve together).
- Focus on the present, minimize the past, and find common ground in the future. (See Philippians 3:13–14.)

Establish Long-Term Relationships with Other Staff

- Spend time talking with other staff members.
- Keep your promises and commitments.
- Be guilty of going the extra mile, while turning the other cheek.
- Always speak well about the other staff person.
- If a conflict emerges, resolve it immediately.
- Dream together about the future.

Serving Others

Kouzes, James K. and Barry Z. Posner. *The Leadership Challenge.* San Francisco: Jossey-Bass, 2002. (Note the team inventories in appendix.)

Murren, Doug. *Criticism: Friend or Foe?* Chattanooga, Tenn.: AMG Publishers, 2005.

Pegues, Deborah Smith. *Thirty Days of Taming Your Tongue: What You Say and Don't Say Can Improve Your Life and Relationships.* Eugene, Ore.: Harvest House, 2005.

18

Working with Volunteers

Speak up for those who cannot speak for themselves....
Speak up and judge fairly.

Proverbs 31:8–9

Now you are the body of Christ, and each one of you is a part of it.

1 Corinthians 12:27

Terry was responsible for the custodial services at Midtown Church, a fast-growing urban congregation, many of whom walked to church from nearby, upscale high-rises. Convinced that the wealthy, white-collar executives would not clean windows or empty wastebaskets at Midtown, Terry continued to hire staff to clean the church.

Then Terry met Clyde, who was washing baseboards with a rag during a Saturday leadership conference Terry attended at another downtown church. Interested in Clyde's work, Terry introduced himself and asked if Clyde was a paid member of the custodial staff. "Nope, just a volunteer," Clyde responded. "Really, is this all you do for the church?" Terry quizzed. "Well," Clyde said, "several of us show up every Saturday, drink coffee, and handle a number of cleaning chores. When we complete one, we check it off the list and move to the next one." As the two men struck up additional conversation, Terry was amazed to discover that Clyde was the president of a successful manufacturing plant.

Terry was never the same. His myth was destroyed by "President Clyde's" spirit of volunteerism and discovery of his spiritual gifts of helps and service. Terry went back to his church with a new attitude about volunteer recruitment. He now believed that every believer has spiritual gifts that need to be used in the body of Christ. The gifts of helps and service are not limited to paid employees.

Today, Midtown Church has a thriving volunteer custodial program. Terry is a hero of the faith. He has encouraged many people to use their gifts. In addition, they have fun working together and play a significant part in Midtown's ministry. And, the staffing budget has actually been reduced.

Is Volunteerism Worth It?

Volunteers can be demanding and difficult. Some volunteers may think, *I am doing you a favor,* or *you owe me something for what I have done for you.* Others might reason, *If you want me to help you work through all of this bureaucracy and limited budget, then we will do this my way and in my time.* With all of that and more, it is sometimes easier to conclude, "I will do this myself" or "Let's just hire someone to do what we want done."

Nonetheless, God has called ministry leadership to equip the saints to do the work of the ministry (see Ephesians 4:12). The saints include *all* believers, uniquely gifted and called by God to serve him and others. Ministry staff have been invited by God to carry out a presumably messy job.

Volunteerism need not be a messy business. It can be an immeasurable source of joy and celebration when men and women use their God-given giftedness and talents. Indeed, volunteerism is God's plan for the ministry, not just a good nonprofit strategy. Paid staff should never replace volunteers.

Recruiting Volunteers: Three Important Lessons

First, know the person you are trying to recruit. I once heard an interesting cliché, "Today's act of friendship is tomorrow's recruit." There is some truth to that statement, with the proper motives and in the right spirit. People want a relationship with you, the ministry staff member. Take time to get to know people. The saints of God are not objects or your resources to get the job done.

Our ecclesiology must be stronger and more articulate than a Madison Avenue corporate attitude. Relationships come ahead of any task. People need to understand they are more important than the program or project. I am rather sure the phrase "the show must go on" was not birthed in a healthy local church.

Second, ensure that a potential volunteer knows the mission and the purpose of the ministry. Ministry core values should be clear and evident. The program needs to make sense as a part of something larger in the body of Christ.

Third, before you recruit your first person to share ministry with you, believe that he or she can be a meaningful contributor to the ministry with or without your input. Volunteers are gifted by God and want to use those gifts for his kingdom. They can lead. They are capable of creating self-motivated workteams. You can assure those values by:

- Asking volunteers what they hope to contribute to the ministry.
- Inviting volunteers to use or discover their spiritual gifts.
- Encouraging volunteers to pray and seek other

opportunities before committing to your request. While that may be risky, it will result in greater retention.

> **Four Simple Ways to Hold Volunteers Accountable**
>
> 1. **Clear objectives/written deadlines:** Establish clearly written objectives and goals, and provide a final completion date as necessary.
> 2. **Public acknowledgment:** Give applause for people's commitment in the appropriate public arena (for example, names and titles listed in newsletters; articles mentioning names and roles).
> 3. **Peer responsibility:** Place people in teams as a way of creating synergy and holding each other accountable.
> 4. **Follow-up:** Create periodic checkpoints to motivate as well as ensure progress.

Motivating Volunteers toward Meaningful Service

Very few people are delighted with ineffective efforts or incompetence. Volunteers know when ministry is not going well. Without good motivational leadership, they will remain discouraged or simply quit after they have made every possible effort to succeed. To ensure volunteers get the most out of their experience and that the ministry benefits most from their involvement (win-win), the ministry staff member should:

- Give clear directions and expectations which tie into the overall mission.
- Encourage volunteers to pursue their passion and giftedness.
- Allow volunteers to establish their own goals and objectives within the boundaries of the overall objectives of the mission.
- Grant confidence with adequate training and resources.
- Build into the calendar points of celebration and rest.

- Create a flexible work environment by allowing volunteers to create the rules.
- Enhance reputations by creating meaningful roles and titles for volunteers.
- Include volunteers in the life and ministry of paid staff and other leadership.

Honor Volunteers

"Well done, good and faithful servant!" Volunteers love to hear these words of Jesus from the New Testament parable (see Matthew 25:21, 23). As a ministry staff member, think about this message of affirmation from two perspectives. The first is your expectation of a particular volunteer. You desire that they do well, do good, and remain faithful to their ministry commitment while remaining faithful to God and others.

What Volunteers Expect from You

- Belief in a clear simply stated vision and purpose for the recruited task
- A positive spirit and environment to work
- Respect and confidence that they can contribute more than requested
- An opportunity to offer suggestions or opinions to improve on your ideas
- Ongoing encouragement and positive feedback
- To know their name and their story as well as the opportunity to know your story, and together to create a new story
- Honesty, loyalty, and integrity
- Quality and excellence which goes beyond "good enough"
- The opportunity to leave and volunteer in another area of ministry without pressure or guilt
- Permission to lead (when applicable)

The second perspective is that of the volunteer. They desire to look back and see a ministry done well with excellence, reflecting good work(s) and proving their faithfulness, marked by completeness, authenticity, and fulfillment.

Just any "praise" is not necessarily good praise. "Thank you for your efforts" or "Thank you for helping" can almost be an insult to a hardworking volunteer. From the time we were children, most of us were taught to say, "Thank you." It is the most basic response to a kindness performed on our behalf or at our request. However, "thank you" can wear thin after a while. Think about it. "Thank you" alone does not speak to the depth or quality of one's service. "Thank you" may overlook the sacrifice and hardship a volunteer has given. "Thank you" is inadequate for the personal investment of time, talent, and treasure.

Be specific in what the person has recently accomplished. Spend some time with the volunteer and try to resist a hit-and-run moment of praise. Next time, exonerate with, "Good job on …!" or "Well done with …!" or "Way to go! I am thrilled with …" or "You do great work by …" or "Your ministry has brought so much joy to me and others by your …" Fill in the blanks.

Let volunteers know that you really notice what they have done. When you do, you may see some new smiles and renewed joy. Confidence will grow. Added partners in ministry will emerge. And, don't forget, coffee, donuts, or lunch can go a long way, as long as you spend that fellowship time with them.

> ## Encouraging Volunteers Should Become a Lifestyle
>
> Ministry staff will do well to incorporate the following into daily routines:
>
> - Create a prayer list from your volunteer list.
> - Set aside at least one day each week (or month) to send volunteers a note, regardless if volunteer service has been recently performed.
> - Always send a note to people after each meeting. (After every appointment, my administrative assistant places an addressed envelope and a note card on my desk.)
> - Use voicemail, email, and other means to show appreciation.
> - Systematically invite volunteers to meet for coffee, breakfast, or lunch *without* an agenda.

Make Volunteerism Personal

Volunteers are people. They have personal lives. They experience pain and joy just like a paid staff member. During those times, they need encouragement and a personal touch, just like you. During those tough times, call, visit, spend time with your volunteers.

Every volunteer will not be your best friend. Some will. However, every volunteer has a desire to know you and have you know them, some more than others. So, invest in their lives, not just a ministry program or event.

Create Professional Training

As much as possible, train volunteers at the same level of training you have experienced. Create a modest budget for volunteer training courses, conferences, and professional materials. Volunteers need many of the same tools the paid staff member uses for effective ministry. So seriously consider:

- Taking or sending volunteers to your next ministry training conference.

Five Simple Ways to Abuse Volunteers

1. *Listen to me!* Be the "know it all leader" and never ask for the input or opinions of others, just give them work to do.

2. *Work for me!* Demand they do exactly what you expect, in your way and in your time, and if they don't, act upset or disappointed.

3. *Look at me!* Make sure that you are the only "upfront" person, and refuse to acknowledge the hard work and names of others.

4. *Be loyal to me!* Treat critics and complainers like the enemy, and don't invite them to participate again. Create a negative spirit which says, "We don't need you!"

5. *Trust me!* Maintain you are the boss, and remain aloof by running things from behind your desk, being careful to avoid hard work or making mistakes.

- Purchasing the same books and periodicals on your shelf for volunteers.
- Involving volunteers on "vision trips" to visit and dialogue with other ministry contexts.
- Empowering volunteers with a ministry budget to make needed purchases.

Volunteers Take Time

Volunteers are expensive. They take time, lots of time. If they don't, then they will not be around much longer. One of their "paychecks" is time with you, the leader.

Honor volunteers with your time. Focus on each one as a unique, important individual created by God. Let them know you care about them. That may be all they need to move forward with their gifts and talents. Above all, love them and treat them as you would expect to be treated.

When attitudes are bad, there may be good reason. When turnover is high and production low, consider reevaluation of your leadership style or techniques.

Ann C. Humphries, The Prior Report

Additional Reading

Bolton, Barbara. *Care and Feeding of Volunteers: Recruiting, Training, and Keeping an Excellent Volunteer Ministry Staff.* Cincinnati: Standard, 2001.

Haggard, Ted. *The Life Giving Church: Rebuilding Your Church from the Inside Out.* Ventura, Calif.: Regal, 2001.

Maxwell, John C. and Les Parrott. *Twenty-five Ways to Win with People: How to Make Others Feel Like a Million Bucks.* Nashville: Thomas Nelson, 2005.

McGinnis, Alan Loy. *Bringing Out the Best in People.* Minneapolis: Augsburg Fortress, 1995.

Principles for Running a Good Meeting

As a staff member and volunteer team leader, you will be expected to run committee or organizational meetings. The following insights can contribute to a good meeting:

- Announce the times (including end time) and place in advance.
- Send out an advance agenda. Include on it people's names who are expected to attend as well as who is responsible for a discussion item or assignment.
- Create an atmosphere of warmth and focus by providing beverages and/or refreshments; a clean, organized room; and materials at each seat. Be sure you are always the first in attendance to greet and show appreciation to each participant as they arrive.
- Try to open every meeting with a meaningful time in prayer, considering the special and personal needs of volunteers.
- Employ as many questions as possible to encourage open discussion.
- Demonstrate good listening skills, while keeping the meeting on task and moving forward.
- Let attendees know you are well prepared, but not eager to "sell" or "tell" everything you have discovered and learned.
- Create assignments for a future meeting rather than getting bogged down on an enormous emerging task or difficult-to-solve problem.
- Consider giving volunteers an opportunity to run the meeting.

Parrott, Les. *Motivating Volunteers in the Local Church.* Kansas City, Mo.: Beacon Hill, 1991.

Tepper, Joyce. *Big Book of Volunteer Appreciation Ideas.* Ventura, Calif.: Regal, 2004.

Wilson, Marlene. *How to Mobilize Church Volunteers.* Minneapolis: Augsburg Fortress, 1990.

Wilson, Marlene. *Volunteer Orientation and Training.* Loveland, Colo.: Group, 2005.

Serving the Governing Leaders

Like the coolness of snow at harvest time is a trustworthy messenger
to those who send him; he refreshes the spirit of his masters.

Proverbs 25:13

But the LORD forbid that I should lay a hand on the LORD's anointed.

As surely as I valued your life today, so may the LORD value
my life and deliver me from all trouble.

Words of David after again sparing Saul's life,
1 Samuel 26:11, 24

Russ was beginning his second year as chairman of the board of elders. Paul was beginning his third year as middle school pastor. The two had never exchanged more than a handshake and brief pleasantries before their lunch meeting that day.

Paul had a few apprehensions about this appointment. Why did Russ insist they meet the week before Paul's middle school retreat? Paul had heard about Russ's direct, forthright style of leadership. He was not hungry when the server came for their order.

Russ indeed had an agenda, but it was a soft one. It was true that several parents had gone to him about the middle school ministry, concerned with some of Paul's impulsive decisions and ill-conceived programs and confident in Russ's ability to effectively intercede. Though they should have gone directly to Paul, Russ decided to hear Paul's story himself. He was simply doing his job as chair.

Over lunch Russ tried to get to know Paul better, to more fully under-stand his passion for the youth in the community. He asked Paul many ques-tions about life and ministry. Paul misunderstood Russ's heart and sincere desire to establish a well-grounded relationship, and became very defensive. This took Russ by surprise.

Paul did not eat his lunch, his stomach was in such knots. In fact, he couldn't wait for the meeting to end. It was the worst day of his ministry; the "honeymoon" was clearly over. In fact, he had his first thought of quitting. When he returned to the church offices, he shared his "awful experience" with two other staff members, who consoled him and shared about a simi-lar lunch meeting they had with Russ. Together, they wrongly judged and maligned Russ's character and actions.

Unfortunately, this story has no "happily ever after" ending. Paul en-dured three years of avoiding Russ. Russ spent three frustrating years un-successfully attempting to facilitate and redirect parents with the middle school ministry problems.

Ultimately Russ fulfilled his term as chair. He is still at the church. Paul eventually accepted a call to another church. Unity, shared vision, and growth were never achieved. These men were not able to serve one another.

Understand Where Lay Leaders Begin

"How did he or she become a governing leader of this ministry?" a staff person may ask with a tone of consternation. Sometimes, knowing the an-swer to that question can save a lot of grief and misunderstandings. It is good to know that your governing leader is in that position today because he or she was a:

- Patriarch or matriarch of an influential family in the community or ministry
- "Favorite son or daughter" born and raised in and around the ministry, with a proven family track record of faithful service
- Natural leader who has volunteered for numerous tasks
- Friend or colleague of a current leader
- Community leader or business professional known for being successful

While these qualifications may not always reflect the most spiritual rea-sons to be in a ministry governance role (on boards and committees), they are nonetheless a reality. Just remember that these people are in governing positions only by the sovereignty and providence of God. They are not the enemy. The next step is to give them your honor, respect, and allegiance.

Offer a Constructive Role to a Governing Leader

Assuming leaders desire to participate in your ministry, consider offering various (if not all) governing leaders a personal role in your ministry. Invite them to be one of the following to help and support you.

- **Ministry coach:** Ask a committed and caring leader to give you open, honest feedback and advice on your leadership style and role.

- **Mentor:** Invite a gifted, experienced leader to help you further develop some of your ministry or leadership skills.

- **Research assistant:** Invite a leader to help you explore and discover trends, ministry models, and future opportunities.

- **Eyes and ears:** Often, leaders will see and hear what you do not. It is important to have objective criteria to proceed with new plans and ideas.

- **Prayer warrior:** This role often begins when a leader says, "I am praying for you." Provide ongoing prayer requests and answers to prayer.

The outcome can be a growing ministry relationship which gives God glory. It is from that place of unity that ministry moves forward to accomplish its mission.

Develop a Sense of History and Understanding

In most cases, the ministry staff person did not grow up in the church or community. You are an outsider and have been hired on staff because of your resumé, clear calling, and the positive influence of your references.

The volunteer leaders in your church have history. Many know nothing else. They have only heard about other churches and their practices or beliefs. You have come from one of "those" churches. That may make you suspect to some.

You and a governing leader may have differing perspectives about your role. One of you may see the role as more visionary, equipping others to do the work. The other may consider the role to be very pragmatic and task-oriented.

Two governing leaders also may have a difference of opinion about the staff member's role. One may see you as a called, gifted, anointed (ordained?) servant of God. Another may view you as a "hireling," an employee of the ministry.

The more you learn about the past and discover current perspectives, the more effective you can lead toward the future. Catch up by walking down memory lane. Become a historian and participant, not a spectator. You will learn to appreciate and better understand the leadership in your ministry and their decision-making process when you:

- Ask "old-timers" to share stories about the "good old days."

- Ask lots of questions about the past and what impacted people the most.
- Take time to read some of the recorded history through old board minutes and other archived documents. I learned much one day by going through a member's collection of saved church bulletins.
- Bring people together who have a sense of history and listen to their conversation.

Communicate to Governing Leaders

Listening comes first with people in authority. Dietrich Bonhoeffer said, "The first service that one owes to others in the fellowship consists of listening to them." Governing leaders have something to say. They expect to be heard. Being a listener will only improve your ability to lead. You will gain new language and insights to unknown areas of ministry.

Ask questions! It cannot be overstated: *learn to ask questions.* Once you know what others are thinking, let them know your thoughts, then your plans. Resist interrupting their flow of thinking and communication process.

Be a team player. When you hear opposition, try to foster a team spirit. Resist ignoring an opposing comment, even with a subtle slur marked

Creating Positive Alliances

Most leadership conflicts are born out of misunderstandings or lack of knowledge. The ministry staff person can manage healthy progressive insights and communication by exercising some of the following:

- Spend time with a governing leader. I can't imagine a leader in your ministry refusing time to establish a healthy relationship. (Helpful reminder: You don't need to be best friends.)

- Add governing leaders to all of your mailings, distributing handouts and other helpful materials you produce. Periodically, send leaders a packet of information on your area of ministry.

- Add them to your Christmas card list.

- Give lay leaders copies of insightful articles or books which have stimulated or shaped your thinking.

- Invite lay leaders to briefly participate in your area of ministry. Invite them to an event—to watch, to interact, to pray, or give a report from the board to your constituents.

- Include governing leaders on vision trips to other ministries or training/learning experiences. (When was the last time a board member attended a children's, youth, women's, or national training conference?)

by a pejorative tone. Respond with, "Help me understand ..." or "If I hear you correctly, then ..." or "If what you are saying is true, then ...." Now you have demonstrated that you just heard what was said.

What Volunteer Leaders Need to Hear from You

Governing leaders and constituents need to hear:

- General ministry philosophy, mission statement, and biblical core values. (Repeat these often.)
- Inspiration and positive stories from the ministry you serve.
- Specific goals and future ministry opportunities.
- Accurate report of successes. (Tell the truth; you will be amazed how many leaders will "check" the accuracy of your statistics or comments.)
- Detailed report of *failures*. (Yes, time to be vulnerable. It is better for you to report a loss or *failure* upfront rather than leaders receiving a secondhand report from disgruntled participants.)
- Honest reports of needs and prayer requests.
- Appreciation for resources and volunteers rather than complaints about lack of funding and incapable volunteers (who, by the way, are often the leader's best friends or relatives).
- A request for feedback. (Ask leaders, "What are you hearing, or what do you personally perceive from my area of ministry?")

Healthy communication can only develop a stronger alliance between you and a governing leader to move forward, and if not today, then in the future. It may also help you conclude, "I am not going any further with this idea … at least, not now."

Report, report, report. Engage governing leadership in your ministry goals and plans by regularly informing them. There is no substitute when it comes to sharing the ministry. While others will talk about your ministry, you will give the best perspective of purpose and direction. No one should be able to passionately share your area of ministry better than you. If you remain silent, others may give a report by default, and you may not be pleased with their story.

Take extra time and effort to prepare written reports. Give leaders something to take with them. This will ensure accuracy of their secondhand report to others. A well-written ministry summary also communicates that you are mature and intentional, that you value the ministry's plans and results, and that you respect the leadership enough to care. Serve your governing leaders with accurate information, memorable insights, and inspiring anecdotes.

Remember, the quality and quantity of your communication will affect the quality and quantity of service by the governing leaders. That service will ultimately support and resource you. Mutual service and respect result in a mission accomplished.

No Surprises!

Very few lay leaders like to be surprised. They want to be the first to hear your ideas, dreams, and future expectations. Without question, it is much easier and seems to be more expedient to plan, dream, and create ministry with other staff or volunteers who work alongside you. However, when that happens, the governing leadership is the last to know. That is when questions, doubts, and divisions occur. That is when you become defensive.

There are advantages to sharing your dreams and opportunities with the governing leadership. Mature leaders with a sense of history and experience will be able to contribute valuable insights that may help you broaden your ministry objective. You may also gain alliances and allegiance from leadership who will become strong advocates in the face of objections and misperceptions from ministry constituents. While all of that may require patience (a fruit of God's Spirit), you will discover:

- Fewer objections from leadership
- A less defensive response from you or others
- A stronger plan marked by forethought and afterthought
- A strengthened dream that may become a reality
- A positive reputation marked by careful process and planning, revealing respect for the ministry's governing body

Finally, win the hearts of your leaders. People do not serve to squelch your dreams (at least most don't). While each leader must examine his or her own heart, the ministry staff member can do much to inspire, inform, include, and invite governing leaders to become a part of the ministry. Create insiders, not outsiders!

Additional Reading

Carver, John. *Boards That Make a Difference* San Francisco: Jossey-Bass, 1997.

Lay Leaders Can Contribute to Your Ministry

"You can't get anything accomplished through the board!" is often reported by ministry staff who need immediate action to an idea. However, with better advance planning and dialogue with leadership, you will gain the following from your governing team:

- Wisdom, greater understanding, and experiential insight from the broader constituency
- Unexpected resources
- Policy support and protection
- Positive promotion and excitement
- Unity and consensus
- Prayer support and personal appreciation
- "Warm fuzzies"

Serving Others

De Pree, Max. *Called to Serve: Creating and Nurturing the Effective Volunteer Board.* Grand Rapids, Mich.: Eerdmans, 2001.

Getz, Gene. *Elders and Leaders.* Chicago: Moody Press, 2003.

Strauch, Alexander. *Biblical Eldership.* Littleton, Colo.: Lewis and Roth, 1995.

Strauch, Alexander. *The New Testament Deacon.* Littleton, Colo.: Lewis and Roth, 1992.

Webb, Henry. *Deacons: Servant Models in the Church.* Updated edition. Nashville: Broadman and Holman, 2001.

www.BoardSource.org

Giving Responsibility to Others

A ruler who oppresses the poor is like driving rain that leaves no crops.

A stingy man is eager to get rich and is unaware that
poverty awaits him.

Proverbs 28:3, 22

Treat people as if they were what they ought to be,
and you help them to become capable of being.
Johann von Goethe, poet, dramatist, scientist

Penny was overwhelmed by the insurmountable tasks facing the senior adult ministry. She kept saying, "I am only one person. I cannot do what you people want me to do." Some of the ministry volunteers could not understand Penny's apparent frustration. What did she mean by "what you people want"?

Sid and Mary loved the senior adult ministry. It was reaching countless needs, including their own personal needs. More and more people were attending the expanding events and bulging Bible studies. Sid and Mary also loved Penny. This wise, gentle couple celebrated Penny's creative ideas and strong work ethic. She was like the daughter they never had. Yet they perceived Penny was working too hard and doing too much by herself.

One day Penny exploded in front of a few volunteers. Mary witnessed the incident and invited her out for coffee, asking if Sid could join them. Penny agreed. After Penny exhausted her feelings and immediate disappointments, Sid asked the all-too-obvious question, "Penny, are you asking people to help you?"

Penny's response was fast and furious, reeling off a half-dozen examples of asking people to help with one task after another. She slumped in her chair not knowing what else to say or do.

Mary broke the emotional moment with a deeper observation. "Penny, you have asked many of us to do numerous tasks, and have provided long lists of things to do. Some of us, not all of us, would love to be responsible with an area of the ministry. We are adults. We run households and businesses. We are very capable of shouldering this ministry alongside you. We want to lead. But you have to let us."

Mary went on, "We are not going to take over. We respect and love you too much. But we might look for excuses to say no to a lot of the little things you ask us to do."

Penny sat in amazement. "You mean you want to do more?" That coffee hour changed Penny's life as a leader. She realized people want responsibility with the authority that goes with it. In rather short order, Penny completely reorganized the senior adult ministry. She not only put gifted people in charge, but gave them authority over budgets, recruitment, and training of volunteers. Penny found a new joy and refreshment in her role and ministry.

Now an army of volunteers come to Penny asking permission to start new ministries. Volunteers realize that Penny has a high value on their ability to lead, not just to work as a labor force. As soon as a volunteer's new idea is in alignment with the overall mission and purpose of the senior adult ministry, permission is granted.

Penny has a new frustration. She cannot attend all of the committee meetings she is invited to by her adult leaders.

Delegating Tasks or Responsibility?

Most everyone knows how to delegate a task. We learned that in early childhood: "Mommy, will you tie my shoe?" or "Daddy, will you help me with my homework?" As adults we request, "Will you move those tables? Would you please drive the van this weekend?" Task delegation comes naturally. Often it works and gets the job done. However, we are called to do more than just get the job done. As the body of Christ, we are called to work together, and encourage believers to responsibly use the gifts God has given in order to accomplish the mission (see 1 Corinthians 12).

Literature abounds on task management and empowerment. This chapter is not about delegating a task, but giving away responsibility. The two are remarkably different.

Giving away responsibility also implies giving away authority. For some leaders, that can be threatening or require "out of the box" thinking. Some leadership gurus advocate that good leadership demands risk-taking. Here is your greatest risk: give your authority away to a volunteer leader. That requires a strong leader. Make sure you have thought through all of the implications.

Some might react, "Give away authority! Are you nuts? You will lose control." Indeed you will lose a sense of control. We are not called to be "in charge," but we are given "a charge" to serve God and equip his people. Gifted, capable volunteers want to be empowered to make decisions and pursue their passions while offering their skills, experiences, gifts, and resources with a sense of responsibility and authority. If you give them responsibility, they want the authority that goes with it. The authority you can give them is yours. You and I are not any different; we desire the same authority that goes with the responsibility.

It is at this junction that delegation of authority becomes one of the most crucial and critical avenues to pursue in ministry. Carefully, thoughtfully, and wisely executed, it can determine the future course of a growing, expanding ministry. Ignored, the staff member will become overwhelmed and volunteers will feel used and useless.

Boundaries for Giving Away Authority

The following boundaries are important to help ensure that giving away authority is not perceived as reckless abandonment from responsible ministry. Volunteer leaders must:

- Be able to articulate the overall ministry's mission and core values.
- Accept and adhere to the ministry's written policies and guidelines.
- Know exactly what outcome is expected and what will be inspected by the ministry leader. (A ministry leader must be careful not to withhold information from a volunteer that may breed frustration or potential ministry failure.)
- Understand that, while they are granted permission to lead, they are responsible to not incur additional responsibilities for staff or the budget to ensure their success, without a prearranged commitment and understanding to make those additions.
- Create their own leadership teams and lead their organizational meetings. (That means that the ministry staff person is not in charge of the meeting, though he or she may attend.)
- Remain accountable to the ministry staff leader through good communication.
- Expect periodic inspections from the ministry staff leader.

This level of delegation is serious ministry. We are talking about the kingdom of God, not just a human program created by high-energy people. Effective delegation of authority demands prayer. God must be seen in the lives of those sharing ministry.

Delegating Authority Requires Training

Unless they have unusual pioneering skills and an adventuresome spirit, people typically best lead others to where they themselves have already been. You can best ensure a leader's success by taking them where they can bring others. That, in essence, is effective training.

That will mean personally mentoring a future leader, whether volunteer or paid. Let them observe your ministry style and leadership skills. Bring them into your ministry journey. Share a ministry project together. Include them in your life.

Budget to send the leader to a leadership training workshop or related conference. Provide resources, books, and other materials. Encourage the leader's growth and don't worry about instant productivity. Quality training takes time.

Give Away Your Ministry

You have been entrusted with certain responsibility by your board or supervisor. It can be difficult to know what areas of authority to give away to others. Work with your supervisor and consider the following as a few principles you may be able to use to empower others:

- Ask other leaders (your immediate supervisor, other staff, or volunteers) what they think you should not be doing.

- If a program or ministry is someone else's idea, give it away.

- Has the current ministry outgrown your capacity? Have you run out of time? Admit it and give it (or portions of the ministry) away to others.

- Do you find yourself in a routine rut? Train others and give it to them.

- Has a ministry continued with the "same ol' same ol'"? Recognize the need for a fresh start, with fresh leadership.

- Are you doing this ministry only to feed your ego? Prayerfully consider giving it away.

- Can another do this? If the answer is yes, then give it to a gifted person.

- Are there areas of ministry where you are no longer:
    Excited ... like you once were?
    Refreshed ... to the point of renewed and encouraged to "do it again"?
    Innovative ... with new thinking and fresh new ideas?
    Motivated ... to dream a new dream and go a step above and beyond?

I remember a leader once said, "If I knew I only had ten years remaining in ministry, I would spend nine years preparing and one year doing." I think you get the point. There is little substitute for training, and while on-the-job training may be good, you will need to judge if it is the most effective.

Delegating Authority Requires Wisdom

Some people cannot handle authority. Some ego inflated personalities will confuse authority with power and abuse the privilege of leading others. Irreparable damage may be the result. Wise and careful delegation to the "right people" will detour unwanted disasters.

The following are a few guidelines for empowering the right people:

- Learn to acknowledge the leader's commitment to the mission and core values of the ministry. Has this person come to lead or become a part of your mission?
- Know firsthand the leader's integrity and seek to learn his or her outside reputation. Spend personal time with the leader. Take a day trip or work together, just the two of you, on a difficult project or conflict situation. You will learn much.
- Observe past performance and reliability. If an awkward history appears, ask yourself (and maybe others), does this reflect a one-time event or is a pattern emerging?
- Consider the opinions of others. Always check with people who have worked with the leader in the past.
- Learn how the leader treats family members and people with whom he or she has close relationships.
- Be careful of self-promoting, self-aggrandizing individuals with secret agendas and short histories.

Delegating Authority Requires Good Communication

When giving away ministry, be sure to let others know you have done just that. I remember a time when others assumed the ministry staff person

> **Reasons Why Some People Do Not Delegate**
>
> - I just don't want to.
> - I don't know how to.
> - I fear not being needed by others.
> - My identity may suffer if I give this away.
> - I enjoy doing this too much.
> - No one else can do this as well as I can.
> - I have not figured out what I am going to do if I give this away.

was responsible for an area of ministry. He had given away that particular responsibility but no one on the staff or board was aware of the transfer. The volunteers were embarrassed. The ministry staff person had a mess to clean up. Bottom line, delegation should not be a covert or secret operation.

There Are Times When You Should Not Delegate

Yes, there are times when you are the only one who can or should be responsible. The short list of ministries that only you should do may include: evaluations; ministry reviews; holding direct reports responsible and accountable; returning phone calls directed specifically to you; handling direct criticisms; dealing with certain conflict; and making difficult decisions that you need to own. Indeed the list is longer.

Sometimes only you can make the determination which responsibilities, tasks, or roles you cannot give away. Experience will be your best friend and the counsel of others should be considered. Until then, consider these few suggestions:

- Don't give away ministry for which you must give a personal account to the board, committee, or your personal supervisor. Don't give away what was specifically assigned and expected of you and you alone. A leader has every right to say, "We expected *you* to do that! That is why we pay you."

Guidelines for a Volunteer Policy Manual

I don't like policy manuals any more than you. However, they are a necessary protection tool for your volunteers. They need not be long, but they must be respected and observed to effectively empower others. The following guidelines should be included in a volunteer manual:

- Clearly written values, mission statement, and objectives for the ministry
- Job descriptions for each volunteer leader
- Legal requirements and reporting procedures
- Recruitment and training guidelines
- Budget information with fiscal management tools and procedures
- Procedures for emergency and crisis intervention
- Guidelines and process for ministry approval and communication

Be careful of so many details in a manual that a person cannot breathe to be creative and effective. No micromanaging!

- Don't give away ministry too early. It may appear you don't care or don't have a healthy work ethic.
- Don't give away ministry because it is failing. Some responsibilities are on your shoulders.
- Don't try to give away ministry just because you don't like what you are doing. Every area of ministry is not always going to be "fun." Volunteers are called to make sacrifices; model that same lifestyle without complaining. Some days you do not have the luxury to pick and choose your role.

Giving Away Authority Means Giving Respect

If you empower another person in ministry, you give them enormous respect. With that level of respect comes trust. You are saying, if not aloud then certainly by your action, "I trust you. I recognize in you the ability to lead and handle this area of ministry. I believe in you!" Those words alone are empowering and life-changing.

Trust and respect involves cutting the cord of control. That is the first step.

The second step is giving the necessary permission a person needs to lead. It says, "You may go wherever you believe God is leading us (not just you) and this area of ministry." A new kind of freedom is granted.

Finally, trust and respect give away valuable resources. Place high value on every area of your ministry. Raise the standards to kingdom standards. Giving away ministry says, "I can trust you with this equipment, or these funds, or these people."

When you raise the bar and give ministry to another, your personal or ministry's reputation may be on the line. What has been a "pearl of great price" is now in the hands and care of another. God did that with you. Now you are bequeathing that same gift.

When you start giving away ministry like this, people will begin to grow and will in turn draw other people who will want to lead. Be ready—your ministry may grow exponentially. Be careful to take care of the people God entrusts to you.

Additional Reading

Adams, Jay E. *Shepherding God's Flock.* Grand Rapids, Mich.: Zondervan, 1986.

Barna, George. *The Power of Team Leadership: Achieving Success through Shared Responsibility.* New York: Random House, 2001.

De Pree, Max. *Leadership Is an Art.* New York: Dell, 1989.

Serving Others

Heller, Robert. *How to Delegate*. New York: Dorling Kindersley, 1999.

Miller, Calvin. *The Empowered Leader: 10 Keys to Servant Leadership*. Nashville: Broadman and Holman, 1997.

Reed, Bobbie and John Westfall. *Building Strong People*. Grand Rapids, Mich.: Baker, 1997.

www.mindtools.com

PART 5

Leaving a Legacy

Building Godly Character

All a man's ways seem right to him, but the Lord weighs the heart.

To do what is right and just is more acceptable to
the Lord than sacrifice.

Proverbs 21:2 – 3

The grace of God ... teaches us to say "No" to ungodliness ...
to live godly lives.

Titus 2:11 – 12

I believe there is an urgent call for leaders to
demonstrate the character traits of Jesus.

Rod Handley, Christian Management Report

Clark had been in ministry for more than twenty years. He was a brilliant theologian and caring shepherd. When Clark preached, it was like listening to the voice of God. People wanted to get close to their pastor. He could say and do no wrong. In fact, he was *always* right. He was right in his sermons, weddings, funerals, and in the board room. No one could tell Clark otherwise. Nor could they dispute his ability to handle the Bible or challenge his convincing arguments. When anyone tried, his caustic tongue would put an unsuspecting debater in his or her place. Eventually people were not as enamored with Clark's ability from behind the pulpit. Too many knew his heart and arrogant spirit. Before long, individuals, families, and small groups began to leave the church. Today, Clark has a handful of people who don't bother to disagree with him. He will be with those few until he retires in two years. He will never be wrong.

Perry served at the ministry center for nearly seven years. His accounting skills and background could have earned him a lot of money in the business world. Perry kept the ministry books in impeccable order. Perry also kept a secret addiction. His vice became so expensive it cost him everything: his wife, children, house, new car, and savings account. What he embezzled from the ministry center wasn't nearly the price of his losses. It angered him to think that everyone made such a big deal out of a few hundred dollars and he is still very bitter. It makes no sense to Perry that the leadership would not restore him to his job, especially after they said they forgave him.

Lois was the most gifted musician her church had ever known. There was hardly an instrument she could not play. When she sang, her pure and powerful contralto voice penetrated every heart with gospel lyrics from a biblical text. There was only one person who did not enjoy Lois's music—her husband, Wes. Wes knew the real Lois. Her life at home was not the same as at church. She did not sing the same sweet songs. Later everyone was to learn what Wes suspected, but could never seem to prove. Lois's ongoing affair was now public. Wes's marriage disintegrated. The music left that church for a long, long time.

Godly Character

Lifelong ministry begins with you and God. I will never forget when my seminary president, Dr. Vernon Grounds, said, "Godliness is when others look at the quality of my life, and they begin to think about God." That has been a powerful (and occasionally incriminating) definition. That definition not only applies personally to my life, but the community of believers with whom I identify.

Paul exhorted his spiritual sons Timothy and Titus to aim at godliness as if there was no other target in sight. Godliness will be seen, or it won't. God invites you to "train yourself to be godly" (see 1 Timothy 4:7).

That level of training requires perseverance and hard work. Godly living does not come naturally or easily. There are no automatic formulas or built-in mechanisms that cause the world to see that we belong to God and God alone.

I remember interviewing a marvelously gifted and loving believer of Jesus for a church staff position. When I asked the reason for applying for the new position, the potential candidate responded, "It will cause me to live closer to God; then I can better help others." It just doesn't work that way, does it?

A new title and position on a ministry staff does not come accompanied by a close relationship with God. Your first day in ministry did not instantly draw you as close to the Good Shepherd as you may have anticipated. When Paul writes, "Make every effort to ..." (Ephesians 4:3) and Peter writes, "Make every effort to ..." (2 Peter 1:5), they are both saying, "Living the Christian life requires hard work." Dr. Gary Meadors, professor of New Testament at Grand Rapids Theological Seminary, calls this kind of perseverance "moral sweat." He's got that right.

While some things of the "old man" disappear and new desires create a new thirst and hunger for God, we still need to establish disciplines in our lives that draw us close to God's plans and will. Later in this chapter we will discuss a few of the essential disciplines that accompany ministry. While not exhaustive, they provide a good launching pad for further growth.

> ### Becoming People of Godly Character
>
> If we're going to become people of genuine and authentic biblical, Christlike character, then we need to do the following:
>
> - Commit to following the example of Jesus Christ.
>
> - Vigorously pursue biblical character qualities.
>
> - Engage in regular conversation with people on what you have been learning.
>
> - Do a personal inventory of your own character by seeking godly counsel and advice from other godly people who will take on the challenge of Ephesians 4:15: "Speaking the truth in love, we will in all things grow up into him who is the Head, that is, Christ."*

Ungodly Character

I have never known a ministry staff person to leave the ministry because of his or her lack of theology and giftedness. Those two areas of the minister's life are usually determined before a position on a ministry staff is granted. However, I have witnessed too many leave the ministry because of moral failure or character flaws.

Moral failure is the far easier to discern. God has established certain godly characteristics for the leader to follow. Adultery, thievery, and other biblical sins may disqualify a person from ministry in an instant. A senior leader or ministry board does not need to ponder long and hard on what God requires, plainly written in black and white.

However, character flaws are harder to get a handle on. Unkind, less-than-gracious actions are perceived as uncomfortable at the time and

---

*Adapted from Rod Handley, "A Vast Emptiness," *Christian Management Report*, April 2002, p. 31.

Words You Might Hear from Godly Ministry Staff

- "I am sorry."
- "I apologize; would you please forgive me?"
- "You were right and I was wrong."
- "You have helped me so much in my relationship with God and others."
- "I have been praying for you."
- "God recently showed me something wonderful in the Bible, and ...."
- "Thank you for sharing that with me; may I pray for you right now?"

quickly sidestepped. Selfish actions or unhealthy motives often go undetected. Ornery attitudes and subtle maneuvers of sabotage may fly under the radar, resulting in no obvious or immediate harm or consequences. Only the most discerning and objective leader will be able to identify and properly deal with this kind of faintly detectable behavior.

As a ministry staff member, at times you will become the target of ungodly behavior by volunteers, board leaders, other staff members, or members of the congregation. In some cases you will find yourself chafing under these unmerciful actions. Rather than chafing, you can respond in kindness, tenderheartedness, and ultimately forgiveness (see Ephesians 4:32).

On the opposite side of the coin is your *own* ungodly behavior toward other people or the mismanagement of ministry gifts and resources. Such will require personal examination. Ask God to reveal and restore your heart to the right place (see Psalm 139:1, 23–24). Get on your knees. Ask God to forgive your sin-filled and selfish heart. If those thoughts have led to sinful acts (gossip, slander, unkind disengagement, or negative detachment), don't justify them or hope that time will heal. In most cases time may only further irritate an injury. Go to your sister or brother and do what is right, before you continue forward in ministry.

Godly Disciplines

A balanced ministry employs a variety of ministry and personal disciplines. The place to begin is with you. It is hard to lead others in prayer if you are not experiencing a vital prayer life. It is hard to teach the Bible if you are not a student of God's Word.

As a ministry leader, you will find no lack of resources on Christian disciplines and spiritual formation—from the ancient Desert Fathers to contemporaries including Richard Foster, Eugene Peterson, and Kenneth Boa.

This chapter cannot begin to supply the wealth of wisdom and insight to living the life of a godly leader in ministry.

The following are a few areas to pursue. Begin with personal spiritual disciplines before attempting spiritual disciplines in ministry. Note that each is marked by the word *time* because time is what each one will cost you. And it could result in your best times, personally and in ministry.

Personal Disciplines

Time with God in his Word. *Lectio Divina* (Latin for "sacred reading") or time in God's Word includes reading and listening to the Bible, Scripture memory, writing your own paraphrase of a biblical passage without in-depth study, and devotional reading aimed at the heart. While your role may require biblical study and research to teach a lesson, share a devotional, or preach a sermon, it is never a substitute for the time needed for God to speak to you and you alone with no other agenda. This is God's appointment with you. In fact, you may want to write it into your calendar as just that!

Time in God's Word may include reading through the Bible. It may mean reading the same passage over and over, day after day. You may find yourself on a journey in pursuit of one word, a word that you hunger and need, such as grace, or healing, or faith, or hope.

Time in prayer. I like Leith Anderson's definition of prayer the best: "Prayer is alignment with God."

Shaping Moral Character

The Bible, of course, speaks often to character issues through both positive and negative records of historical men and women as well as through actual teaching. Consider, for example, these various truths speaking through Proverbs 6:16–19:

- *Purity and Piety* say, "Keep your eyes accountable and where they need to maintain focus." (verse 17)

- *Truth-telling* says, "Tell the whole truth rather than holding back or exaggerating." (verse 17)

- *Humility and Submission* say, "This ministry is not all about you and your designs (pride) and you are not in charge (power)." (verse 18)

- *Contentment* says, "You don't need more. Better is not always bigger." (verse 18)

- *Integrity* says, "Get to work, quit taking advantage of people, and stop privileging yourself with 'personally deserved' perks. Be careful how you treat the people around you." (verse 19)

Prayer is our time to align our minds, dreams, intentions, plans, emotions, motives, and so much more of who we are with God. If we don't, our lives will wobble down life's road. That makes for a rather uncomfortable journey.

Others will observe, then comment, "I am not sure I want to ride with you."

God desires that we pray, that we speak to him, loudly or quietly, even to the point of silence. Prayer may include fasting. Learn that lost discipline. Our current culture does not seem quite sure what fasting is all about. It is time to learn, practice, and teach others.

Prayer may include long periods of meditation. Just do it. God will lead you through a marvelous adventure of quiet and powerful thoughts about him and his ways. Eavesdrop on the prayers of others. Some believe the more spontaneous a prayer, the more spiritual it is, but that is not necessarily the case. Try writing your prayers on occasion to be more thoughtful and intentional with your words. Some of your prayers will be confessions, admitting to God that you have not been in alignment. Agree with God about your life.

Time to think. The people I have met in ministry all have one thing in common—they have a lot on their minds. It is good to discipline ourselves to sort out all of those thoughts.

With a great deal of amazement, my wife and I watched a recent reality television program that exploited the inability of people to keep their lives in order. All of their collected "junk" and "treasures" were either sold, given away, or organized in new boxes, closets, or creative shelving units. The personal application is simple. I have much in my mind and heart that needs to be organized, removed, or given away.

Getting away to organize the mind clutter requires time and a legal pad. Put the date on a calendar. Go to a retreat center, local library, someplace where you can avoid noise and distractions. Hide in a corner and start writing your thoughts, dreams, frustrations, plans, goals, and the names of people in your life. Look at your lists. Pray through each item or person to properly value each one. Reduce the lists to a manageable page to keep in front of you, until the next retreat day.

Time to exhale. We all need to exhaust. That may happen in your quiet moments with God. It may mean shouting to the Lord, literally! It may result in singing a "new song" that God places in your heart. You may find yourself exhausting some feelings, frustrations, or topics of confusion to a trusted mentor or friend.

Sharing with another requires a higher level of trust than most people find comfortable. This discipline should never be treated lightly. It should never be a casual encounter with a less-than-Spirit-guided confidant.

Every year I meet with six other ministry friends from throughout the Midwest. We've known each other for fifteen-plus years and find comfort in each other's friendship, confidence, and company. It is a safe place, a place to exhaust and then be loved and accepted. These ministry brothers pray for me as I pray for them; none is impressed by where I have been or what I have done. It is mutual accountability, but it requires discipline, because it would be easy to curl up in a ball and say nothing to anyone.

Ministry Disciplines

Ministry disciplines are really no different than personal disciplines. The community of believers needs to exercise their spiritual lives. There are two realms to consider.

First, each person in your area of ministry needs to discover personal disciplines they can utilize in their own private world. They should be able to watch and learn from you.

Second, the community at large needs to exercise disciplines to meet your biblical mission and its objectives. Corporate disciplines will create unified strength, character, and vitality. Here are a few ways that can happen as a community:

Time in God's Word. This happens through more than just preaching and teaching. Encourage your community to memorize Scripture—as it is or through spiritual songs. Develop times of praying through Scripture. Commit to developing every ministry program on biblical values, principles, or truths. Teach people the discipline of asking, "Is this project or ministry what God wants us to do? Is what we are doing in accordance with the truths of the Bible?"

Time in prayer. Teach your community to fast and pray. Continually ask the question, "Are we a community that prays or a praying community?" You decide, then figure out how to become the latter.

Time to think. Planning retreats or mapping days are effective ways to bring ministry participants together to think, dream, talk, and design ministry for the future. Begin by identifying what already exists. From there, identify your mission, where you need to go, and suggestions about how to get there. Let people talk. Ask good questions. You might be amazed what people suggest. The unity and excitement will become contagious.

Time to exhale. Like any good exercise program, there is the need to exhale. People need to let off some steam; it's natural and healthy. Too often, it is avoided.

Once or twice a year, create a safe environment for people to share their thoughts and feelings. Ask questions. Give people permission and encouragement to talk. Resist becoming defensive. Write everything on a large white board, newsprint, or overhead projector (that is when they feel heard). When everyone is "exhausted," stop and pray about each listed item. Next, respond to the community with a commitment to appropriately address every item.

Additional Reading

Bounds, E. M. *Powerful and Prayerful Pulpits.* Grand Rapids, Mich.: Baker, 1993.

Crabb, Larry. *Soul Talk.* Nashville: Integrity, 2003.

Dodd, Brian J. *Empowered Church Leadership.* Downers Grove, Ill.: InterVarsity Press, 2003.

Foster, Richard. *Celebration of Discipline.* New York: HarperCollins, 1978.

Hinthorn, Aletha. *Leaders God Uses.* Kansas City, Mo.: Beacon Hill, 2002.

McNeal, Reggie. *A Work of Heart: Understanding How God Shapes Spiritual Leaders.* San Francisco: Jossey-Bass, 2000.

Myra, Harold and Marshall Shelley. *The Leadership Secrets of Billy Graham.* Grand Rapids, Mich.: Zondervan, 2005.

Young, Ed. *High Definition Living.* West Monroe, La.: Howard, 2003.

Selecting and Becoming a Mentor

As iron sharpens iron, so one man sharpens another.

Proverbs 27:17

Of the leaders I have known, few have been willing to be vulnerable.
It's dangerous ... it might get you killed! Still leaders ... should possess
an open heart, value innocence, curiosity, listening skills, embracing
warmth, compassion, acceptance, caring, shepherding, exposure.

W. Ward Gasque

Associate pastor Lee Brown had just completed preaching a sermon at Christ Church of Lakeville. After the message, an elderly woman approached Lee with an enormous smile and twinkle in her eye. "Reverend Johnson, that was one of the best sermons I have ever heard." (Reverend Johnson was the senior minister at Christ Church.)

Lee kindly responded, "I'm sorry, I'm not Reverend Johnson, but thank you for the compliment." The woman wasn't convinced. "Yes you are, I listen to you on the radio all the time. I'd know that voice anywhere. You're Reverend Johnson." Lee did not know what to do, but politely nodded as the confident parishioner turned and headed for the church foyer.

About a year later, Lee heard a similar comment after he spoke at another church. "Your preaching reminds me so much of Reverend Johnson." Lee could only again say thank you, with a deep sense of gratitude, knowing that his senior pastor was well regarded as a gifted communicator. Over the next few years, Lee could not escape numerous comparative comments.

Finally Lee realized what was happening when his wife commented, "You are starting to laugh like Mike Johnson." Lee was taken back. While by that time he had served several years on the same staff, he had never been formally tutored or mentored by his senior pastor. Nevertheless, Lee had picked up many of the preaching skills, leadership abilities, and now the whimsical mannerisms of his pastor. Lee had indeed been mentored.

Lee learned one of the most significant lessons watching his senior pastor interact with his family. Lee cannot forget the affectionate and respectful demonstrations of how to treat one's wife in public. The senior pastor's children were likewise prized and valued in the company of others.

Years later, Lee still is occasionally compared to his former pastor. Mentoring sticks. Learned skills and life's little lessons can last a lifetime. They certainly have for Lee. And Lee is grateful for what he saw modeled and now imitates.

Good Leaders Are Always Mentoring

I have heard a number of leadership clichés, such as: "You can never not communicate" or "You are always leading, even when you choose not to." I would like to add another, "You are always mentoring." Someone is always watching you and taking notes. Others are learning your style, watching your character, imitating your actions.

Mentoring is hardly a new science or leadership art, despite its recent press. Every parent mentors a child, both positively and negatively. Mentoring is simply teaching skills and developing abilities to carry out certain responsibilities. It is what yoke-fellows are all about, the younger learning skill sets from the older.

When you accepted your ministry staff position, you not only accepted a greater sense of accountability and responsibility, but you placed yourself under an enormous magnifying glass. Some have referred to the life of the ministry leader as living in a fish bowl. Volunteers and ministry participants are watching you constantly.

> ### Two Powerful Quotes*
>
> We all need truth-tellers in our lives. Do you have someone who will "speak the truth in love" to you regarding your life and ministry?
>
> **John Ortberg**
>
> Nothing can be more cruel than the leniency which abandons others to their sin. Nothing can be more compassionate than the severe reprimand which calls another Christian in one's community back from the path of sin.
>
> **Dietrich Bonhoeffer,**
> *Life Together*

---

*From *Rev* magazine, May/June 2003, p. 44.

With that reality, it is wise to become intentional about the "messages" you send your protégés. You are teaching lifestyle, skills, and strategy, whether you want to or not. As a leader, you cannot escape this added role and responsibility to others. In fact, the people around you will subconsciously say, "When you are down, we are down. When you are up, we are up!"

Choose a Mentor

As a ministry staff person, you are never too old or too late to identify a role model in life and ministry. While you may never experience the approach of a gifted leader offering a mentoring relationship, consider the offer seriously if one is extended. If not, take personal initiative to seek out a mentor/coach for your life and ministry.

Before selecting a mentor, ask yourself the following questions:

- Where would I like to be in about five years?
- What are my greatest underdeveloped gifts and areas of passion?
- Who models those gifts the best?
- Would that leader be available and willing to spend time with me?
- Are my selection motives political or pure?
- Has the possible mentor demonstrated with me or others an ability to be open and vulnerable with his or her personal life?
- Am I ready to be told the truth about my giftedness, personal life, and calling?

The next step is to pray. Ask God to lead the "right" person into your life. You want someone godly and gifted. You also want someone who will be honest and upfront with you.

Spend some time observing and developing a casual relationship with the potential mentor. Ask others about his or her background and experience. Learn all that you can about the model of leadership you aspire to attain.

Finally, ask the mentor for a commitment of time and personal involvement. Ask how often they would be willing to meet with you. Then adjust your schedule accordingly. Don't be afraid to suggest several learning outcomes with personal goals and objectives. However, don't overwhelm a mentor with every area of your life and ministry. It is best to consider one or two areas of personal development.

Understand that the individual you approach may be new to a mentoring relationship. Not every ministry leader has taken the course, "How to Mentor 101." Proceed slowly. Set an end time and easy "out" for both of you.

Signs That You May Need a Mentor

- You have a deep desire to grow and develop to the next level.
- Ministry has become routine and stale.
- Others identify in you a loss of passion or energy.
- Very few people are pursuing you.
- Your life has become out of balance and at times chaotic.

There is great wisdom to an exit strategy. In time, your mentor will lose objectivity and the relationship will be marginalized at that point. You will know when the dynamic becomes static. Actually, that can be a good thing because it's a small indicator that mentoring has occurred. Celebrate the time and input. Redefine your relationship and roles.

Your mentor is a special gift from God. However, he or she will most likely not be the only person who shapes or molds your ministry life. *No one size fits all.* Enjoy each mentor; one at a time. Celebrate the men and women God brings into your life. I thank God for Bob, Chuck, Jerry, Leith, Ed, and most of all, my wife, Donna. And I keep learning and seeking input from others—including Rex, Don, Craig, Leland, and Fred—and, God willing, still more down the road.

Become a Mentor

Wouldn't it be nice if someone came up to you and offered their time, resources, and personal involvement in your life and ministry to help you grow? Again, that may never happen. But you can make it happen in someone else's life.

First of all, not everyone thinks that you would be a great role model. Eat that humble piece of pie. Having said that, begin to consider a future leader with whom you have a rather natural connection.

The next step is to be aware of your strengths and weaknesses, and that you will mentor both. However, since real mentoring is primarily about skill development and character shaping, realize that more is caught than taught. Discern which personal skill sets will be helpful to a potential protégé.

Begin the selection process with those who share the same ministry passion. Perhaps they are volunteering in your ministry right now and may already look to you as a leader and example. Now it is your turn to observe them. Ask the following questions:

- Does this person share with me similar passions and interests?
- Does this future leader demonstrate some of my gift sets and abilities?
- Do we seem to share some compatibility beyond formal ministry?

- Is there evidence and interest to learn more, work harder, and grow?
- Does this person seem to "hang around" more than others?
- Do I have the time to invest in the life of another?

As you narrow the candidates, spend increasingly greater amounts of time with your potential protégé. Grow the relationship, recognizing that time is your best friend. At a Spirit-led juncture and during a natural teachable moment, ask permission to have input and personal involvement in the protégé's life and ministry. Assuming that is granted, a more "formal" mentoring or coaching relationship can begin. Just remember, it cannot be forced or hurried.

Mentor One at a Time

Finally, don't try to mentor more than one protégé at a time. It seldom works. If you are a ministry staff person with full-time responsibilities, you simply don't have time to adequately and effectively pour your life into more than one person.

A number of years ago I received a special grant to develop a model of ministry mentoring. Twenty-three ministry staff leaders were asked to mentor three future leaders apiece. Each agreed to the same coaching principles within an established deadline. At the end of the "experiment," everyone without exception reported effectiveness with only one person. That outcome was never predetermined or suggested to the mentors. It just naturally happened. We all learned a valuable principle in the process. (The only exception to mentoring more than one person at a time seems to be ministry

---

Ten Questions a Mentor Should Have Permission to Ask ... At Any Time

If a mentoring relationship is to effectively mold and shape both skills and character, the following personal questions can create a foundational fiber that will penetrate to the core of healthy development:

1. What are you reading and pursuing in your personal studies?
2. How is your personal time with God meaningful and significant?
3. What experiences and opportunities do you sense you are lacking?
4. Are you encouraged or discouraged with your personal development?
5. Are your relationships with your husband or wife, children, and family healthy and rewarding? If not married, how are your friendships?
6. Are you finding victory or struggling with specific sins and temptations?
7. Do you see the need or desire for minor or significant changes?
8. What are your greatest fears and joys at this time?
9. Do you harbor any deep resentment or bitterness toward another person?
10. What can I do for you?

leaders who have mentoring others as a part of their job description and responsibilities.)

As you will learn if you haven't already, mentoring takes time. It requires a special focus, personal attention, and almost always becomes more involved than originally anticipated. But don't run from the opportunity. Know there is a great reward and joy as you watch another grow.

Additional Reading

Anderson, Keith R. and Randy D. Reese. *Spiritual Mentoring.* Downers Grove, Ill.: InterVarsity Press, 1999.

Biehl, Bobb. *Mentoring: Confidence in Finding a Mentor and Becoming One.* Nashville: Broadman and Holman, 1996.

Davis, Ron Lee. *Mentoring: The Strategy of the Master.* Nashville: Thomas Nelson, 1991.

Engstrom, Ted. *The Fine Art of Mentoring.* Brentwood, Tenn.: Wolgemuth, 1989.

Graves, Stephen R. and Thomas G. Addington. *The Fourth Frontier.* Nashville: Word, 2000.

Hendricks, Howard G. and William Hendricks. *As Iron Sharpens Iron: Building Character in a Mentoring Relationship.* Chicago: Moody Press, 1995.

Longnecker, Harold. *Growing Leaders by Design.* Grand Rapids, Mich.: Kregel, 1995.

Stanley, Paul and Robert Clinton. *Connecting: The Mentoring Relationship You Need to Succeed in Life.* Colorado Springs: NavPress, 1992.

Making It for the Long Haul

Make level paths for your feet and take only ways that are firm.
Proverbs 4:26

It's tough to be a pastor today! Perhaps, tougher than it's ever been!
Leslie B. Flynn, How to Survive the Ministry

Don't quit. Never give up, give in, or give out. Pray and obey. Find courage and motivation in the blessed hope of a coming Christ, a heavenly home, the victor's crown, and eternal joy.
Anonymous

Then Jesus told his disciples a parable to show them that they should always pray and not give up.
Luke 18:1

"I quit" sounded so good to Robin. Those two little words were going to set her free; she believed a new life with greener grass was just around the corner.

The gripes, complaints, and lack of commitment from disrespectful volunteers at the parish center were off the charts. Volunteers came late, left early, or never showed up at all. Morale was terrible. The work was not getting done. Now, even guests and visitors commented on the negative spirit and ungrateful attitude, it was so apparent.

Jody, Robin's assistant, was just as frustrated as Robin by the pessimism and air of gloominess created by unhappy, unpaid workers. Every day it was their task to maintain a bright atmosphere and keep the lid from blowing off a veritable cauldron of heated emotions and inflammatory comments. Something had to change.

One afternoon Jody suggested to Robin that maybe they were doing something wrong. At first Robin rebelled against such an outlandish comment: "These people are rude and offensive to everyone who walks in these doors. They treat our needy parishioners with disdain, looking for paybacks for their meager hours of service. What do you mean, *we're* doing something wrong!"

Jody responded with a spirit of calm that exuded profound insight and wisdom. "Robin, I think you just identified a big part of the problem. Our volunteers are wonderful people and they are looking for some kind of return on their investment of time and energy. We're not providing it. We are only managing the animosity with guilt and duty. We are treating them as a work crew. We have not honored and celebrated them as a hardworking ministry staff."

Robin quickly settled down and began to reflect. Jody was right. They had taken advantage of people who were sacrificing their time and resources to make the inner-city ministry a viable outreach to needy people. They were not complaining about the work or the environment as much as they were unfulfilled by a lack of approval and appreciation. They were not feeling a part of the center.

The two leaders initiated immediate changes after that. Jody brought in donuts and coffee. Robin started acknowledging volunteers' birthdays, wedding anniversaries, and "employment" anniversaries. They created a suggestion box. Jody ordered quality logo T-shirts, hats, and sweater vests. Each day they gathered volunteers together to hear a story of how the center had helped a person with special needs. The volunteers noticed their suggestions being implemented and began suggesting more changes.

Before long, the old complaints began to disappear. Volunteers worked longer and harder. Today Robin doesn't even think of those two words "I quit" anymore. In fact, she is thinking of ways to expand and further develop the parish center.

Overcoming the Urge to Quit

Staying for the long haul is not easy. When ministry raises unanswered questions and doubts, life can become very emotionally charged; doom and gloom often prevail in most every event, conversation, and relationship. We have all been there. At such tough crossroads, we ask: Do I stay put? Do I leave? Is my ministry done? Will I discover untapped potential if I stay? Will I bury a future opportunity to grow if I don't leave?

If you are at the point of quitting, it may be time to make one of those infamous "lists."

Identify the things that create a desire to quit. Those may be on the tip of your tongue and in the frontal lobe of your mind. What have you heard yourself saying to others over the last few weeks and months? Write them down. Read them back. Erase those that are ridiculous. Begin praying through the phrases that are rational and reasonable. Don't discount your feelings. They are there to tell you something is wrong.

Once you have completed the list of reasons to leave, *identify the things that would make you want to stay.* This list may be short. Nevertheless, write them down. Each reason may speak loudly and profoundly into your situation at this turning point. Review the list. Take time thinking and verbalizing your objective reflections. Does this list make sense? Compare the two lists.

Make a Few Adjustments

As you consider remaining in your current position, it is possible that you may need to make some bold, new moves (perhaps even reassignment) or at least some minor adjustments. Begin by examining your job description. Remaining stuck in all of the original assumptions at the point of hire may not be realistic. You have changed. Most likely the ministry has changed. A significant question will always remain, "Am I a match with the current and future ministry?"

Before you make a drastic career decision, you may need more information than you currently have. First ask, What can I change about my situation? Then ask, Am I willing to make those changes? If the answer is yes, go for it. If the answer is no, it may be a signal to talk to someone you can trust.

If making a few changes does not move you in a positive direction, ask the important question, What can't I change? The answer(s) should drive you to a discussion with leadership or volunteers who can make or assist you in making the necessary adjustments or changes in your role and responsibilities. Ask if they are willing. If so, your spirit and theirs may be renewed. If not, at least you have gained important information that will help you take the next step.

Finally, ask yourself some personal questions:

- Do I expect too much from myself or others?
- Am I avoiding some difficult people, situations, or needs?
- Am I living in fear of change?
- Have I lost respect and trust in leadership and volunteers?

- Have I become "lost" in the busyness of routine and keeping my head above water?

Overhaul and Re-create Your Role and Identity

Re-creation is a part of the redemptive process that God does in our lives. Overhauling your role and identity can work for you *and* the people around you. While you are limited in some respects by your job description and the role your ministry has called you to fulfill, there nevertheless are some healthy ways to re-create the role you already have.

Renew your relationship with God and the people around you. Ministry is about people and God. Have one or more relationships weakened or soured? Is there distance where there was once closeness? Reconnect.

It may be time to refresh and renew important relationships which have been taken for granted or slowly eroded over time.

Sometimes a new title is all it will take. I have seen many respond with renewed interest and respect when a title was changed from *assistant* to *director.* It gave a greater sense of responsibility and authority. It demonstrated new confidence in the ministry staff person. And, in most cases, people rise to the title and apparent new role.

A different office setup/fresh environment can breathe new life into your spirit and attitude. It is amazing what a little remodeling can do. Other participants will sense the positive change and newness.

Ask permission to get away for a few days. Take some extra time to think and pray through your ministry role and objectives. Ask God to pour "fresh wine into an old wineskin." He can do that. Often he does.

Add some new resources to your ministry. Read a current rel-

> ### Live Beyond the Circumstances of the Day
>
> God calls us to make the most of each day and to learn to be content, regardless of the circumstances (see Ephesians 5:16; Philippians 4:11). That kind of living and ministry requires a different perspective. Consider:
>
> - What God did one year ago and five years ago. Recall his goodness.
> - The current needs of the people entrusted to your care. Think about them.
> - Eternal values, which go far beyond today's situation. Think ahead.
> - Reentry with a fresh, new love for the ministry and the people around you. Don't forget or discount the call of God on your life.
> - The lives that have been changed by your current ministry. Celebrate your spiritual children and grandchildren.
> - The body of Christ belongs to Christ, not you. He is the head, you are a servant.

evant book. Subscribe to a new journal or periodical. Attend a ministry conference.

Sign up for a course at the local college, university, or seminary. Make new discoveries in your area of passion at a professional level of higher education. Learn a new discipline. Stretch yourself. Become a lifelong learner.

Discover an interest not related to your ministry role. Many leaders are burned out and ready to quit due to overload and over-ministry. Sometimes previously uncharted territory—a new hobby or new pursuit—can create excitement. This may take courage for the overextended staff person. It could mean major changes and giving up some areas of ministry (see chapter 20). Ask a good friend or trusted colleague to help you find a new balance in your schedule and priorities.

Overview of the Big Picture

It is my conviction that most ministry leaders leave their positions without seeing the big picture. At the time of resignation, they seem to only see the trees in the forest. Those trees are unhealthy and many should be removed. However, the big picture can reveal a healthy prospect and vision for the future. It is important to step back and take another look. Learn to develop an unblinking view of reality, creating resilience with sober judgment.

Seeing the big picture may require some corrective lenses. Those may come from other, more objective observers. Ask people what they see in your current ministry. Their perspective may have redeeming value. In our chapter-opening story, Jody could see what Robin could not see. That created a new perspective for both.

Connect with people in your ministry who have never grown beyond being spectators. It may be revealing and refreshing to hear some new stories and get out of the rut of the same faces and same issues which slow you down from day to day. Discover what God is doing in the lives of others because of the ministry.

Celebrate what you see and hear. When was the last time you and your

> **Four Areas of Need That Will Keep You Going Strong**
>
> 1. **Safety and security:** Can I speak honestly and not lose my job?
> 2. **Independence and interdependence:** Can I work in an environment which celebrates autonomy as well as integrated ministries?
> 3. **Belonging and becoming:** Do I feel a part of the whole and am I growing within the ministry's context?
> 4. **Friendships and fulfillment:** Do I enjoy the community I work with while pursuing my passion and using my gifts and talents?

An Overhaul of Your Personal Life May Redeem Your Ministry

Sometimes when our private worlds are out of order, everything else is impacted and negatively affected. Here are a few suggestions to reorder and reorganize you, before you do the same to your ministry:

- Establish a new time and place to meet with God.
- Exercise.
- Get some sleep. Try a little advice from *Poor Richard's Almanac*, "Early to bed, early to rise, ..."
- Write, journal, put a "legacy box" (memorable pictures, stories, tokens, etc.) together for your children or other family members.
- Reconnect with your family.
- Take the initiative to add some new friends to your Christmas card list.
- Forgive someone against whom you have harbored ill feelings. Let go of the baggage.
- Add some new books to your reading list. If you have not been reading, read. If you haven't picked up a novel in twenty years, try a recommended one.
- Get away on a trip. Find a new hobby. Attend a play or concert. Learn to play the piano. Do something you have been putting off for a long time. Go ahead, "smell the roses."
- If married, reestablish a healthy dating life with your spouse.
- If single, get out and do something with a friend.

---

team authentically and exuberantly celebrated the work of God in your lives and ministry? Sometimes that level of joy is renewing and invigorating, sustaining you into the future.

Overhaul Your Current Goals and Objectives

It may be time for some fresh goals. When we first step into a new ministry role, our focus tends to be rather short-term. Anything we accomplish at the beginning is celebrated by many. However, we don't live in the short term.

Long-term goals and objectives will bring your dreams, thoughts, and spirit into the future. A good ministry friend of mine created a concept called the "imagination team." While short-lived, the I.T. stimulated some new thinking and concepts which carried a number of us into future days with a spirit of optimism and renewal.

Create your own "imagination team." You have nothing to lose and much to gain.

Write down your new dreams, ideas, and concepts.

Reinvent Some of the Little Things in the Ministry

We all agree that sometimes less is more and it can be the little things that count, that people notice most. Consider a few of these random suggestions and ideas. Consider your own. Reinvent.

- Change the name, title, or slogan for a ministry program, publication, or event.
- Redraft the layout or format for your publications. Breathe new life into printed materials.
- Remodel a room with paint, new window coverings, new carpet, and some artwork on the walls.
- Remove the bulletin board and replace it with a programmed plasma screen (you will be amazed how inexpensive this can be ... start saving, or create a project with a few techies).
- Give a ministry a break from rigid routines. Take a *Shabbat* or time-out.
- Rewrite the lyrics to a song or piece of the normal memorized liturgy. Bring into the worship service ancient liturgy never used.
- Resurrect something "old" which may reflect your core values. Bring back to life a "prayer meeting" or a "choir" (yes, I did say that) or an evangelistic "program" which involved many people and touched many lives. Now, go down the church's memory lane and find a meaningful point of history and revitalize it.

Create a slogan or two, which will become a motivating mantra for the next leg of the journey.

Trust God.

Pray. Wait for the exciting results. And remember, God "is able to do immeasurably more than all we ask or imagine, according to his power that is at work within us" (Ephesians 3:20). If that doesn't keep you going, I don't know what will.

A Biblical Picture of Long-Haul Principles Lived Out

> *Now the priests who carried the ark remained standing in the middle of the Jordan until everything the Lord had commanded Joshua was done by the people, just as Moses had directed Joshua. The people hurried over, and as soon as all of them had crossed, the ark of the Lord and the priests came to the other side while the people watched.*
>
> **Joshua 4:10–11**

Additional Reading

Blaine, Allen. *Before You Quit: When Ministry Is Not What You Thought.* Grand Rapids, Mich.: Kregel, 2001.

Leaving a Legacy

Ezell, Rick. *Ministry on the Cutting Edge.* Grand Rapids, Mich.: Kregel, 1995.

Flynn, Leslie B. *How to Survive in the Ministry.* Grand Rapids, Mich.: Kregel, 1992.

Larson, Craig Brian. *Hang In There to the Better End.* Grand Rapids, Mich.: Baker/Revell, 1996.

McLaren, Brian. *Reinventing Your Church.* Grand Rapids, Mich.: Zondervan, 1998.

Schaller, Lyle E. *Survival Tactics in the Parish.* Nashville: Abingdon, 1977.

Considering a Major Change

A man of understanding keeps a straight course.

Commit to the Lord whatever you do, and your plans will succeed.

Proverbs 15:21b; 16:3

No direct biblical texts address the question of changing churches.

Gary Meadors

Scott placed the receiver from the kitchen phone back in the cradle and began to share the forty-five-minute conversation with his wife, Lisa. The caller was the pastor of a church in a nearby city whose search committee for associate pastor had actively pursued Scott over the last three months.

At first, Scott said he was not interested. That did not seem to deter his committed pursuer. As he continued the dialogue with the pastor, a chemistry and affinity began to develop between them.

Scott had just completed five years of youth ministry at Covenant Bible Church and was well loved by the youth and parents there. However, the ministry was not growing and Scott was not growing. He was beginning to wonder if he had lost his passion for youth ministry, even though he greatly enjoyed working with the kids. Yet, he persevered with integrity.

Lisa was concerned that Scott was not using his ministry gifts of teacher and shepherd. The leadership at Covenant Bible Church needed Scott to be an effective administrator. Many times he would be asked to coordinate church-wide events. While he could do these things well, he longed to be more of a shepherd to the people. That became their major discussion as a couple.

What complicated the issue even more was the fact that two other churches had also expressed interest in Scott. Each one was offering better financial packages as well as outside ministry opportunities. One church was located near a seminary, and further theological training definitely intrigued Scott. All three churches were asking him to share the pulpit ministry and shoulder the pastoral care ministry.

Though Scott and Lisa prayed and prayed, they could not seem to make a decision. They were stuck. They had not sought out the other churches. They had not received criticisms or complaints from their current ministry. Their motives, attitudes, and work had been exemplary in every way. They did not want to be tempted by more money or opportunity. They simply desired to be the servants God had called them to be.

Finally, Scott and Lisa met with the pastor at CBC. They talked, prayed, and cried together. When they finished, Scott's pastor encouraged him to move forward to the church in the nearby city. Are you not surprised?

How Do You Know When It Is Time to Go?

Even the best of jobs come to an end. While the previous chapter in this book encourages longevity in ministry, staying long may not always bring the greatest joy and fulfillment in ministry. Not everyone can be spared the agony and difficulties of management's notions and impulses. Sometimes, godly wisdom says it is best to move on to another role.

In many respects there is a natural life-cycle to any role in ministry. Ministry changes, people change, and you change. You will grow and discover new passions, strengths, weaknesses, and obstacles. You will dream new dreams while a new vision for ministry may emerge. From the will and heart of God, you may discover he has something else, something different, something more significant today than what you may have considered a year ago. You need to respond to that leading and yearning in your life.

As you consider resignation, advice will come from all sides. "Quit while you are ahead," is an old corporate cliché. With that comes a bit of wisdom. Others will say, "Hang in there," "The grass is never greener on the other side," "Ride it out and see what happens." Again, there may be wisdom in doing just that.

Some will look for the finger of God to write the message clearly in the sky whether to stay or leave. Fleeces will be attempted, time lines developed, many people consulted. After all the voices and counselors, your answer may be crystal-clear *or* you may still wonder, "Do I stay or leave?"

It All Depends

Such a critical decision seems to come down to three things: God, you, and your situation.

It depends on what *God* is saying to you at this time in your life and ministry. God could be saying to you it is time to move. No one else may be repeating those words. Listen well to God. Trust him.

It depends on what is going on inside of *you*. Are you growing? Do you have hope? Are you defeated? Are you healthy? Listen well to yourself, your emotions, your ability to think and reason. If you are right with God, trust your heart.

Finally, it all depends on your *situation*. Only you can best determine your fit. If the ministry is healthy, are you able to bring it to the next level? If the ministry is floundering and struggling, are you gifted and called to bring healing and renewal? Listen carefully to what "the ministry" is trying to say. Trust the voices of reality.

> ### Less-than-Best Reasons to Consider a Move
>
> While each staff person needs to personally and carefully evaluate his or her reasons for moving to another ministry, the following should *not* be the primary reason for a change. In most cases these scenarios have internal resolutions.
>
> - Burnout or current stress
> - Envy or jealousy of another's ministry
> - Unfulfilled dreams or expectations
> - A few difficult people who are "love busters" in the ministry
> - Unexpected losses, program failures, or decline in numbers
> - Breakdown in communications or relationships
> - A bigger and better ministry opportunity
> - One or two people have suggested you make a change

In other words, there is no one single, clear, hard-core answer to the question, "How do you know when it is time to go?" Some will know through the still, small voice of God. Is that mystical? For some, yes. Nonetheless, it may be very clear. Some will discover God's will through the pages of the Bible together with the conviction of God's Spirit. Others will discern the need to make a move after listening to trusted friends and family.

Check Your Motives

James, the brother of Jesus, powerfully stated, "You do not receive, because you ask with wrong motives" (James 4:3). If you are contemplating a move, take an "M.I." (Motive Inventory). Ask yourself:

- Will this new opportunity advance my ministry career?
- Am I leaving because I can make more money?

- Am I running from unresolved issues?
- Have I been treated unjustly to the point of resentment and anger?
- Do I simply not like it here anymore?
- Am I feeling restless and anxious?
- Is my ego inflated with the dreams of a bigger, better place to serve?
- Do my thoughts of this new opportunity mostly raise material visions?

Unless your heart convicts you of having a wrong motive which causes an abrupt stop to your plans, keep moving forward. While answering yes to any of the above may not be a reason to stop planning, keep your heart in check, so that you may serve the Lord wholeheartedly.

Indicators That It May Be Time to Leave

Just as we pay attention to the fuel, oil, and engine lights on our car dashboard, we do well to observe the indicator lights of ministry. When the lights go on, sudden peril is not imminent. It is simply time to pay attention to future health and development. The following list, by the way, is not inclusive:

1. *God has clearly and obviously called you to another ministry.* If God says it is time to move, the ministry staff member must respond. When does God call? I can't tell you. How does God speak? In different ways.

So, how do you know the clear voice of God? Remain close to God through a life of devotion and personal worship. When he speaks, you will know. If God's voice is clear, other godly people in your life may be able to discern a divine calling (remember Eli and Samuel, see 1 Samuel 3).

I recall suggesting a friend not pursue a call to another ministry. He was convinced that God was leading him. He just knew it. He resigned

Healthy Reasons to Consider a Move

While longevity is always the better side of wisdom, the following may be compelling reasons to consider a major change:

- I have experienced the clear and obvious call of God.
- I desire and need to use my personal gifts and talents.
- There are special family needs and extenuating circumstances.
- I have brought this ministry as far as I can.
- The ministry's values and vision have changed; mine have not (or vice versa).
- I can no longer respect my leader(s).
- This role is no longer a healthy situation for me.
- My friends have suggested I consider a change.

and moved to a new location. I was wrong. God significantly used my friend in the new role.

2. *Your spiritual gifts are not being used.* Paul urges members of Christ's church to not neglect their gifts. Gifts are apportioned by the Spirit of God for each member to do the work of the ministry. Are your gifts being used in your current ministry?

A colleague of mine is a gifted communicator. He could not deny his spiritual giftedness to pastor and preach. It was clear, based on his gifts, that he needed to leave his current role and pursue a senior pastor position. Within months, God called him to the pastorate of a rapidly growing church.

3. *This ministry needs someone else to bring it to the next step.* "I have gone into neutral. I have been on a plateau far too long. The ministry is suffering. I am suffering. The values or mission of the ministry have changed, while mine have not."

Do any of these comments sound familiar? If they do, it may be a blinking light on your ministry dashboard, indicating time for a change.

Dean (not his real name) was "wearing two hats," but was unable to do either ministry job effectively in the fast-growing church where he served on staff. He approached his senior pastor for help, only to be told: "You are young, you can handle it." That day, in Dean's heart and mind, he resigned. He left the church within a year, and the church was "forced" to hire two people for the two roles. The ministry continued to expand. Meanwhile, in another city, Dean grew rapidly in his new role.

4. *You are unable to regain respect for leadership (after much time and effort).* When trust in a ministry leader is replaced by disrespect or loss of respect, it is difficult to regain confidence and collegial interdependence. Yes, it can and sometimes does happen. Yet, the relationship may never be the same. It could be a flashing warning light. Pay careful attention to your "respect" gauge.

5. *Staying in this role is obviously not healthy for you or the people around you.* Are you under a lot of stress? Having trouble sleeping at night? Do you suffer from high-anxiety moments with subtle panic attacks? Are you sensing a growing level of resentment toward people? Are ministry results lacking? Are you a victim of encouragement deficit? These questions form a cluster of warning lights. When any one goes on, it is time to pull over to the side of the road and take inventory.

The questions continue. Is your marriage struggling under the pressure of ministry demands? Is the burden of ministry negatively impacting your friendships and family? Are your children showing signs of disdain and

<table>
<tr><td>

**Lessons to Learn from a
Departing Colleague**

While you are determined to stay put, another staff member has just announced his or her resignation. You can learn a lot from this departing partner in ministry, who has "nothing to lose" by being honest with you. Give your colleague permission to be honest with you to learn and grow by asking the following:

- How would you suggest I can grow and improve as a leader?

- Have you noticed any blind spots that I have missed?

- How could I better interact with people?

- How is my ministry perceived by other staff, leadership, volunteers?

- Is there anything I have done to offend you?

- Do you believe it is time for me to consider leaving?

</td></tr>
</table>

apathy toward ministry? Sometimes we don't even recognize our own frailty and weakness. The once obvious warning signs are no longer obvious.

Ministry often means helping those who cannot help themselves (the unhealthy). That demands that you maintain good health and personal vitality. As the flight attendant instructs passengers, "Place the oxygen mask on yourself first, then on the child next to you." If you are not getting enough ministry oxygen, it may be time to make a change.

6. *Several close colleagues suggest that you consider a change.* A close and cherished friend will most often speak the truth in love. Recommending that you consider a resignation may indeed be the wound of a friend (see Proverbs 27:6).

Carefully pause to consider the motives behind such advice. Make sure your personal counselor has your best interest in mind. Discern whether or not a trusted friend is advising out of jealousy, envy, selfishness, or unresolved bitterness.

If there appears to be a unity among your spiritual brothers and sisters, take their counsel to heart. Respect this warning sign. Listen to those who love and respect you.

Announcing Your Resignation

At my last resignation, my senior pastor Ed Dobson announced to the church congregation that I would be leaving to be the president of the seminary which was quite literally across the street. The next week, I was given a brief opportunity to share with my supportive church family the brief story of my journey. I asked for their permission to continue attending the church (which Donna and I have done). I also requested that the elders lay on hands and send my wife and me into this new adventure in ministry. They did just that. We did not burn our thirteen-year bridge of meaningful ministry at Calvary Church.

A resignation should not be a moment of sensationalism, but a time to glorify God for his leading in the life of his servant. It is a time to celebrate, not to shock; a time to pray, not to create division or inflict wounds on a congregation. It should reflect good forethought and planning, and serve as an opportunity to bless the ministry and provide future hope. Consider the following:

- Appraise your supervising leader of your plans and potential of leaving as soon as possible. While this may be difficult in some situations, it demonstrates respect and honor to those who have been colleagues and shared ministry with you.
- Talk through a reasonable time line in order to fulfill duties and responsibilities of your current job. How long should you stay once you decide to leave? Ask your leadership team for input on that decision.
- Share one-on-one with as many people as possible. Don't grandstand the announcement.
- Be open and honest where you are going and explain how God has led you.
- A written announcement (letter to the constituency or congregation) is sometimes a helpful tool to remove emotional edges and clear up many unanswered questions.
- Don't ignore or refuse a going-away celebration. Not everyone enjoys this event, but it helps some people bring closure to your departure.

When you leave, you leave. Give room for your successor to lead. Resist and refrain from derogatory or inflammatory comments, even if your resignation was forced or by mutual consent with the leadership. Do all that you can to uphold and honor the reputation of Christ's body of believers.

Additional Reading

Cionca, John. *Before You Move: A Guide to Making Transitions in Ministry.* Grand Rapids, Mich.: Kregel, 2004.

Ducat, Diane. *Turning Points: Your Career Decision-Making Guide.* Upper Saddle River, N.J.: Prentice Hall, 2002.

Meadors, Gary T. *Decision Making God's Way.* Grand Rapids, Mich.: Baker, 2003.

Winseman, Albert L., Donald O. Clifton, and Curt Liesveld. *Living Your Strengths.* Washington, D.C.: Gallup, 2003.

Finishing Well

Let love and faithfulness never leave you; bind them around your
neck, write them on the tablet of your heart. Then you will win favor
and a good name in the sight of God and man.

Proverbs 3:3 – 4

Who can say, "I have kept my heart pure; I am clean and without sin"?

Proverbs 20:9

Few leaders finish well. The ones that don't finish well predominantly
lost it in the middle game, not in the end game.

Robert Clinton

Now director of his own ministry, Luke completed seven years of service as an associate at Fellowship Church. Luke worked hard while at Fellowship. He followed his job description to the best of his knowledge and ability. He tried to do everything that was expected and never made waves. Whether he performed a task or led a ministry, people enjoyed and celebrated what he did and how he did it. Overall, Luke was respected by other staff and leaders in the church. Those he served hated to see him leave.

On his last day, Luke left something bigger than a job well done. He left a new paradigm at Fellowship Church. His personal lifestyle, godly character, and commitment to excellence raised the level of respect and honor for the volunteers and staff he served. His philosophy of ministry set a new standard. The biblical values that he instilled were tried and tested. It wasn't a program Luke bequeathed. It was a legacy. A new heritage had been established.

The ministry today moves forward. The volunteers who remain at Fellowship Church will accept nothing less.

What did Luke do? He taught. He modeled. He led. He faithfully served from his heart. He did not waiver or cave in to what he did not believe. He lived out Proverbs 3:3 – 4.

Leave a Legacy

Live and serve with a clear sense of destiny and a deep conviction of your calling before God and others. While it is difficult to give a clear formula for knowing one's specific "calling" in ministry, there are a number of things that an associate can do to create a sense of personal worth and value as a servant of Christ.

I have discovered there are four basic steps to consider when finishing well. While they may not be foolproof, each one can bring a sense of fulfillment to you and to those you serve.

1. *Listen well to those who observe your life and work.* If we are able to discover our spiritual gifts through the open and honest feedback of those we serve, then the same can be true of our general area of service and calling. When you "bless" another and they tell you that they have been "blessed" by your life and ministry, consider the power of that feedback. Don't treat it lightly. However, if you have been working hard at a role or task and hear little or no feedback, or you know the feedback is patronizing, listen to that as well. Should you make quick responses to and draw immediate conclusions from a few comments? No. But, keep listening. What you hear will become a picture of your legacy.

2. *Be rather certain of your spiritual gifts and skill sets.* It is important for you and the people you serve to be able to articulate the gifts and abilities that God has given. It instills confidence in you and others, creating a healthy, vibrant ministry context. Modeling your gifts and ministry skills will teach others to do the same. Your ministry will expand beyond the written job description. A legacy begins to emerge.

3. *Humbly identify your strengths and weaknesses.* You know what they are. And if you don't, ask. It won't take long for people to share the good they see in you. Perhaps they'll also share comments about needed improvements. Consider every comment. Take each one seriously. Then learn to celebrate. Thank God for the strengths and acknowledge openly what you cannot do.

It is not a problem to admit weakness. It also is affirming to the people you serve because they soon realize that their feelings of inadequacy are normal. Now you serve together as true peers, and your volunteers move

<table><tr><td>

Eight Barriers That Will Keep You from Finishing Well*

1. **Using people:** When people are manipulated, kept at a distance, and treated as a means to the end.

2. **Power plays:** Top-down management and political games.

3. **Family dysfunction:** Ignoring, mistreating, or avoiding your family relationships.

4. **Mishandling funds:** Lack of integrity or respect for the finances of the organization.

5. **Sexual impropriety:** Including inappropriate relationship, pornography, or casual and inappropriate sexual contact.

6. **Loss of integrity:** Promise-breaking and creating unhealthy alliances.

7. **Pride and arrogance:** Nothing more needs to be said.

8. **Discontent and avoidance:** Lack of contentment, while avoiding risks and change.

</td></tr></table>

forward celebrating their God-given strengths instead of worrying about their weaknesses.

4. *List your core values, convictions, and passions.* This final step will take time. But it is worth the effort. Ask yourself the following three questions (also see chapter 2). The results will be a legacy driven by biblical values, providing a secure foundation for your volunteers or staff to establish their own ministries. Indeed, others will embrace such a legacy and move forward long after you are gone.

- What do I believe? What biblical support drives that belief?
- What am I willing to die for? What am I not willing to lose?
- Who am I committed to? Who do I think about, pray for, and hope to impact?

Do you have answers to these questions? If you do, then your legacy is beginning to emerge. Proceed faithfully and carefully.

How to Leave Well

Leaving a current ministry staff position is not something to be done haphazardly. There are a number of aspects to keep in mind.

Maintain a Vibrant Personal Relationship with God and Others

Very few people will remember the programs you created, the songs you sang, or the talks you gave. However, most will never forget the life you lived. People will remember if you were kind, easy to be around, or delightful

*Adapted from Robert Clinton, *Leadership Network Explorer.*

when engaged in a personal conversation. They also will remember if you were frequently abrupt or standoffish. They will remember if you were available or if you closed the door to your office and your life. After you leave, people will comment on how you treated them. They will know whether you used them for your own agenda, or honored them as children of God.

Let me repeat the words of Dr. Vernon Grounds that I quoted in chapter 21, "Godliness is when others look at the quality of my life, and they begin to think about God." That's what we need to be remembered for—godliness. If the quality of your life causes people to think about God, then you have left a spiritual legacy. That is a life worth living.

In Ephesians 4:1 the apostle Paul writes, "Live a life worthy of the calling you have received." It is out of a godly life that God will bless.

Leave Behind One or More Lasting Contributions

Think about the things that last. Think about your own past experiences in life, family, education, or work. What do you remember about the key leaders in your life? What do you recall as most memorable? What was positive? What was negative? What would you imitate? For what do you wish to be known?

Beyond personal issues, think about the mission and the people you serve. What does each need to go forward? What can you leave behind to meet those needs? Leaving a legacy is about meeting the needs of people who could not meet those needs alone. Tie your activity to these lasting treasures.

Don't Get Lost in Your Ministry

In 1 Timothy 4:15–16, Paul encourages young Timothy to give himself to important ministry values (teaching, preaching, reading the Bible, using his gifts, and so on). He then reminds Timothy that everyone needs to see his progress and growth.

We can become so absorbed in the minutiae of ministry that what we do only affects today, with little regard for tomorrow. While sweating the details is important (we need to take care of the little things), we need to wisely not lose sight of the big picture and the future impact of what today will bring.

Don't get so involved in doing ministry that you lose sight of who you are. God does not desire that we be so driven that we find ourselves far away from our original passion and calling. He desires that we go home each day content and fulfilled in what was accomplished today that will impact tomorrow. Learn to say, "I accept today as God has designed, minus nothing and plus nothing."

Leave No Bridges Burning

Most do not finish well because of unhealthy relationships with other people. Very few leave ministry because of faulty theology or incompetence. Doctrinal disputes generally can be overcome through theological study. An ability deficiency can be remedied through skill training. But a breakdown in relational skills requires much more than a few classes or personal coaching. In order to finish well, some associates may need to initiate healing in relationships that have failed. Consider the following three principles:

- *Seek forgiveness.* If it is not obvious or apparent, ask God to help you identify who you have offended. Go to the person (Matthew 5:23–24), offer an apology, and ask forgiveness.
- *Offer forgiveness.* You know who has offended you. Forgive that person (Matthew 6:14). That means letting go of the offense. It means holding no record of wrongs, no longer identifying another with what they have said or done to you. The slate is clean, the topic never to be discussed again. No gossip. No slander.
- *Seek to bless those who have blessed you.* Undoubtedly during your ministry, people have blessed you. Have you said, "Thank you"? Do people see you as ungrateful for their contribution in your life? Have you received their good gifts and human resources (and more), but never shown gratitude and appreciation? Bless them. Speak well of them. Finish strong.

Make a Healthy Transition*

1. Make an ending and let go of your former role. You are now committed to something new. Everyone else sees it that way. So should you. Resist doing what you did. You have resigned. Don't forget to leave.

2. Use your neutral zone for health, strength, rest, and renewal. Get away for a few days or longer. Do something you have long wanted to do. Read a new book. Renew some former acquaintances. Spend time with people to laugh, pray, and dream about tomorrow.

3. Start some new habits and patterns of growth. Honestly attempt to revise your style of leadership or approach to relationships. Find a new format for personal management. Reinvent yourself. Seek counsel. Ask for help to grow and learn. Talk to someone who finished well.

Leave Everything in Order

You may be the only person who really understands and knows your area of ministry. There may be some

*Adapted from William Bridges's book, *Transitions: Making Sense of Life's Changes.*

processes for programs that you designed alone or a long time ago. Pass on your knowledge and expertise. Consider leaving a written document of what you know and what you did in your job. Leave a clearly defined legacy of information to those who remain and will follow your leadership. Provide the kinds of tools and ministry assistance that will create an ongoing retention of what you started.

On the other hand, some things may need to die. Identify those things. With the support of your supervisor, put them to rest. Don't feel like everything needs to continue just because you started it. People who will take your responsibilities may need to exercise their own styles and personal touches. Leave room for their creativity. It may be better than what you did. But improvement on what you started is still leaving a legacy.

Leave a list of your duties and responsibilities.

Leave a list of people who served with you, along with their duties and responsibilities.

Leave with those who remain a description of the ministry as you see it, including the values, vision, and dreams that you shared. It is their responsibility to handle things now. Not yours.

Leave a legacy by following God's call in your life, with godliness, speaking well of others and giving all glory to God.

Additional Reading

Clinton, Robert. *Focused Lives: Inspirational Life-Changing Lessons from Eight Leaders Who Finished Well.* Altadena, Calif.: Barnabas Books, 1995.

McNeal, Reggie. *A Work of Heart: Understanding How God Shapes Spiritual Leaders.* San Francisco: Jossey-Bass, 2000.

Thomas, Gary. *Sacred Pathways.* Grand Rapids, Mich.: Zondervan, 2000.

PART 6

Managing Life and Ministry

Creating and Managing
Communication Tools

He who answers before listening—that is his folly and his shame.

Proverbs 18:13

You are always communicating. Your silence speaks loudly.

There are no misunderstandings; there are only failures in communication.

Adapted from a Senegalese proverb

None of us has a crystal ball, and we are not very good at guessing the direction of your ministry. This seems to be your ministry since our input has not been requested, so at the least, tell us where you are taking us, please!

A ministry participant

B arb was shocked when a board member shared some rather negative comments about her made by Rachel, another staffer at the local crisis pregnancy center. She thought Rachel was her friend.

It all started more than a year ago when Barb was expected to make a furnishing purchase for the counseling rooms and her calculations were wrong. Unable to cover the expense with a donor's gift, she had to dip into the operating budget to absorb the balance of the purchase.

Clearly Barb's error and responsibility, she quickly made the center's business manager and finance committee aware of her miscue. After a lengthy discussion on how to avoid such problems in the future, Barb humbly apologized and the matter was forgiven.

Recently, while Rachel was talking to one of the volunteers, she offered her interpretation of what Barb had done to expend additional dollars on the furnishings. She focused on how Barb had blown it, but never mentioned Barb's apology or the board's forgiveness.

Later the volunteer discussed the matter with a board member, who was quick to make the exoneration clear. Then the board member shared the incident with Barb.

As other individuals were questioned by the board member, each story became a bit fuzzier. Rachel did not want to own the communication malady. Further discussions were strained and difficult.

Barb lost trust. Rachel distanced herself. Ever since, the two colleagues have been very guarded in what they say and share with each other.

Communication Is Expected

What volunteers and paid team members want most is to know where leadership is headed, where they are being taken. They expect you, as a ministry staff member, to deliver honest, clear, concise communication. People will disconnect quickly if they sense you are not sharing truthful, relevant, and important information with them.

Preaching or teaching pastors can report their activities and share their heart through sermon illustrations. As a ministry staff associate, you will often need to find other creative ways to share your life, heart, vision, and ministry results. That may require extra effort on your part, but the means are numerous: newsletters, reports, open forums, letters, phone calls, email, visits, meetings, and more.

Communication is a two-way process; there are no substitutes or shortcuts to face-to-face, life-on-life exchanges. Even efficient means of information-giving may not always be effective. Email and voice mail often appear efficient and in some cases they may be effective. But when modern electronic methods of information delivery are overused, a rather cold, impersonal communication style results.

Listening Is an Art

A capable leader should seek to spend more than 50 percent of his or her time listening to people. The key is asking good questions, striving for clarity, input, and the heartbeat of others. Skillful listening will make you a better leader, providing you with better feedback and input from your ministry participants. Problems can actually be solved by listening!

Some areas to improve your listening skills may include maintaining good eye contact, responding to what the speaker has just said, trying hard to not interrupt, and removing potential distractions (for example, cell phones, other people, and daydreaming).

Listening may be the hardest work in communicating with others in ministry. As leaders with defined roles, specific responsibilities, and high expectations, it is easy to talk too much. Will Rogers curtly stated, "Never miss a good chance to shut up." Knowing when to remain quiet is a valuable leadership trait. Learn to restrain or refrain from:

- Always thinking out loud
- Making negative comments about other people
- Spinning off on personal "rabbit trails"
- Commenting on every topic and item
- Quickly jumping in with opinion or anecdotes
- Answering every question (which can appear arrogant or controlling)

Most leaders fail by not having a plan for communication. Often communication just happens, becoming a rather serendipitous flow from topic to topic, person to person. The frustration is not landing anywhere with clarity, resolution, or solutions.

Creating a Communication Strategy

You are responsible to communicate to your ministry participants the values, vision, purpose, and objectives of the ministry. That will not happen without you. Church consultant Don Cousins says, "Where there is a lack of communication, there is a lot of imagination." If you do not communicate, ministry participants will imagine all kinds of things. A plan to communicate is a necessity, keeping various specifics in mind.

Your Role

The place to begin is knowing and believing the importance and influence of your role. Even if you have been only recently appointed as ministry staff member, you have been empowered and commissioned to represent an area of ministry with a certain level of authority. People will initially trust you to know the facts and tell the truth.

You also have the ways and means to supply information. You have permission to release the governing board's open discussions and decisions.

Ten Tips toward More Effective Communication

1. Return voice mail and email as soon as possible. Establish a time each day to check your incoming messages. Have your greeting reflect when you will get back to people, and then keep that commitment.

2. Take casual notes when you are on the phone. It will keep you focused on the conversation and assure the caller that you are listening as you refer to items previously stated.

3. Avoid pejorative, cynical, or critical language in written communications. People do read between the lines. Put in writing the positive messages. Confront face-to-face the negative messages.

4. Learn to write like you speak.

5. Learn to speak to groups like you do with individuals.

6. Write down your first and last sentences when speaking to a group. The remainder can be delivered from an outline. The greatest struggle for someone not used to speaking in public is starting or ending a talk.

7. Avoid ambiguous and nebulous language in your communication. Remember that people like to know the details.

8. Solicit feedback from your team and give feedback to them on the ministry results and direction.

9. Establish a pattern and personal commitment of "no surprises."

10. Avoid quarrels.

You have access to the ministry's mailing lists, office equipment, and personnel. You can get the job done.

Regular Tools

Haphazard attempts to communicate will not be most effective or efficient. People appreciate routine communication tools: they look for their newspaper on the porch each day, they anticipate receiving a bulletin at every church worship service. Scheduled communication tools go a long way toward building a healthy ministry.

Routine Information

Some information needs to be communicated on a routine basis. Many people need ongoing reminders of both obvious information and less obvious changes. For example, staff leaders may change and people may miss that one-time announcement. A regular staff listing will notify them of that important change.

What to Talk About

Believe it or not, people want to talk to you. At times it can be difficult to know what to discuss at a lunch meeting or informal meeting with another ministry staff person or volunteer. The following are a few suggestions for developing engaging conversations to build trust and confidence within working relationships:

- Evaluate and serve compliments on a recent project or program.
- Ask questions about background and current family or personal events.
- Be sure to remember birthdays and anniversaries.
- When a volunteer is having a personal crisis, ask questions and listen.
- Talk about future dreams and objectives.
- Ask for constructive input on your personal concerns or questions about an area of ministry.
- Discuss and share personal hobbies, recent books, or articles.
- Create a shared experience to discuss and evaluate (attend a conference or event together).
- Consider leaving the person you're meeting with some kind of a communication take-away, such as an article, brochure, or book for further information.

A list of routine information may include:

- Prayer requests
- Monthly or weekly calendar of events
- Finance and attendance reports (perhaps including names and photos of new members)
- Purpose (mission) statement
- Staff and leaders' names and roles
- Addresses, websites, phone numbers, and email access

Periodic Information

Some items do not need to be communicated on a regular basis. Periodic communication tools may be in the form of a quarterly or annual report, or a quarterly or annual calendar issued to ministry participants. Perhaps you may want to send a personal letter to motivate people with your passion and commitment to the ministry.

Some periodic information may include:

- Updates or stories from ministry participants or leaders
- Overviews of future mission or ministry opportunities

- Reminders of ministry core values and vision
- Discipleship tools for personal growth

Special Information

Occasionally it is important to supply breaking, relevant information. For example, an innovative idea or new program may require a special communication piece; a significant ministry addition or adjustment might be best communicated by letter, brochure, or special announcement. Remember, because typically not everyone is in attendance for a verbal announcement, it is always wise to consider a written communication to those absent. One church I know of regularly communicates key information with a video or written announcement on the ministry website.

Special information may include:

- A staff or leadership member's addition or deletion (resignation or dismissal)
- Any change in a regularly scheduled meeting (service) time or location
- A major ministry event
- A major crisis
- Unusual opportunities requiring a major decision

Communication Requires Forethought and Afterthought

- Think before you speak. Weigh all the options. Ask, Where will this message lead us?
- Plan before you write. Your words will go a long distance.
- Consider the needs of your audience. They did not show up just because of you. They will process your communication according to their personal agendas and interpretations.
- Remember there are two sides to the brain, left and right. Not everyone thinks or processes information like you.

Soliciting Feedback

Most of the previously mentioned communication tools flow from leadership to participants. The reverse information exchange (participants to leadership) is equally imperative for best communication practices. Unfortunately, this is the one area where ministries are not generally effective.

A few ideas to provide informational and personal feedback include:

- Carefully written surveys
- Personal meetings, asking people the same questions and tabulating the results

- Open forums (regularly scheduled, so as to not solicit negative feedback only during difficult or crisis times)
- Focus groups of people selected at random to provide open feedback on new ideas or concepts
- Advisory councils of select or key volunteer participants to provide routine feedback on ministry progress or new innovations

Soliciting Commitments for Leadership or Development

Nearly every ministry seeks volunteer participation at some point. As you seek commitments from these people, ask yourself questions such as: Are expectations clear? Do participants know the resources you will provide? Do they know the details of times, commitment, and personal costs? Do they know how to get out of the commitment with grace and dignity?

Once people commit to serve in a ministry area, give proper orientation. Be sure they are respectfully informed, introduced, and proper connections are completed. Provide adequate training and materials to get the job done. Allow for early feedback to ensure the best fit has been made.

Strategize how the committed volunteer can further grow and develop. Every volunteer and staff member wants to have the question answered, "How am I doing?" Provide meaningful opportunities for ongoing feedback through meetings and personal interaction.

Meetings with your volunteers should be routinely scheduled. Hit-or-miss meetings do not endear people to you or the mission.

Finally, provide a stable environment with dynamic interaction among members. Let people know you care by your honesty and time.

Sidestep Ministry Politics

It is easy to get swept into political agendas. An article by Jeffrey J. Fox entitled "How to Become a CEO" inspired the following suggestions to avoid unhealthy discussions among colleagues or volunteers:

- Don't gossip or listen to it ... either walk away or courageously suggest the inappropriateness of the discussion.
- Don't share a negative comment or innuendo about another person in the ministry.
- Be cautious agreeing with people who are pushing an agenda contrary to the ministry's values or vision.
- Learn when to say "no" or "I don't know."
- Be careful spinning numbers and reports on ministry with exaggeration or inflammatory comments.
- Avoid comparing one ministry with another.
- Tell the truth.

Meetings

Meetings can be a powerful tool for communication. Or, they can be a horrible waste of people's time. Take advantage of regularly scheduled meetings.

You attend meetings and lead meetings. The meetings you attend may be led by the chair of your governing board or a senior leader. Participate by listening and responding. Become positively engaged in the process. Prepare complete written reports on your area of ministry and request permission to pass them to all meeting participants. Maintain current information and updates on your area of ministry.

In meetings that you lead be sure to provide clear written agendas, which hold members accountable. Mail or distribute these to all participants in advance, including any information (articles, reports, etc.) necessary for meaningful discussion. Encourage members to read and come prepared to discuss important agenda items. Place people's names on the agenda, especially if they need to report on a particular assignment. Communicate when the meeting will start and when you expect it to end. Be sensitive to allow adequate time for meaningful discussion.

Begin or close your meetings with prayer. A passage from the Bible or devotional reading may provide an appropriate focus for the ensuing discussion. Plan to maintain a missional focus during your time together.

For some people your meeting is a big deal. It can be one of the most significant times in the month that they have to connect with others. Consider participants' need for coming together before canceling a meeting, regardless of the length of the agenda.

The Barriers to Effective Communication

I know you believe that you understand what you think I meant to say, but I'm not so sure that you fully realize that what you think you heard is not what I meant to say.

Anonymous

Additional Reading

Kassian, Mary A. *Conversation Peace: Improve Your Relationships One Word at a Time*. Nashville: Broadman and Holman, 2004.

Ludden, Marsha. *Effective Communication Skills*. Second edition. Indianapolis: JIST Publishing, 2002.

Marks, David. *Communication and Interpersonal Relationships.* Brunswick, Me.: National Writing Institute, 2000.

Powell, John. *Will the Real Me Please Stand Up? Twenty-five Guidelines for Good Communication.* Allen, Tex.: Resources for Christian Living, 1990.

Self, Donald. *Marketing Communications for Local Nonprofit Organizations: Targets and Tools.* Binghamton, N.Y.: Haworth, 2001.

Vassallo, Wanda. *The Church Communications Handbook.* Grand Rapids, Mich.: Kregel, 1998.

Managing Time and Money

Honor the LORD with your wealth, with the firstfruits of all your crops.

In the house of the wise are stores of choice food and oil,
but a foolish man devours all he has.

Finish your outdoor work and get your fields ready;
after that, build your house.

The rich rule over the poor, and the borrower is servant to the lender.

Proverbs 3:9; 21:20; 24:27; 22:7

A sluggard does not plow in season; so at harvest time
he looks but finds nothing.

Go to the ant, you sluggard; consider its ways and be wise!
It has no commander, no overseer or ruler,
yet it stores its provision in summer and gathers its food at harvest.

Proverbs 20:4; 6:6 – 8

Someone once said, "You can best know a person by reviewing
their checkbook and personal calendar."

Steve was never good with money. Growing up in an affluent culture, there was always enough money from family or friends. He never had to think about paying the bills. Even if he argued with his parents, money problems just went away.

While in college, Steve opened up his first checking account, though his checkbook never seemed to balance. Besides, as long as his monthly bank statement was in the black, he simply put money in and took money out. A few times he received ugly notices from the bank, so he would just make another deposit.

Now, Steve is a staff member with a parachurch youth ministry. Everyone loves him. However, the people in the business office shake their heads every time a check request or expense report arrives from Steve. If it is not late, it is incorrect or incomplete. Their ongoing lectures don't seem to help or phase his less-than-best accounting practices. When it comes to money, Steve doesn't get it.

To make things worse, Steve's immediate supervisor doesn't quite get it either. While he detests the business office memos regarding his staff member's practices, he basically ignores them. With a cavalier spirit from the top-down, Steve is encouraged to keep focused on reaching teens and not to worry about money. Steve heeds his manager's advice.

A few weeks ago, Steve was not invited to participate in a leadership summit. When he pursued the reason, he got an honest answer: his lack of wise stewardship caused the governing board and senior leadership to question his maturity to lead. After the frank discussion, Steve was still not invited.

Oh yes, Steve has a record and reputation of being late for most of his appointments, if not missing them all together. It is all catching up to him. Steve's example of handling time and money has affected his ministry.

You Are God's Steward of Time and Money

God has called us to be good stewards. Whether through biblical parables (note the parable of the talents, Matthew 25:14–30; the unmerciful servant, 18:23–35; the ten virgins, 25:1–13; or the wise manager, Luke 16:1–13) or direct biblical command (see, for example, Exodus 20:15, 17; Galatians 5:13; 6:7–10; and Ephesians 4:28; 5:15–17), he is concerned how we spend the resources of time, money, space, people, and more. Time and money are gifts from God. Time and money are gifts *from* your ministry and *for* your ministry. Spend them wisely.

Managing Time

What then is time? If nobody asks me, I know; but if I were desirous to explain it to someone that should ask me, plainly I know not.

St. Augustine

Unless he manages himself effectively, no amount of ability, skill, experience, or knowledge will make him effective.

Adapted from comment made by Peter Drucker

Managing Life and Ministry

Managing time can be difficult. Consider some of the many clichés about time: "I don't have enough time." "It just takes time." "Money is time" (there's one to think about for ministry!). "Time flies." God says, "Redeem the time" (KJV) or "Make the most of every opportunity" (NIV, Ephesians 5:16), so clearly he places a high value on this limited commodity. Interestingly, this present culture, more than previous generations, places an inordinate value on time.

While time is lucid and dynamic, it should be treated with value and respect. It is a part of eternity. We dare not treat it lightly or casually. We are all managers, stewards of what God gives us. So, how should we manage time?

Managing Personal Time

It is important that you attempt to separate your personal time from your ministry time. While it is impossible to make that separation on some days and during certain ministry "seasons," ultimately it is essential to your physical, mental, spiritual, and family health to guard your personal time. Learn to not feel guilty when you set aside time at work to pay attention to a personal item, any more than you would setting aside time at home to pay attention to a ministry agenda which cannot be avoided. When that happens, without making it a big deal, let someone know how you have spent your time.

Buy a watch. I have a ministry friend who does not own a watch and who often reminds me of that fact, with a silly grin. He is usually late to most meetings. As I wrote this paragraph, a pastor friend stopped by to visit. He smiled when I told him my current topic, then pulled up his sleeve—no watch. We both laughed. However, he uses his cell phone as his time manager and that works for him.

Buy a calendar, paper or electronic. Again, use the tool that works for you. I am amazed how long I initially existed in my ministry role before I bought a real calendar. I was young, more impulsive, and had a rather light schedule. I could actually remember when my three appointments were during any given week. Not today. Three appointments a day would be a light schedule. My memory is not that good.

Coordinate your calendar with your spouse. Protect your days off. Plan vacations, anniversary celebrations, birthdays, soccer games, and more. Don't allow those special days or events to get squeezed out of your life by failing to include them on the calendar.

Determine if you are a morning or evening person. If you're not sure, ask your spouse or best friend—they will know, trust me. Then, let others know your time preferences. If you are not a morning person, don't schedule early morning breakfast meetings.

I have a close ministry friend who, as an associate pastor, seldom arrived in the office or started his ministry day before noon (except as needed). Yes, you read that correctly. Of course, he then worked till ten or eleven o'clock at night. He knew his biological clock, and his ministry cohorts as well as his wife and family learned to adapt accordingly. Find what works for you (and what your supervisor will accept).

Managing Ministry Time

Remember, God is not going to ask you, "How much time did you work?" or, "How many hours did you put in while serving on planet Earth?"

> ### Time Wasters
>
> - Doing it all yourself, not asking for help or denying delegation.
> - Procrastinating.
> - Constantly changing your mind and "moving things around."
> - Spending too much time on the nonimportant, especially small-talk conversations and meetings.
> - Taking on more projects than feasible, spreading yourself too thin.
> - Refusing to organize because it feels nonspiritual and less than spontaneous.
> - Avoiding accountability like the plague.
> - Not saying no.

God has given you time as a resource to complete the work he gave you to accomplish. Ask yourself, "How did I use that gift for God and for the ministry this week?"

Seriously, do your own time study. Don't wait for a ministry leader to ask for your time report. You will be amazed on the hours spent in ministry, hours on personal agendas, and hours wasted … gone forever.

That said, ask your supervisor or governing team to make clear how much time they expect you to give to the ministry. Depending on your role, it may even be wise to ask how they see that time broken down. Does leadership expect you to be in the office, on the road, visiting people, studying?

Create useful calendar tools for ministry participants. Whether it is a wall calendar, newsletter, poster, or website, design ways for people to know when something is happening. And, if time or date must be changed, make the change with sufficient advance notice … enough said. Let others clearly see that you respect their time.

Write it down. If you just made a verbal promise to meet with someone or you committed to care for a detail item, make sure it is logged in a PDA or written on a calendar or "to do" list (or whatever recording method works best for you). Don't rely on your memory, especially the longer you are in your role and the more responsibility you acquire.

Ten Tips That May Indicate You Need to Better Manage Your Time

1. You know that you procrastinate.
2. You are often frazzled to get things done, and you do not procrastinate.
3. You complain you have too much to do (you did not say no).
4. The work day begins with no plan for action ... it just begins.
5. People question where you are and how you are using your time.
6. You have begun avoiding change, risk, and new ideas.
7. You seldom read helpful books or articles, even though you mean to.
8. Your new habit is avoiding people to get your work done.
9. Work is not fun and you find yourself watching the clock.
10. Your spouse or best friend says, "You are too busy."

Years ago I asked a layperson in our church how he managed his three companies and busy life. I will never forget his response, "At the end of each day I write down five things I will do tomorrow. When tomorrow comes I don't go home until I get those five things done. Some days I go home early, others late." My friend found the system that works for him.

In addition to my thin, shirt-pocket-size, annual calendar, I always take several three-by-five cards everywhere I go. I am always writing things down. Ideas, promises, suggestions, names, phone numbers all go on one of the small white cards, which then finds its home in the single nine-inch leather organizer that I carry. That works for me.

So, what system works well for you? Find your personal style and then stick to it.

Here are a few other helpful tips:

- Learn to think backward from a deadline. Keep asking, how much time will it take to reach a particular goal? Be realistic.
- Handle things once. I learned this valuable tool early on in ministry: *File it, pass it on, throw it away, or take care of it.* That mantra has been a time-saver and, I am sure, a life-saver. It should be that simple.
- If possible, have someone (such as an administrative assistant) be aware of or coordinate your ministry schedule. If a lack of funds prevents hiring this assistance, consider one or two capable volunteers. After resisting this idea for years, I finally caved in—it is one of the best management decisions I've ever made.
- Set aside time to talk with key people or get away to pray, plan, and dream. You and only you can make room for these strategic times of input. If you don't place them as a priority on your calendar, everything else, including the tyranny of the urgent, will crowd them out.

Managing Money

*If everything seems to come by simply signing checks [or using credit cards],
you may forget that you are at every moment totally dependent on God.*

C. S. Lewis

The man who loves money is the man who has never grown up.

Robert Lynd

*But mark this: There will be terrible times in the last days.
People will be lovers of themselves, lovers of money.*

2 Timothy 3:1–2

Where Do You Live?

My pastor, Ed Dobson, said it well in one of his sermons, "Living above your means is slavery. Living at your means is selfish. Living beneath your means is stewardship."* Those three principles are more than thought-provoking, they are essential insights to guide every expenditure and financial decision.

As a ministry staff person, I think I can make three safe assumptions about your salary or paycheck. First, you could be making more money with your skills and education in several other professions. Next, you think a lot about money. Finally, you are financially overcommitted or always stretching to make it from month to month. I recall one staff person who said to me, "I am just one month away from losing my house." That is an awful place to live.

A parent recently shared that her collegiate son attended a Campus Crusade for Christ conference on the East Coast. She was thrilled when he called and said, "Mom, I just made a commitment to Christ that I will not desire to ever become a wealthy man." I think I would call that a "vow of moderation." That is a great place to live.

"Don't let your *outgo* exceed your *income* for danger that this will become your *downfall.*" That pithy statement is really quite profound. Some days it sounds so simple. Others it can be scary and create horror in our drama of everyday finances.

You may need to embrace or commit to a different lifestyle than you dreamed or imagined at this point in your life. Live away from debt, the

---

*For more on this topic from Dr. Edward G. Dobson read *Simplicity* (Grand Rapids: Mich.: Zondervan, 1995).

controller of life and breath. Live with contentment and learn to live simply. Watch out for the traps of cultural consumerism. Avoid the sin of covetousness and greed. You will be glad you did. And when you do, it will show positively to those entrusted to your care.

Be honest. Admit to your spouse or accountability partner if finances are a problem. Get help if you need financial assistance. Let your board or senior leader know if you are struggling financially (it may be time for a well-deserved salary adjustment).

Finally, pray and then tithe! Commit your finances to the Lord, once you have followed and lived obediently to biblical stewardship principles. Enjoy the amazing discoveries of how God provides.

What Principles Guide You?

The same principles that guide your personal financial planning will most likely guide your ministry response to finances. If you plan to buy a car or house and save the money for it, you will do equally well in planning a ministry facility or mission trip.

As I review the three guidelines of planning, giving, and limiting, consider your personal management of money while I refer to ministry management. One of the requirements of an "overseer" is to manage one's family well and not be a lover of money (see 1 Timothy 3:3–4). While the specificity (bishop, elder, or deacon) of this biblical mandate may not apply directly to your situation or role, it still might serve as a worthy standard and foundation to establish.

Planning

I have already said much (maybe too much?) about planning. Yet as the topic is found throughout the Bible both in principle and practice, it cannot be ignored. Are you a planner? Are you spontaneous?

By the way, spontaneity can be a good thing, a strong leadership quality that enables you to act quickly in the midst of a sudden need or crisis. But in a leadership role, being spontaneous most of the time is not how the troops want to be led.

People want to have a general if not a clear sense that there is a "road-map" to follow. They prefer a prescribed plan and time frame in which to accomplish their mission. That sense of "going together" and accomplishing a mission is also God-given, part of our DNA. (Actually, spontaneous leaders have a plan and are very much in control … it is usually a last-minute plan and they are often the only ones who make and communicate it. Nevertheless, that is their plan.)

Advanced planning of a schedule and budget are not ends in themselves, only means to the end. Planning a schedule lets people know where they need to be, when they need to be there, and encourages their commitment and support in advance. Planning a budget assures followers and leadership of how they are going to get there. Without one or the other, a ministry endeavor can either get lost or stalled along the way.

Communicate both schedule of time and budget of funds to your people. Money and schedules do not need to be a covert operation. If people understand the budget, they will not wonder or question why they are having chicken for the banquet instead of prime rib. If they see in advance the full ministry calendar, they will not be upset when an event causes a personal sacrifice of time.

"I am not a planner. I'm a lot like Steve in the story," you say. If so, empower someone in your ministry who *is* a good planner, then learn to submit to that person's plans and details. Doing so will strengthen your leadership, not undermine it.

Giving

Are you perceived as a giver or a taker? Have you fostered such a spirit of giving in your ministry that others are likewise inspired to give from their heart, soul, mind, and strength? If you and your team want to consider a great biblical passage on giving, there's no better one than 2 Corinthians 8–9.

At Grand Rapids Theological Seminary we have determined to become givers, not takers, and have designed an entire ministry to give to our alumni, not ask them to give to us. With that sincere spirit of giving, they are giving to others. God is supplying all of our needs. We are not surprised.

I have watched some ministries that hoard resources for their own means struggle from year to year with finances and attendance. I have observed other ministries give away inordinate amounts of funds and people to other ministries, yet they never seem to lack funding or have a problem filling seats.

"You cannot outgive God" is one of those power phrases that seems to guide personal financial choices in giving. I believe the same applies to a ministry. Give away your ministry. Then see how God responds. You will not be surprised.

Limiting

Do you know how to put the brakes on? Do you know when to say, "Enough is enough"? Can you find contentment with what you have, not always wishing or wanting more? That becomes a personal issue first, then leaks out into your ministry direction and decisions.

One way to limit funding is by following the budget; another is having others hold you accountable. A third way to create healthy limits is by developing an annual plan within your resources and living with it. It does not need to become a hardship to say no. As you can see, now we are back to planning. Planning, giving, and limiting become a cyclical process.

What Example Do You Give?

Whether you realize it or not, many people will observe your expenditures and watch your budget. Some will be quick to point out your balance line; others will patiently wait to see how you come out at the end of the fiscal year. Here are several questions to consider:

- Do you request last-minute expenditures?
- Do you request expenditures before you know the budget balance?
- Do you give any thought to whether the ministry really needs this item or can afford this expense?
- Do you follow the best accounting procedures, granting permission and healthy accountability to those responsible for the ministry's finances?
- Are you perceived as one who treats money in a casual or cavalier manner, with little respect for living within your budget?
- Do you create expenditures on your own or do you discuss purchases with others?

Does leadership see you as a good steward, responsible with the funds entrusted to your care and authority? If not, you may be finding resistance in other areas of ministry. For example, your time management and how you are using other resources (space, equipment, personnel, etc.) may be questioned. Or there may be a lack of respect for your ability to lead or make decisions.

Here are a few things you can do to create a positive influence and gain respect from the trustees or stewards in your ministry:

- Communicate with someone in leadership before you authorize a ministry expenditure. Set a dollar amount limit above which you will always seek accountability.
- Regularly ask the treasurer or accounting personnel to give you updated records on your budget balance.

- Make requests for expenses as far in advance as possible. Develop this as the norm. So, when unexpected expenses do arrive, they are perceived as the exception.
- Pray about money.
- Make a concerted effort to seek the best prices or bid for an expense.
- Apologize immediately when an expense is too large or goes over the budget.
- Never surprise ministry with an unauthorized expenditure.

Make money a matter of prayer. Ask God to provide. Show respect and gratitude to people who give to the ministry. Develop a mind-set that says, "The budget creates a privilege to do ministry" not "The budget is the ministry's obligation for me to do my job." Many people will see and notice the difference.

Additional Reading

Covey, Stephen R. *First Things First*. New York: Simon and Schuster, 1994.

Covey, Stephen R. *The Seven Habits of Highly Successful People*. New York: Simon and Schuster, 1989.

Engstrom, Ted W. and Edward R. Dayton. *The Art of Management for Christian Leaders*. Waco, Tex.: Word, 1976.

Finzel, Hans. *The Top Ten Mistakes Leaders Make*. Wheaton, Ill.: Victor Books, 1994.

Miller, Kevin. *Surviving Information Overload*. Grand Rapids, Mich.: Zondervan, 2004.

Managing Difficult Relationships

It is to a man's honor to avoid strife, but every fool is quick to quarrel.

An unfriendly man pursues selfish ends; he defies all sound judgment.

> Be sure you know the condition of your flocks,
> give careful attention to your herds.
>
> *Proverbs 20:3; 18:1; 27:23*

The fallen, the frivolous, the captious, the indifferent, and even the malicious must share our love. We must love them to Jesus.

Charles Haddon Spurgeon

David was well known in the business community—adventurous, self-taught, an ingenious entrepreneur. David also had significant influence (or call it political capital) in the church at which he and his wife were members.

When Dan, the new associate pastor, arrived he became David's personal project. David's mission was to become the new staff member's ministry mentor. He taught Dan the church's history, core values, mission, "tribal rituals and taboos." Actually, the two had some wonderful times together over lunches and visits in each other's homes.

After a few months, David started making certain requests of Dan. Initially, they were rather harmless and Dan agreed to them. Then requests became more frequent. Requests turned into demands. Demands became laced with threats.

Finally, the day came when Dan refused to handle a situation the way David expected (demanded). David blew up. Dan listened to David's rage and ranting for two hours over the phone, too scared to hang up, fearing what his "mentor" would do to hurt his or the ministry's reputation. Dan thought he could reason with David, but found he was speaking with an unreasonable person.

Shaken by David's tirade, Dan went to his senior pastor to share the awful story of horrible accusations and unkind comments. The senior pastor knew exactly what Dan was talking about, having been David's target of control and manipulation before Dan arrived on staff. He too was fearful of this man's power and influence.

As David's invective spirit and threatening outbursts continued, Dan struggled with what to do. Quitting sounded tempting. "Taking David on" would clearly (in Dan's mind) result in vocational suicide. Prayer became the only option. He prayed for his own patience and kindness toward David.

Dan learned to ask God for wisdom, especially when David was on the other end of the phone. In time, he learned to establish several physical and emotional boundaries with David. He always offered to pray with David after every encounter that David initiated. He limited David's visits and calls to forty-five minutes instead of the hours that would otherwise be lost to such interactions.

In time, David moved on—literally, to another state and vocation. Dan learned some good lessons. He survived David. Guess what? Other "Davids" appeared in time.

Different People

God created us in his image with unique backgrounds, experiences, talents, gifts, and temperaments. He made that clear when he referred to the church as a combination of different body parts, describing one of us as a foot, another as a hand, still others as eyes, ears, and so on (see 1 Corinthians 12:12 – 31). We are all different. And those differences sometimes can make it difficult for people to work together.

I find it amazing that among any three people, two combinations will get along with each other very well but one relationship will not work. In other words, if Jane, Susan, and Mary are working in the same ministry, Jane and Mary may work together well and Susan and Mary may work together well. However, Jane and Susan may not do well when it is just the two of them.

Obviously, relationships can become very complicated and there often are no simple answers or solutions to bring everyone together in perfect harmony. Staff members are responsible to God for their own attitude toward the people in their ministry. Each one must respond to the foibles of others with godliness and spiritual maturity. The first place to look when a conflict presents itself with another staff member, volunteer leader, or ministry participant is in our own heart.

In this chapter I have attempted to identify six different types of difficult people. While not inclusive, the following overview is fairly representative of those you likely will meet somewhere along your ministry journey.

Types of Difficult People

Selfish People

Selfish people are just that, selfish. They are self-aggrandizers routinely promoting their own cause and jockeying for political position. They love power, controlling the immediate situation, whether sitting behind the desk or standing up front.

Selfish people always share their story first. Their agenda is the only agenda that really matters (to them, at least). If they are not in the spotlight or in charge, they usually disengage and remain critically passive on the sideline (they typically don't become loud, ugly, or angry). They enjoy living in their own world. Your world doesn't exist, unless they can get into your world and be a key player. They never ask questions about you, nor do they acknowledge your role and ministry. You are there to serve them. It is that plain and simple.

In time, other people begin to see a lack of integrity and legitimacy in selfish people's exaggerated claims. Something is not believable. They cannot be fully trusted.

Resolve: You will most likely not change their heart, mind, or behavior. Love them. Pray for them. Seek ways to sincerely and honestly honor them. Set careful boundaries so that you are not manipulated or controlled by their self-seeking agenda. Forgive.

Apathetic People

We've all heard someone occasionally say, "I don't know and I don't care." Unfortunately, some folks really mean that! Such people act as anchors to hold back your ministry. They show no concern about the passion or mission that is driving you and others forward.

Apathetic people show up at events, do the bare minimum, and exit. They don't speak, other than privately to others. Though not overt troublemakers, their negative tone and attitude eventually begins to drain the enthusiasm of others.

Resolve: Spend time with these people. Ask questions to discover their personal delight and encourage them to pursue that area, even if it means going somewhere else or creating something just for one person. Be patient. Be joyful. Give them some of your joy.

Opinionated People

They are usually right—just ask them. Exceedingly analytical, they love to ask pointed questions, nearly impossible to answer. They appear to have a predetermined agenda, and they seem to want it to be yours. You would love to run the other direction. While at the beginning of an interaction they can appear to hold their cards very close, they are looking for an opportunity to divulge their entire hand.

Highly opinionated people are very observant, well read, and selectively interactive. They may appear obstinate, curt, even hostile, but underneath that strong opinion is a sense of loyalty and earnest desire for your best and that of others. Though they respect the system, they have little patience for it if it is broken or malfunctioning. Answers and solutions which reflect their core values are most important to them.

Resolve: Listen to opinionated people; don't blow them off. Seek to understand their core values and their opinions. They hold those opinions for a reason.

If they openly disagree with you and ask tough questions, work through the answers together. Explore options to expand their opinion. Humbly resolve that they may just be right; if so, use that input to further the mission. If they are wrong, or their opinion is not germane to the development of the ministry, agree to disagree and move on with respect for each other's point of view.

Bitter People

Bitter people are those who haven't gotten what they wanted in the past or what they hope to find or achieve in the present. The bitter root in their lives can cause all kinds of havoc (see Hebrews 12:15), often leading to uncontrolled emotions, slander, and hurtful actions (see Ephesians 4:31).

In many cases, bitter people are self-perceived victims of their environment or circumstances. Highly competitive, they often envy or feel jealous of their best friends or those who appear to be successful in ministry to the point that they carry grudges and become angry (see the next profile).

With bitter people, there is something missing. While we cannot fill that void, we can pay kind attention and share the fruit of God's Spirit to this one held captive in a harbor of losses and unclaimed adventures.

Resolve: Invite bitter people into your world. Help them make new discoveries and find new joys. Let them know that they can move forward from their loss and that there is more to life and ministry than trying to reclaim the past.

Treat them as valued partners of the team. Let them see their contribution. Assist them in discovering their spiritual giftedness and place in the ministry family. Honor them. Bless them.

Hostile People

You may be familiar with the saying, "Angry people win." I have found that to be true. When we were kids, we called such people "bullies."

Very few of us enjoy someone's uncontrolled anger. When displayed in ministry, we tend to quietly back off and cave in to that individual's demands or desires. Our highest value at that moment becomes peacemaking.

Hostile people usually hold a grudge toward someone. The "someone" may be different from day to day. Clearly they live with unresolved issues—sometimes petty and inconsequential, sometimes quite significant—and they need to demonstrate control to prevent further losses or failures. Neither have they learned forgiveness.

> **The Seven Sins That Can Make You a Difficult Person**
>
> - Pride
> - Envy
> - Greed
> - Lust
> - Anger
> - Gluttony
> - Sloth

In most cases angry people have been hurt by someone sometime in their life. Because typically they have carried that hurt for a long time, it has a way of frequently reappearing. In his book *Making the Timeless Timely*, Rabbi Samuel M. Stahl says, "We think that holding a grudge against someone who wronged us will make us feel better. Yet, in reality, keeping a grudge can debilitate us."

Debilitated hostile people are not easy to be around, especially if they've found a way into your ministry.

Resolve: Be kind to the hostile (see Ephesians 4:32). Seek to understand why they live the way they do. Understand that their tarnished image came from somewhere else, not from you. Set boundaries on the physical drain they may cause. Tough love may be the lone resolve, if that is the only language they understand.

In the meantime, don't let them rob your joy or let them take your focus off your mission. And don't take bullies' attacks personally. Remind yourself that their power play is shortlived and not durable.

Troubled Supervisors

What if the difficult person is your boss or immediate supervisor? You know, the one who has become impossible to work for because he or she is always overdemanding and under-appreciating.

It may be he or she is a very unhappy person. That unhappiness and lack of personal fulfillment may go back to childhood, current family relationships, or the inner realization they are in the wrong place with the wrong role. They may be suffering with personal discouragement or physical pain; they may have bad news they can't or don't know how to report to you. Consider the many reasons they could be struggling, and don't rule out the possibility that the struggle may be with *you*.

> **A Few Ways to Earn Respect Among Difficult People**
>
> - Make personal promises to serve them, then do it.
> - Loosen up and create some casual downtime together to share stories.
> - Always be honest; never exaggerate or play political games.
> - Pray *with* them, not just *for* them.

I have learned to observe that supervisors who are promoted above their giftedness or experience become difficult to serve. They are not sure of their own strengths and abilities. Their weaknesses stare them in the face every day. Unsure of where they are going, they frustrate those attempting to follow.

Resolve: It is important to not distance yourself from this type of supervisor. It will only reinforce their personal insecurity and fears, and make them more difficult to understand and share ministry with.

Try to overcommunicate. Initiate more time listening and learning with your supervisor. Ask thoughtful questions as appropriate.

Lead upward if necessary, by helping your leader gain a better grasp of what needs to be done. Do everything you can to personally offer support and encouragement. Don't go behind their back, especially when they are in pain.

Loving People

Servant Care

Remind yourself that God has placed the difficult person(s) in your ministry. That means he has entrusted them to your care. So, show you care. Express sincere concern for the needs of the people around you.

One might want to define ministry as a "contact sport." A serious priority should always be given to nurturing others. That is why we are here. That is why Christ died. That is why we struggle and wage war with an evil one, to bring people into the forever family of God.

While we love to minister to grace-filled, compliant, uncomplicated people, the world is not so tidy. James, the brother of Jesus, requests that we not be respecters of persons by showing favoritism (see James 2:1 – 10). Often we apply that passage to the rich and poor. Yet, "our neighbor" (verse 8) is whoever God brings alongside us. That includes difficult people. Frankly, they are often the ones harassed and helpless, living as sheep without a shepherd, because very few shepherds want anything to do with them.

At this point I want to offer one word: grace. Show grace. Offer grace. Abundantly provide grace to the difficult people in your ministry, as Christ did for you.

Cultivating Kind Relationships

Cultivating relationships with difficult people requires bringing grace to an entirely new level — no longer offered at a distance, but upfront. It is grace at its closest, so close it can be a painful experience. Maybe that, in part, is what Jesus meant when he invited us to pick up our cross and follow him.

Again, you may not be able to change the mind or behavior of a difficult person. But you can be a minister of grace, close-up and personal. Here are a few suggestions to initiate a kind relationship as a ministry staff person:

- Send an occasional note of kindness and encouragement.
- Include a difficult person in your personal or ministry plans.
- Seek out their opinion and insight on a simple question. Affirm their good insight.
- Speak well of them to others.
- Go out of your way to be first to extend a greeting and warm welcome rather than avoiding them.

Have a genuine redemptive concern for difficult people. Again, we can't change them, but God can. Instead of firing back a reason to make a wrong right, or trying to settle the score, consider less bullish responses. Focus on how to bring these people into the ministry. Never find yourself saying, "We don't need that person here." Let them make that decision.

My friend Jim Smoke has often said, "We present our arms in one of two ways to people, folded against our chest or wrapped around theirs." What good advice. What a great way to show mercy and kindness.

Building Respect for Others

Everyone wants respect. That's a given. But some don't receive much respect, and maybe that is why they become difficult—they are seeking so hard, too hard, to earn others' respect.

Showing respect means acknowledging another's giftedness or the simple fact they are created in the image of God. Everyone can be complimented and respected for something. Think about it. Now, deliver it.

Building respect translates into giving. Give your time. Give attention when someone wants to talk to you. Give whatever resources you have available; resist hoarding them for your own agenda and success. Give up your own ego, even if theirs is larger than yours. Ego battles are ugly and messy.

> **Showing Respect to Others**
>
> - Give credit where credit is due.
> - Honor others in a public forum.
> - Invite others into the early stages of a plan or process.
> - Visit and give positive feedback in a routine time frame.
> - Ask how you can help and seek to do just that, either by granting support or removing stressful burdens and obstacles.

Respect demands fairness. If someone deserves to be honored, give honor where honor is due. If you want to create a difficult relationship, ignore the work and giftedness of another.

Give a cup of cold water, even to the difficult people. They want to be refreshed. Offer the same to them as you do to others. As you refresh their spirit, watch them grow.

Additional Reading

Allender, Dan and Tremper Longman III. *Cry of the Soul: How Our Emotions Reveal Our Deepest Questions about God.* Dallas: Word, 1994.

Bevere, John. *Forgive and Build Bridges.* Lake Mary, Fla.: Strang, 2001.

Cloud, Henry. *Changes That Heal: How to Undertand Your Past to Ensure a Healthier Future.* Grand Rapids, Mich.: Zondervan, 1992.

Palmer, Parker. *The Active Life: A Spirituality of Work, Creativity, and Caring.* San Francisco: Jossey-Bass, 1999.

Richardson, Ronald. *Creating a Healthier Church: Family Systems Theory.* Minneapolis: Augsburg, 1996.

Shelley, Marshall. *Well-Intentioned Dragons.* Minneapolis: Bethany House, 1994.

Smedes, Lewis. *The Art of Forgiving: When You Need to Forgive and Don't Know How.* Westminster, Md.: Ballantine, 1997.

Managing Overload

Do not wear yourself out to get rich [to get ahead];
have the wisdom to show restraint.

Proverbs 23:4

A simple man believes anything, but a prudent man
gives thought to his steps.

Proverbs 14:15

So many people have been living stressful lives for so long that they've
become desensitized ... like living in the flight path of O'Hare Airport.

Dan Baker

From the beginning the ministry team at Village Church had agreed that Sharon was to be paid for twenty hours a week to oversee the weekly drama productions. No one had asked her to do more than that. But she did. Very upset because of working extra hours without reimbursement, she felt unfairly treated, and now she had suddenly resigned.

New to the staff of Village Church, Mitch had worked with a few dramatic productions in a former ministry context and also had some drama experience in college. Mitch was called into the senior pastor's office.

"Mitch, we need you to direct the weekly dramas for our services. We start again in two weeks, after Labor Day. You are the only staff person who can help us," pleaded the pastor. "Do I have a choice?" said Mitch. "Not really," responded the pastor.

Mitch had never seen drama in the services at Village, he and his wife having arrived at the beginning of the summer when the drama ministry was taking a break. He felt very inadequate, especially with the unknown. Nonetheless, he met with the drama team and began to find scripts, recruit more actors, and conduct rehearsals.

The first few weeks were rough. Mitch put in many extra hours. He worked late at night, carrying home armloads of drama sketches to find appropriate materials. After several months, however, it became a part of Mitch's rhythm and routine. Small concessions were made in his job description and permission was granted to comp the extra time invested.

What's more, Mitch found a new joy in this unexpected opportunity. New friends were made, new talents were discovered, and a new ministry was born. The initial overload was past, as Mitch managed balance in both his personal schedule and physical energy. The "extra" time and effort was well worth it.

Overload Is a Reality of Ministry; It Should Not Become the Norm!

"This is an all-out team effort; we all need to come in early and stay late." "It's that time of year (holiday, special event, close of the fiscal year, etc.) that dictates everyone puts in 125 percent." Such comments are fairly common in the business world, and the ministry world is no different. Sometimes overload cannot be avoided, and extra hours and extra work are expected of some, if not all employees.

Ministry is dynamic. Seldom is there a static format or routine schedule for the ministry staff person. Overload can be a prescription for either zeal or, of course, for burnout. As long as these occasional long days, weeks, events, and extra responsibilities are managed as temporary and not a license for a ministry leader or supervisor to abuse or take advantage of willing staff members or volunteers, all generally goes well.

Healthy management starts with awareness. As a staff member, you need to be aware of the kind of time and energy you are giving to ministry. As noted elsewhere in this book, it's an excellent idea to take a personal inventory of your hours and work habits. Assess what you are actually doing as compared to your written job description. Is there alignment? Is there misalignment? Are the wheels beginning to fall off?

Everyone needs to maintain balance in every area of life. That balance will grant the necessary tools and equipment to manage the overload days and weeks. A healthy staff person in a healthy ministry context will be able to say no to too much stress and navigate through very difficult times when "extra" is expected and needed.

Being honest with yourself and your supervisor is essential. Though you are aware of the overload, is your supervisor aware of it too? Does he or she really understand and realize how many hours you are giving to the ministry over and above your expected work week? The supervisor has only one way of knowing the truth … and that's you telling the truth.

The ministry staff member needs to regularly read and monitor their emotional, physical, and spiritual gauges. Pastor Bill Hybels of Willow Creek Community Church has preached this commonsense message at ministry conferences from coast to coast. His 1991 *Leadership* article "Reading Your Gauges" indicates how easy it is to miss the warning lights on our emotional gauge while we head toward a ministry meltdown. As ministry staff, we are more programmed to maintain physical health and spiritual health, not emotional vitality.

Handling the Addiction of Ministry

Just saying no is not always the answer. Ministry cannot be denied. It is our calling. God has gifted and placed us where we are to share the good news of Christ's gospel, the message of love and grace to lost and hopeless people. While we cannot say no to ministry, we can accept the fact that God does not expect us to sacrifice our health, families, or moral and spiritual lives for the sake of ministry.

Say yes to the highest of priorities, to what is required on your job description, to your strengths and area of giftedness. In addition, say yes to your spouse, children, and friends. Say yes to a hobby, day off, and vacation time. Say yes to something you enjoy without that becoming a new obsession.

Avoidance is not an option. Ministry will always be there. You can't walk away from ministry and pretend that the tensions you leave behind today won't exist tomorrow. There is always one more person who needs to be encouraged or rescued. The phone does not stop ringing and there is always another knock at the door.

Ministry cannot be avoided. We must believe that God is sovereign and will gift us with sufficient spiritual gifts, time, and resources. While it is clear to God and us that there is always a need for more laborers (see Matthew 9:37 – 38), God has not assigned us double duty.

Ministry needs to be faced head-on. Again, realizing it will not get done today and still be there tomorrow, plan accordingly. Start each day with a list. End each day leaving a list of the things that you will do tomorrow … and only tomorrow.

Boundaries are essential. God's ministry boundaries need not become complicated. He has granted us certain spiritual gifts to serve him. We should seek and strive to operate within the framework of those gifts, our passion for people, and the guidelines of our job description and the ministry's mission.

We will do well to recognize and respect the biological clocks and limits that God has granted us. God originally designed and granted the *day* for work and the *night* for rest. Sleep and food are essential to a healthy life and ministry. Family, friends, and our personal relationship with God are our responsibility. Those priorities need safe borders to guard them from intrusion by unhealthy and unreasonable overloads.

Written annual objectives and monthly (even weekly) goals to meet those objectives provide healthy boundaries in managing a busy ministry schedule and its demands. That "little bit more" may not be necessary. It may bring a "wow" from your spectators or participants, but ask if

> ### Quick Hints to Personally Manage Burnout
>
> - Leave the task of ministry "there" before you go home. Work at that.
> - De-personalize negative comments and a negative environment. Try it.
> - Ask others for help and personal support. Open up.
> - Have a feast on the "good old days." Think back and rejoice!

it is ministry to people's needs or a production to draw attention for your own needs. Don't get caught or stuck with *bigger and better* or *new and improved.* Those words are a guarantee that you will never get out of that rut.

Accountability is imperative. Because we are too weak to plot a course to safety on our own, workaholics and ministry "enthusiasts" need accountability. We need to listen to our spouses, children, best friends, and those who are healthy in authority over us. Perhaps we may even want to form a ministry accountability group.

Many senior ministers are held accountable for their time and resource management by the ministry's governing board or, in some situations, a special task force or accountability group endorsed by the board. An associate minister should not be exempt, unless the supervisor is willing to take full responsibility for monitoring and assisting the ministry staff member toward healthy use of time and resources.

If you decide to create an accountability group, seek godly men and women (preferably couples if you are married and single adults if you are single, or a mixture of both single adults and married couples) who love you and understand the ministry's core values and mission. Appoint people who are mature and experienced in managing others. Look for honesty, care, and those who will demonstrate tough love for you, your family, and ministry.

Symptoms of Burnout

- I don't like my job anymore.
- Physical and emotional exhaustion are more frequent.
- I think often about doing something else.
- Isolation from others is preferred.
- I feel overworked and under-appreciated.
- It is easy to be focused on ministry outside of my job description.
- There is confusion between burn-out, stress, and depression.
- I am more emotional and sensitive than normal.
- I relish excuses to avoid going to work.

Permission should be granted. The place to land when you're constantly feeling stressed and overworked is in your supervisor's office. It is here that you request the unwritten rules or guidelines for comp time. Without complaining, your request may sound something like this: "I have just put in ten consecutive twelve-hour days to prepare and execute our annual retreat. May I take a few extra days off next week as comp time?" Ask. It should be given. Don't just give yourself a number of days without gaining permission. Once granted, you may then ask if you need to always request permission in similar situations.

In some cases, you must grant yourself permission. For example, if you are gifted in one particular area of ministry, you may be requested to share your expertise and service in other areas of ministry. Knowing your own regular workload and with healthy boundaries in place, sometimes you will be able to say yes and other times you will have to say no.

Just be sure to share a team spirit and participate in other areas when you can. Don't be like "Dale," a gifted speaker and staff member in pastoral care ministries in a medium-size suburban church. When asked by another staff person to teach a single adult Sunday school class, his response was, "Sure, but you will need to pay me out of your budget." Dale is clearly not a team player. His mercenary needs outweigh his heart for ministry.

"Permission granted" needs to be available to help balance the scale, not pad your checkbook. It's available to encourage your emotional IQ, to serve your family, and to promote a normal healthy life, protecting you from unnecessary overload and resentment which can later turn into bitterness.

Handling Overloads from Others

It is natural when poorly organized, procrastinating supervisors are under pressure to pass that stress and tension on to the ministry staff. Their objectives are not being met and they need your help. Besides, they seemingly rationalize, they are paying you to serve. The pressure is on. You feel obligated to say yes.

At such times, you need to be diplomatically honest and straightforward. If you are not, your resentment will come through. While you may offer to help with some overload this time, your healthy boundaries might also say without guilt, "Next time I would love to help you, if you give me more information and enough advance notice. But I have this evening scheduled (playing board games with my children)."

There are times when you will be taken advantage of because of your giftedness or willing spirit to serve. Beware. Be careful. Be honest. Speak up and offer to work together for a better plan to get things done in a more orderly, timely manner. The other option is to boldly say, "Maybe we can't do *that* at this time."

> ### Quick Tension Managers
>
> - Take a minute to pray.
> - Write a thank-you note to someone in ministry.
> - Make a casual call to a friend or phone home.
> - Take a brisk walk outside.
> - Share a quick snack with a coworker.
> - Take the long route home or back to the ministry place.
> - Listen to one of your favorite tunes.
> - Read a newspaper article.
> - Visit a coworker and "waste" a minute of their time on small talk.
> - Find a quiet spot to relax and think about something else.
> - Write down the things you will do tomorrow.
> - Write in your journal.

Occasionally, a fellow staff member will become overwhelmed and burdened with unexpected problems or a ministry overload. If he or she asks for help and you say yes, just be sure you are not creating an enabling system for a staff person who is not a good planner. Sometimes, a failure may be a wakeup call to be a better manager. You cannot "save" everyone.

Taking a Step Backward Is Not an Awful Idea

If you find yourself overextended, there is one other alternative when you cannot manage through some of the above suggestions. It may be time to take a step backward. You may have stepped into ministry over your head.

Some have called it the "Peter Principle." Occasionally, ministry staff are promoted beyond ability, experience, and giftedness. In due time, it catches up with the staff leader. He or she feels trapped and faces an increasing sense of overload.

Were you most fulfilled in your former role? Do you still have a passion for the people in that ministry position? Is it reasonable to go back to that role and regain renewed effectiveness in ministry?

If overload has led to significant ongoing stress and burnout, to the point of depression or frustrating activity, consider a step back. Take a break. Get good counsel. Pray. Take courage and move forward by taking a step backward.

Additional Reading

Hart, Archibald. *Adrenaline and Stress.* Revised edition. Nashville: W Publishing, 1995.

Hart, Archibald. *The Crazy-Making Workplace.* Ann Arbor, Mich.: Vine, 1993.

MacDonald, Gordon. *Ordering Your Private World.* Anniversary edition. Nashville: Oliver Nelson, 1995.

Swenson, Richard. *The Overload Syndrome: Learning to Live Within Limits.* Colorado Springs: NavPress, 1998.

The Ministry Staff Spouse

He who fears the Lᴏʀᴅ has a secure fortress,
and for his children it will be a refuge.

The righteous man leads a blameless life;
blessed are his children after him.

Proverbs 14:26; 20:7

We ought to be such husbands [spouses] that every husband [wife] in
the parish may safely be such as we are. Is it so? We ought to be the
best of fathers [parents]. Alas! Some ministers, to my knowledge, are
far from this for as to their families, they have kept the vineyard
of others, but their own vineyards they have not kept.

Charles Haddon Spurgeon
in Lectures to My Students

Donna was raised in a picturesque Midwest town close to a beautiful inland lake, which led boaters out to Lake Michigan. She grew up with one sister and parents whose love for her was never questioned. At age six, God became real to her while attending a vacation Bible school. From that day forward, youthful memories captured a deep and profound love for him.

Donna's early childhood introduction to Jesus Christ as Savior began a lifelong journey and desire to serve Jesus and others in "full-time ministry." While she could not fully envision or even clearly articulate that life of service, the longing never ceased.

"Going forward for the Lord" almost became a mantra and never-ending quest for Donna. As a teenager, she became very involved in a church youth group and the ministry of Youth for Christ. During a summer youth ministry trip to Puerto Rico, at age sixteen, she cemented and yielded her life to full-time ministry, again not knowing exactly what that would mean. She took advantage of every conference, Bible study, prayer group, and mission team opportunity, and attended Cornerstone University in Grand Rapids, to grow in her faith and learn how to better serve Jesus.

On that same team to Puerto Rico was a young man who would also make that same commitment to serve God. Yes, they later dated, married, and began an adventure in ministry. He started as a youth pastor and continued in associate pastoral roles. Donna explored every opportunity in ministry as a ministry staff spouse. Doors opened. Doors closed. Yet, the two remained faithful to God, each other, and people in five different ministry contexts. Donna's dreams were becoming real. Her lifelong prayers were answered one after another.

It wasn't until becoming an adult that she began to better understand the role of her family of origin, her marriage to a young man with the same desires, and the convergence of education, talents, experiences, and gifts. All of these marvelous events and gifts from God pointed to the early dreams and heartbeat to wholeheartedly serve Jesus Christ.

Donna also realized early in her marriage that it wasn't just her husband, the staff member, who had been called to vocational ministry, but that she shared the same invitation from God. She served alongside her spouse. Shared ministry wasn't about titles, money, or roles. It was all about God and people.

After thirty-one years of serving as a ministry staff spouse, Donna's call is just as real today as it was as a child. She realizes not everyone experiences God's plan in the same way over the same time frame. She knows how important it is that her relationship with God and ministry can make an enormous difference in her spouse's life and ministry. And it does.

Family Is a Priority

God never intended a family be sacrificed for the cause of the ministry. Just the opposite is true. Family is a model for ministry. Husbands are to love their wives as Christ loved the church (see Ephesians 5:22 – 33). Wives are to honor and respect their husbands in mutual submission to one another, as to the Lord (see Ephesians 5:21, 33). Children are a gift from the Lord — to be valued, cherished, nurtured, and loved. These imperatives are God's priorities.

Making family a priority is essential and needs to be demonstrated in very practical ways. Protecting a day off, family vacations, family traditions, children's events, and "date nights" are not options. Let your spouse and children know they are more important than the people in your ministry. The "rules" need not be more complicated than that.

NOTE: *I have asked my wife Donna to write the rest of this chapter. As you may have figured out, the story at the beginning of the chapter is hers. In my mind and heart, there is no one else who could share more valuable insights on this crucial topic.*

You and God
You Belong to God

In her book *High Call, High Privilege* Gail McDonald shares her personal quest for the secret of the spiritual life. As she shares the story of a missionary, she quotes the overseas minister, "A fire untended soon turns to useless ashes." Gail began to think about that statement and began a personal journey through the Bible, only to realize that God had given a powerful principle for her spiritual life. The moment she trusted Jesus Christ as Savior, the Holy Spirit placed a fire within her, and it was her responsibility to tend that fire.

That principle results in serving Jesus Christ. Gail helped me, a ministry staff spouse, to realize, accept, and find great joy in the privilege that is mine to serve Jesus and others alongside my spouse. I am humbled, grateful, and privileged to know God has chosen me to tend a spiritual fire as his servant.

When I was only six years old, God had powerfully and unusually placed in my heart a personal calling. Knowing and believing that life-truth freed me to realize I, not just my husband, was called into ministry. What a discovery, God had called me. I was now free to pursue that calling.

My freedom to serve has freed my spouse in his own service to Jesus Christ. We are both sold out. Our time is his time. Our priorities, gifts, and resources belong to God first, then to each other, then to our family and others.

Fortunately, I was never jealous of the extensive time that ministry demanded. I have learned to not regret a phone call in the middle of the night; hours spent at the hospital; long walks alongside people in their grief; church weddings, funerals, picnics, and other events; the major investments of discipling others and lesson and sermon preparation; and more. I was okay with it all. Why? I had a personal call.

I've talked to many women through the years who have been married to a ministry staff spouse and viewed the ministry as their husband's "job."

They had no sense of calling to ministry themselves. As I heard many share negative feelings about ministry, my heart was grieved over their missing out. I so wanted them to know my joy in serving Jesus as a ministry staff spouse. Indeed, I want ministry spouses to discover we are all ministers, with the glorious opportunity to serve Jesus Christ, whether paid or unpaid, married or single, with a title or without.

Your Expectations Are from God

In other words, *you be you*, just as God has designed. Early on in ministry I found myself exhausted trying to be someone else. I could not measure up or keep up with the demands of others. I could not just be me.

In the 1970s, as I was preparing for ministry, the "rules" for being a pastor/ministry wife were poorly defined. I sensed I was in big trouble right from the beginning because I didn't play the piano. I assumed (and it had been modeled) that to be a "good" ministry wife I had to play the piano; teach Sunday school; sing in the choir; have a perfectly planned Sunday menu for guests; work in the nursery; lead the women's ministry; give devotionals at a moment's notice; be an eloquent, humorous, theologically correct public speaker; always dress perfectly for any and every occasion; parade into the room perfect children (who knew all the answers to the questions the Sunday school teacher would ask); maintain a perfect looking home; and the list goes on. Whew! Some of you may think I'm making this up, but that was the way it was.

And though I know the above are sometimes considered the "expected role" of a senior pastor's spouse, I discovered it is seldom different for the ministry staff spouse. Because that was all I had ever been shown and knew, and because I bought into that mind-set, someone was suffering. That someone was me. I was hurting over not meeting other's expectations. I was stung by the comments of other ministry spouses and their

---

Your Personal Commitment to Ministry

While there is nothing mystical or magical about a "call to ministry," if you resent or find apathetic feelings toward your spouse's role as a ministry staff member, consider the following:

- Ask God to renew and align your heart toward your spouse's ministry.

- Pray every day for your spouse and the specific ministry events in his/her day.

- Be interested in (talk about) your spouse's ministry activity.

- Volunteer to use your gift in your spouse's ministry.

- Create a safe haven in your home as a place to do ministry and/or a place to get away from ministry.

expectations. Subtly, my self-image wasn't *my* self-image. It was someone else's.

Now, I must admit, I'm a people pleaser at heart and genuinely love to serve them to make them happy. Some reading this might want to label me as a codependent or use some other pathology to describe my personal DNA (help yourself). However, I realize many people in ministry can fall into that trap.

Eventually I learned to realize and accept that the expectations I live under must first come from God. He has given wonderful "rules for holy living" in Colossians 3:1 – 17, which include these words: "Set your minds on things above, not on earthly things. For you died, and your life is now hidden with Christ in God.... Therefore, as God's chosen people, holy and dearly loved, clothe yourselves with compassion, kindness, humility, gentleness and patience" (verses 2 – 3, 12). These are the expectations I want to live by, because they are God's. I have learned to resist and reject many of the things that others within the ministry thought I should be able to do or be.

I have learned and embraced being Me. I knew if I wasn't going to be Me, sooner or later the real Me would come out anyway. Through the years, my one piece of advice to ministry wives is to be YOU.

No One Else Can Be You

I can't tell you how refreshing and freeing it is going into a ministry setting as yourself. No pretense. It doesn't go without saying that I've always wished I could beautifully play the piano, but that wasn't part of God's plan for me. Instead, he's allowed me to use my voice through singing, speaking, and leading worship. As the psalmist writes, "[You are] fearfully and wonderfully made" (Psalm 139:14). Be the wonderful YOU that God created you to be for his honor and glory.

Your Job Is from God

Whether you're just beginning your ministry journey or if you've been in ministry for a while, let me encourage you to identify your giftedness. As you give yourself freedom and permission to be all that God created you to be, it's also important to know the spiritual gifts he's given to you. God's Word is clear: every believer has at least one spiritual gift (see 1 Corinthians 12:4 – 11).

It was in our ninth or tenth year of full-time ministry, as we served on the pastoral staff of Wooddale Church in Eden Prairie, Minnesota with Pastor Leith Anderson, that he taught a powerful course on discovering one's spiritual gifts. I particulary like Leith's definition: "Spiritual gifts are jobs from God."

While attending that course, a lightbulb went on! I didn't have to live a life of spiritual frustration! I could serve the Lord within the giftedness he had designed personally for me.

I found my job from God. It wasn't my husband's job. It wasn't the job the church gave me. It didn't come from other people. It was God's job description for me to be one of the many shepherds of the flock, teaching, showing mercy, and encouraging the sheep.

When we receive a special gift, what do we often do with it? Depending on the gift, I treasure it, display it, use it, share it. Isn't that exactly what God wants us to do with the "gifts" he's given us? He wants us to take great delight in them. Do you want to experience peace and joy in ministry? Serve within your gifts!

I often sit back and wonder how beautiful it would be if we all could work within the giftedness that God has given to us, instead of desiring or being jealous of someone else's gifts or talents.

> ### Discovering Your Spiritual Job from God
>
> - Pray and ask God to help you better understand the spiritual gifts described in the Bible. (Read 1 Corinthians 12, Romans 12, and Ephesians 4.)
> - Read books on discovering your spiritual gift. (I highly recommend *19 Gifts of the Spirit* by Leslie B. Flynn.)
> - Take a spiritual gift inventory. (See recommendations at the end of the chapter.)
> - Observe how other people have discovered and use their gifts.
> - Get involved in a ministry that interests you.
> - Don't be afraid of growing and discovering your gift through "trial and error."
> - Listen to what other people say over a course of time. Are they indicating they perceive one of God's spiritual gifts in you without you necessarily trying to demonstrate that gift? (That is a good sign God is at work through you!)
> - Dedicate yourself to develop the gift you sense God has given you.

You and Your Ministry Staff Member

You Belong to Each Other

From our first day in ministry, Doug and I have always approached it as a team. Many times in a ministry context our names were used together. Frankly, we both learned to place a high value on that dual identity. I'll never forget in one of our churches when someone said out loud in a business meeting, "When you get Doug and Donna, you get two for the price of one." I suppose you could read into that statement either a compliment or a criticism, though I certainly think the former was intended.

I can think of two reasons why we were often perceived as a team. First, Doug continually encouraged me to participate alongside him in ministry. By including me, he let others know we were a team. Second, I chose to be involved because I knew my gifts and where I could best be used. That doesn't negate the fact that much prayer went into each ministry opportunity we shared.

We find throughout the Gospels that Jesus modeled team ministry. The twelve disciples had one another. In addition, we find ministry teams among Paul, Silas, Luke, Barnabas, and Timothy. Married couples? Priscilla and Aquila worked together as a team to support the apostle Paul.

When I think of ministry, and I think about God's requirements for husbands and wives to love and respect one another, I believe spouses need one another in ministry. Ministry can be lonely enough, without your spouse engaged with you in God's work.

Consider these benefits of team ministry: When one is down, the other is there to lift up. We draw from one another's strength. Can you imagine any

---

You and Your Spouse: Ministry Teammates

The following ten ideas can encourage and build unity and oneness as partners in ministry:

1. Talk together about life, family, and ministry. Learn to develop a sense of intimacy, sharing your life and ministry in ways you don't share with others. Call each other throughout the day.
2. Pray together, and pray for each other when you are not together.
3. Invite your spouse into an area of your ministry. Share something in ministry, as little as the effort may be.
4. Read the same books and attend outside ministry experiences together.
5. Agree and decide how to open your home to ministry opportunities.
6. Discover creative ways to include your children in your ministry.
7. Celebrate your spouse's strengths. Give open and constructive feedback.
8. Learn to be versatile and flexible in your schedules and lifestyle. While you need to have healthy boundaries and established routines, remind each other that ministry is dynamic, not static.
9. In light of number eight above, protect your day off.
10. Date, vacation, and "Shabbat" together.

team sport being played with one person? I think ministry has always been a "team sport," from the very beginning of creation.

And of course, no one knows my weaknesses or shortcomings more than my husband (except maybe our daughter) and vice versa, but we help each other through them. We're able to add another dimension to the ministry since we know one another so well. We seek ways to complement each other. We don't take for granted the need to help one another.

You Can Be a Cheerleader

It is a great joy to share ministry with my spouse. I can't think of anything better. I genuinely believe one of my most important roles is to be Doug's strongest and loudest cheerleader. It comes easily, naturally, to cheer for something or someone you believe in.

I'm sure when you think of a cheerleader, all sorts of images come to mind. I suppose the most memorable to me is making a lot of noise and jumping up and down. While I am not a "loud" person and don't usually jump up and down, I do talk a lot about the ministry in positive, affirming ways. I tell Doug when I am proud of him, reassure him when something went well, and share the good things others have said. And, yes, I am honest to let him know the things he needs to know to help him grow and mature in ministry.

We all know ministry can be tough. There are times when your spouse may be overlooked and underappreciated. There are days when he or she will come home discouraged, cherishing the thoughts of last week's contact from another church with a ministry offer. Some people will say unkind things to your spouse. Others will say nothing. Late at night, your spouse will come dragging in the door, simply weary in well-doing. He or she may work all day ... alone ... for several days. Whatever the situation, be a cheerleader, a source of joy and encouragement. Some days your kind voice will be the only good news audibly heard.

Now, I'm not suggesting that you should go out and fight his or her battles and right all the wrongs. I've always taken the posture that God will fight those battles on our behalf. God keeps the final score card, I don't have to. Wow, that is so freeing.

I'm also not saying during those tough times I haven't hurt right alongside my husband, sometimes more. He needs my support. He needs me to be in his corner telling him to "[be] confident of this, that he who began a good work in you will carry it on to completion until the day of Christ Jesus" (Philippians 1:6)

I have also learned the value of building a cheerleading team. These trusted, godly friends can walk some of the tough journeys with you. God has been so faithful to bless us with invaluable friendships in every ministry. Today we could pick up the phone and call any one of them and they would be there for us.

So don your cheerleading outfit, whatever that may look like for you, and cheer on your spouse. There can be no doubt what a difference it makes if just one person believes in us. You're a team—go, fight, win, to the glory of God.

You Can Pray

One of the greatest ways we can share ministry with our spouse is through prayer. Early in our ministry I read a wonderful book, *Much Prayer—Much Power*, by a great missionary statesman, Peter Dyneka Sr., of the Slavic Gospel Association. This fervent prayer warrior impacted my life with this simple statement: "Much prayer, much power, little prayer, little power, no prayer, no power."

Communication is one of the keys to a great marriage and that's also true of our relationship to Jesus Christ. I think it's key to pray together as partners, but it's also vital that you pray *for* your spouse who serves as a ministry staff member. And you can encourage others to pray for your ministry staff spouse as well.

There is no shortage of resources on how to pray. One day as I began to prepare for a talk on prayer, I went into our home office and counted the books we have on prayer—I stopped counting at thirtysomething. Rather than read everything others said about prayer (I did read a lot), I chose to simply spend as much time praying as studying.

If praying for your ministry staff spouse is a rather new concept, don't worry about how you pray, or how long you pray, or what format you use. Just begin praying. Make a list of prayer requests beginning with his/her personal needs, then adding job responsibilities and special needs.

Ask your spouse what the day holds. Share calendars. Pray when those scheduled moments become real. Keep a list of events. Then, ask your spouse what happened, and assure him or her that you prayed. Believe me, when someone tells you that they're praying for you, that alone gives hope, strength, and confidence. I can't think of a more powerful way to partner and show love for my spouse than being faithful in prayer.

You and Your Children
Modeling Healthy Ministry in Your Home

If you have children, I encourage you to model healthy ministry in your home as well as out of the home. What exactly does that mean? I think it begins by speaking well about the people in the ministry in the presence of your children. It can include praying for ministry needs with your children or sharing the fruit, joys, and celebrations of ministry. Suddenly a door opens for them to the needs and joys of others.

The old saying is so true: "What you see is what you get." It's so important that our children see the same person living at home as they do in your ministry context. Children really do "catch" more than they're taught sometimes. Those young minds form attitudes and opinions which may lead them toward or away from loving God and others.

Doug and I were married for seven years before the Lord blessed us with our miracle baby, Darci. My earnest prayer had been Hannah's prayer from 1 Samuel 1:27: "I prayed for this child, and the LORD has granted me what I asked of him." Ever since Darci was old enough to understand, it has always been a burden on my heart that we authentically practice what we preach and to instill in her the fact that ministry is both a high calling and a high privilege. Don't get me wrong, we weren't perfect; but it was our desire and goal to be genuine and real with our daughter. When we were frustrated and tempted to speak poorly of people or the ministry, we resisted that weakness, especially in front of her. (Besides, it was amazing what she picked up from other children and adults in ministry settings ... things we had to talk about, balancing truth and reality.)

I remember recently for one of my "BIG" birthdays (you will have to guess which), my daughter surprised me with an album she had assembled. In it were thoughts and reminiscences from people we knew over three decades and four churches worth of ministry—whether a personal story, Bible verse, photograph, song, whatever God laid on their hearts.

In her letter asking my friends to contribute to this keepsake, Darci shared how I had been a cheerleader in her life and their lives. Now she was requesting that *I* be the recipient of *their* cheers. The most meaningful moment of this project was learning that my own daughter saw me as a cheerleader in her life and others. She actually had seen me as a positive role model for ministry. That happened at home.

Make your home a safe haven, a place where your family wants to be. Comfortably and casually invite ministry into your home, in whatever way is meaningful for you, your spouse, and your children. Mirror the DNA of the ministry at home. It need not be fancy, difficult, or all-consuming. You do not need to be a gourmet chef or the perfect housekeeper. Ministry in your home, like in your spouse's ministry assignment, is about people and God. And it reaps powerful benefits.

Over the years, when the phone has rung, we've had opportunities to offer the caller a needed place to stay. Some have stayed a night or two; others longer. I can't suggest what works best for you, but may I suggest that you pray how you open your home as a ministry to others. The young eyes and ears in your home will catch much through such modeling, influencing them positively in ways you might not even imagine.

Including Your Children as "Ministers"

King Josiah was only eight years old when he reigned over Judah. Samuel, David, and Daniel were young boys when God granted them ministry opportunities and responsibility. Jeremiah stated, "Ah, Sovereign LORD, ... I do not know how to speak; I am only a child" (Jeremiah 1:6). God does not preclude our children from being ministers and servants of Jesus Christ, even if it only means giving up *fishes and loaves.*

While it may not be God's plan for your children to go into ministry as their vocation, it is our responsibility to teach them to love God (see Deuteronomy 6:1ff), love others, obey his Word, and discover his will for their lives. We encouraged Darci's participation in ministry by often including her in some of our ministry experiences. She watched her mom and dad serve Jesus Christ. Sometimes she participated in music or drama. Other times she became a "sponge" and just soaked it all in.

From time to time, Darci wanted to be involved in her own ministry. Sometimes that inconvenienced our schedule, but God gave us the attitude, "It's okay!" We adjusted our lives to encourage her youthful ministry, whether it was sharing Jesus with friends, going on a mission trip, having summer Bible school in our backyard, or helping her pursue some of her God-given gifts and talents. We did not have an elaborate plan. We just did it.

While we recognized, and Darci helped us to see, some of the liabilities of growing up in a ministry staff member's home, we tried to be a "family in ministry." We often thought through our choices and determined if this or that activity would encourage and nurture our daughter as well as ourselves. While we sometimes missed that objective, we found great joy when we got it right.

Today, Darci is serving as a director of ministries on a local church staff. That was God's plan for her, not ours. She is growing. She is learning and leading. She reminds us of us … many years ago. What a smile that brings to our hearts and lives. But in all honesty, if Darci were loving God and loving others while working in a bank or restaurant, we would have the same smile.

After a recent Christmas Eve service we learned that Darci had designed and developed the program that had richly blessed our lives and many others. As Doug and I were driving home, I whispered a prayer of thanksgiving to the Lord for Darci and her husband, (our son-in-love) Jason, her heart, her passion, and her life. That night, I felt that a ministry mantle had been passed.

Additional Reading

Brestin, Dee. *The Friendships of Women*. Wheaton, Ill.: Victor Books, 1988.

Briscoe, Jill. *Renewal on the Run: Embracing the Privileges and Expectations of a Ministry Wife*. Birmingham, Ala.: New Hope, 2005.

Habecker, Eugene B. *Rediscovering the Soul of Leadership*. Wheaton, Ill.: Victor Books, 1996.

London, H. B. Jr. *Pastor to Pastor* CD Series. Colorado Springs: Focus on the Family, 1999–2005. (See www.family.org/resources.)

London, H. B. Jr. and Neil Wiseman. *Married to a Pastor*. Ventura, Calif.: Regal, 1999.

Omartian, Stormie. *The Power of a Praying Wife* and *The Power of a Praying Husband*. Eugene, Ore.: Harvest House, 2000.

Weaver, Joanna. *Having a Mary Heart in a Martha World*. Colorado Springs: WaterBrook, 2000.

Williford, Carolyn and Craig Williford. *Faith Tango*. Colorado Springs: WaterBrook, 2002.

Free Online Spiritual Gift Inventories

www.christianitytoday.com/biblestudies
www.churchgrowth.org/

PART 7

Practical Advice for Senior and Governing Leaders

Hiring a Ministry Staff Member

The wise in heart are called discerning.

Better a patient man than a warrior.

Proverbs 16:21a, 32a

The leader's challenge: Hiring and cultivating great managers,
the glue of an organization.

Tom Peters

The search committee at Redeemer Church was excited. After reading scores of resumés and screening nearly two dozen applicants, they at last were ready to interview their top candidate. Kelly Swanson looked perfect. One search committee member exclaimed before the interview, "We have our man! Let's just make him an offer when he comes in and forgo all these questions." A few nodded in agreement just before the chair invited Kelly and his wife, Carrie, into the conference room.

Kelly had it all on his resume: His references had given outstanding recommendations; his educational degree was more than the job description required; his graduate degree was distinguished with honors. He had ten years of experience in two different churches. It was apparent from his resumé and correspondence that he could write well. The committee was thrilled when they listened to one of his preaching tapes. To top it off, Kelly and Carrie could identify with the culture of the people attending Redeemer Church, having been born and raised in the same region. They were an obvious fit.

The two-hour interview was filled with serious discussion from doctrine to ministry. It also was punctuated from time to time with moments of uproarious laughter. Once a few tears were shed when Kelly told about the death of his oldest brother. The interview demonstrated he was a mature, capable, and confident leader. There was no doubt he could handle the job of senior pastor.

However, two of the search committee members were becoming a bit troubled. Twice they heard Kelly comment about the price of their house and the exotic vacations they enjoyed as a family. He also spoke of the need for an office large enough to house his extensive library and quiet enough to be secluded away from the other staff for serious meditation and study. That would mean rearranging the church office floorplan, though it was certainly doable.

Then Carrie mentioned how nice it was that the senior minister in their former church was given a car and one entire month off for study, in addition to the regular four-week vacation package. While some committee members dismissed the comments as informational, others saw the remarks as out of context.

Ron, the search committee chair, finally asked Kelly what he was expecting salary-wise. When the candidate threw out his number, the committee was rendered speechless, realizing his amount was significantly higher than what their denominational and regional research concluded would be a more-than-fair package. Kelly's resumé now looked less impressive and the preaching tape not quite as spectacular as it did before. The committee never did discuss money or an offer.

Before You Hire
Hiring Staff Should Be Strategic to the Ministry

Before hiring a staff member, you need to ask and answer a couple important questions: Is the only way to develop this ministry through hiring, or do we have the volunteers and non-paid staff to fulfill this area of our mission? Do we really need to develop this ministry, or are we being seduced to expand this area of service apart from our strategic initiatives?

A staff person needs to be strategically hired and placed for at least two reasons. First, the *mission* must drive the reason for the *position*. Second, the new hire needs to fit the position. It is possible to hire a capable person who's gifted and talented for the role, but not personally qualified for your ministry context. It's equally possible to hire a wonderful, godly person who is not gifted or capable of fulfilling the mission. While these issues may sound rather simplistic, they are vital to the success of the mission and the fulfillment of the person.

Another key question: Will this new position and person fit into what we are already doing? If the right person is brought into a new position that is perceived as external or even unnecessary to the mission and vision, the person will ultimately fail. If the wrong person is brought into the right position, failure is again inevitable. So, the leader must think strategically as he or she considers both mission and person before hiring.

Having said that, always review the validity of a vacant position to your current mission and needs *before* replacing a staff member. Due to strategic changes in the ministry, the position may no longer be needed.

Another tip: hire or rehire from within. It is always wise to survey existing staff to make sure you do not overlook exceptional talent or potential leadership in another area. You may have the right person for the job opening and only need to provide additional training or experience.

I once asked my friend Jim Griffith, the "coach's coach" among many ministry leaders, why he thought some ministries fail. His answer was spontaneous: *the wrong person in the wrong place.* Similarly, management guru Tom Peters once wrote, "Winning ... [means] having the right people in the right place at the right time." Wise counsel indeed.

Hiring Staff Is Hard Work

Hiring staff is not easy. Only by God's amazing grace will you find a shortcut. Finding the right person may require more time than you expected. It may result in ministry not getting done, or in placing higher expectations on volunteers and other staff, including the senior pastor. The temptation may come to settle for "the best we have on our list" or "the most available" rather than continuing to pursue "who we need to accomplish the mission."

I will never forget attending a leadership conference, "Institute for Church Imperatives," sponsored by First Baptist Church in Modesto, California, whose senior pastor, Bill Yaeger, forcefully warned attendees: "Never hire your old cronies." I thought, *Why would I do that anyway?* Since then, I have learned, it is easier to hire friends. I also have learned, it is not always better. Clearly, Bill was right.

When asked to rate themselves, a group of pastors told church consultant George Barna the following: 53 percent considered themselves good at administration or management, and 53 percent (not necessarily the same pastors in the first statistic) said they were above average at developing a ministry strategy. If hiring staff is strategic to the ministry, one may deduce from Barna's survey that a little over one out of two pastors are good at strategically finding the right people for the right job. That also means, of course, that nearly one out of two pastors is *not* prone to do well at hiring staff. Yes, some do this better than others, but a success rate of 50/50 is rather telling.

Two Keys to a Good Hire

Human resources literature offers valuable information about the ins and outs of hiring. Additionally, I have discovered two keys that, if developed well, can provide great results. Simply stated, they are Person and Process. Person refers to the characteristics and qualities you are seeking in the new hire. Process is how you are going to find the right person for the right job. The remainder of this chapter is devoted to exploring those two important aspects of your next hire.

The Person

Godly Character

In his book *Courageous Leadership*, Bill Hybels indicates three qualities he looks for in a hire: character, competency, and chemistry. I can imagine Pastor Bill in his office conducting an interview of a potential new hire—sharing a dialogue on godly living, asking questions about abilities and experience to get the job done, and quietly wondering if he can connect and find affinity with this new person who has just entered his life.

Hiring a person with godly qualities of life, high integrity of beliefs and behavior, and exceptional skill has become somewhat of an art and a science. The scientific aspects can be found in some of the "process" suggestions listed later in this chapter. However, discovering what is deep and personal is a relational skill learned over time and experience. And, yes, there can be risks and at times you will be deceived. That is when you trust God to lead and give you the wisdom to see what you cannot see.

Core Values

Can this candidate embrace the values and vision of your ministry? Does he or she have sufficient biblical background to understand the foundation of your ministry? Does he or she have the ability to see the mission accomplished before it is inaugurated?

While responses to these questions carry varying levels of importance, depending on the position being filled, the questions should be asked nonetheless. For the most part, the leaders in the early church had the Old Testament, the teaching of Jesus, and a "Great Commission vision" for the future. That is not a bad place to start in creating or building your team: the Bible and a vision to reach out to people.

Healthy Attitudes

In the past, hiring was all about education and experience. Today, attitude appears to be at the top of the list when meeting potential staff members. Here are a few characteristics to look for when considering a candidate:

- Shows real enthusiasm for people and mission
- Naturally demonstrates love for God and others
- Exhibits a positive work ethic
- Desires responsibility and is willing to assume a role of authority
- Initiates relationships without being forced, asked, or set up
- Demonstrates an interest in learning, listening, and making discoveries
- Displays humility; service to others is more important than self
- Seeks adventures in problem-solving by listening and stretching resources
- Exudes a humble confidence and creativity to get the job done

Loyalty

I once asked a CEO of a large financial holding company what he looked for when hiring new employees. He said two things that I have not forgotten. "They need to be able to read and write....Next, I expect loyalty to the company and other employees." Employers cannot say enough about loyalty, a quality initially evaluated through careful interviews of a candidate's references and only proven over time. Ask references about the candidate's faithfulness and loyalty to others and ministry. Education and talent are very important, but cannot override personal loyalty.

The Process

A Spiritual Process

It is interesting to read the account of choosing Judas Iscariot's replacement in Acts 1:21 – 26. The disciples qualified candidates according to their personal history and experience with Jesus and the apostles from John's baptism through Jesus' ascension into heaven. Then they cast lots (rolled dice or drew straws). I don't recall that method recently being used in selecting a ministry staff person!

The first deacons were appointed for service in Acts 6:1 – 6. By their devoted followership, they were already committed to the apostles' ministry, biblical teaching, and God's imparted vision to spread the gospel to the world. Beyond that, they were selected because of their godly character (verse 3). Once identified, the apostles simply chose seven men and laid hands on them (verses 5 – 6). This time they did not cast lots.

Practical Advice for Senior and Governing Leaders

Elsewhere in the New Testament we read that Paul instructed Titus to "appoint elders in every town, as I directed you" (Titus 1:5). The word *appoint* (also translated by some as *ordain*) means "to put in charge; to be made or to become." While the qualifications listed in the text are detailed, along with those listed in 1 Timothy 3:1 – 13, God does not specifically tell the early church leaders "how" to appoint their leaders. Did they keep rolling dice? Did they vote? While Paul seems to give final responsibility to Titus, did the process involve one person, three persons, ten persons? We don't know. Apparently, God has given us some liberty to exercise our own process of integrity to find godly men and women to build a staff team.

Take the time necessary to hire the right person. Make your process thorough, both spiritually and practically. In the end you at least will have the confidence to know that you honored God and did your best. The hire will be affirmed in the rigors of your search, and God will be glorified as you have sought wise counsel and asked his direction in prayer.

The Source of a New Hire

Before we discuss some of the process functions, it is good to get an idea of the possible sources for a new hire. Where a person comes from is important to where they are going. Again, core values and mission must be placed upfront. Where you find people with those qualifications may be near or far.

Hire from within. As mentioned earlier, sometimes the best hire has grown up in your ministry or he or she has been a volunteer for the last several years. If that is the case, you have had opportunity to build a relationship, test core values, and observe competencies. You know the person's family as well as personal history, strengths, and weaknesses. Likewise, the loyalty question is probably already answered, one way or the other.

Certainly that doesn't mean the candidate won't have deficiencies. But can that lack be compensated for by further training? And is there time to learn additional skills or traits while getting the job done?

Even if the potential candidate is already in your ministry context, go through a "formalized" search process. This will protect you from making a bad choice. The process can surface or remove some personal issues that may be connected with your relationship, whether good, bad, or indifferent. You also help the candidate to graciously reject the offer or process without making it a personal issue between the two of you.

Hire from outside. When it is obvious to all that your candidate is not near, the search needs to go far. In fact, some experienced leaders would suggest that the search be extended beyond your immediate ministry context to assure your ministry community that the person close to you is the best hire and not just a convenient one.

When I was hired into my current position at Grand Rapids Theological Seminary, I came from Calvary Church, which was literally across the street. I am grateful that the search was long and extensive and that I was not the first candidate nor on the original list of possibilities. That way no one ends up wondering whether a thorough enough search had been conducted.

Hiring from outside is more costly both in time and finances. However, it need not be more risky, provided you do your homework and take the necessary time to build at least an entry-level relationship with your new hire. Again, measure the candidate against the job description and his or her own history and merit.

Finally, hiring from the outside can bring fresh insights and perspectives that may be invaluable in growing your ministry. Your new staff member's eyes and ears can help you see and hear what you have taken for granted. Don't be afraid of someone from the outside.

Network to find potential candidates. Even if you are not planning to hire someone in the near future, create a list of trusted friends and colleagues—whether from shared educational pasts or current or former ministry experiences. Then, should the need arise, you will have a ready resource to consult. It is possible they have even concluded a recent search and can recommend worthy candidates to you.

Besides that valuable network, don't forget to:

- Keep praying. God will lead you.
- Ask your staff and volunteers.
- Post the position at various Christian colleges and seminaries.
- Identify certain "gatekeepers" in the area of ministry being pursued. For example, if looking for a youth leader, contact such organizations as Group, Young Life, or Youth Specialties.
- Ask someone who is computer savvy to start a search on the web. Warning: the volume of information may become overwhelming.
- Keep talking to others. Word of mouth is often the best.

When the word gets out that you are hiring a new staff member, be prepared for resumés to come without solicitation. Send a note to each one, acknowledging receipt of their resumé and confirming that a search committee member will get back to them in the future.

Resist impulsively contacting an inquiring candidate. Bring them through your process. When they are clearly not on the priority list, be sure to send them a courtesy note just the same. Be forthright when notifying a person that they do not meet the criteria established by the search committee.

A Hiring Process

I have read scores of hiring procedures and processes. Most are good. However, you only need one. While I have titled this section "A Hiring Process," I don't presume for a moment that this is the most complete or best format for you. I have simply taken some of the best discovered practices and now share them with you. It is your job to fit the hiring process to your particular ministry context. Don't be afraid to tweak it along the way. It will improve. Most of all, your hiring process will be yours.

Some ministries are large enough to have human resource departments. Other ministries have a senior pastor or executive director and governing board searching for their next staff person. Some leaders have a history of hiring staff, while other leaders have no experience at all.

Regardless of the size of your ministry or experience, you will do well to draw some clear lines in the sand. What will you and your search committee *not* settle for? What items in the job description are nonnegotiable? Determine early on what type of person you are looking for and the job description you desire to fulfill, then stick to it, apart from God's leading otherwise.

Start the search with a well-written job description. Often this is the first printed material a potential candidate will thoroughly review. The potential staff person wants to know the following: your expectations, the required qualifications to do the work, the job's responsibilities and authority, and reporting relationships. Each of these categories should be clearly spelled out in the job description.

The search committee is an important factor in a successful hire. If we

---

Ministry Employer Expectations of Employees

The following are expectations by most ministries in our current culture. This short list may help you evaluate potential candidates:

- Able to form partnerships with other staff and organizations (or is at least desirous of such)

- Embraces your ministry's core values and mission

- Demonstrates increasing flexibility and the desire to work hard and smart

- Willing to accept honest feedback from other employees, supervisors, and ministry participants

- Displays initiative and innovation without being prodded or told what to do

- Surrounds himself or herself with mentors and other resources in order to be a lifelong learner

agree that hiring is hard work and takes time, then having a qualified search team is imperative. The role and function of this committee is not just to interview and recommend a final candidate to the proper governing body (or person making a final decision). They should engage in the labor of prayer, making phone calls and visits, reading applications, performing reference checks, and remaining as objective as possible.

Choose a team of five or six men and women (or couples) who have time and flexible schedules as well as a working knowledge of the specific area of ministry. Meet regularly to pray and review the process. Give copies of every candidate's resumé and references to each member of the search committee, perhaps creating a "notebook" for each committee member.

A preliminary package most often becomes the first official point of contact with a potential candidate. The packet should thoroughly represent your ministry and the expectations of the role being considered by the candidate, and might contain the following:

- Personal letter of interest from you, the senior leader (Include your dreams.)
- A well-written, clear, concise job description
- Current informational brochures or literature on the ministry
- Information on your community/city from the chamber of commerce
- One or two pages of written values, vision, and mission statement(s), ministry opportunities, and the ministry's theological (doctrinal) position
- A job application form legally requesting important information (Check with an HR person or legal counsel in your community or state for the best application template and then carefully adapt the form to fit your context.)
- Names and phone numbers of people (references on you and your ministry) that the candidate may want to contact (This is optional at this point, and may be granted after a first interview, nevertheless, important to the process.)

Reference and background checks require a lot of hard work. After reading a person's resumé, I would always begin with reference checks, not a call or visit to the candidate. There are two types of references to check. The first is obvious: the names the potential candidate provides on the resumé. Of course, you expect to get a good reference, but regardless, they are important.

Second, call those places of previous employment or ministry service listed on the candidate's resumé. Ask who worked with this person, or who can give some information to assist your search. Be upfront and honest. Remember, you are not on a covert operation, just seeking as much information as possible. Ask each reference if there is someone else who knows the candidate and if that person can be contacted for more information.

When I became a candidate at Wooddale Church in Eden Prairie, Minnesota, I was amazed how much they already knew about me and my family. I learned of several people they had contacted whose names I had not provided. I was pleased. Also, when I was a candidate for my current role at the seminary, I was delighted to hear that a female staff person at my current place of ministry was contacted without my knowledge and asked about our working relationship. Obviously, both search committees had done a thorough job of investigating my history and reputation.

Background checks usually include a criminal and motor vehicle report. The candidate needs to sign a waiver to release this information. You may want to add, with the candidate's permission, a financial credit history. Again, seek legal counsel for these proper forms and procedures.

Train your committee members to ask all references the same questions. You can only be objective if you have similar data from several references on several potential candidates. Craft seven or eight questions with a final question, "Is there anything else which would be helpful for us to know about this potential candidate?" (Crafting the questions is a good process for your search committee to work on together.) Let each reference know how many questions you have and approximately how long the interview will last. If the necessary amount of time is not available during the first contact, ask for a phone appointment.

Resist email references. Written responses are fine, but are not as helpful as a voice-to-voice reference check. If you run into a reluctant reference, fearful of sharing personal information or concerned about defamation of character, ask positive questions about the candidate's strengths and accomplishments. If the answers are few and vague, then you may have what you need from your reference.

> ### Peter Lowe's Three Qualities of Great Employees
>
> In his website, Peter Lowe suggests three simple qualities for great employees. Though they seem simplistic, they definitely are worth consideration. (Check out www.successmagazine.com.)
>
> 1. Smart
> 2. Hardworking
> 3. Loyal

Reviewing and prioritizing possible candidates is one of the most valuable tasks in the search process. First of all, it assumes you are considering more than one person. Prioritizing calls everyone on the search team back to your ministry's core values and the candidates' strengths and weaknesses. Keep a current list of possible candidates, with objective criteria that can assist the team with a rating scale. For example, you may want to create a list similar to the following, rating each area for each candidate with a $1-5$ system, 5 representing the highest value.

- Years or months of experience in ministry
- Educational background specific toward the job
- Skills and competencies
- Comments by references
- Unusual criteria which sets this possible candidate apart from others
- Affordability
- Overall impression

A visit is best made after the above work has been done, whether the person is currently involved in your ministry or unknown prior to your search. The visit with the potential candidate now changes the ground rules from highly objective to upfront and personal.

The first visit may be on the potential candidate's "home turf." Or, it may be on yours. That will be your call, based on finances, time, and level of confidence by your search team.

Plan the visit well. If the candidate is coming to you, be a good and generous host. Think through the details. Imagine yourself coming to visit your ministry. You may even consider the costs of child care the candidate may incur to make this visit.

If you are going to the candidate, make your own travel arrangements. Try not to place any unnecessary or unrealistic responsibilities on the candidate. Remove any potential conflicts, tensions, or edginess to your first "official" yet informal encounter.

Interviews are crucial to the process. This face-to-face experience will make or break the process with any given candidate. There are two important aspects, the meeting itself and the questions you ask.

The meeting: Create a warm and friendly environment. That may be a restaurant, a relaxed setting in a neutral meeting room, or someone's home. Let the nature of the job and your ministry context dictate the best place to meet. Also, schedule a beginning time and ending time for the interview. Try to make the first encounter meaningful, but not overbearing. Grow into this new relationship.

Practical Advice for Senior and Governing Leaders

Include the right people. Especially, if both men and women are involved, make sure the candidate or candidate's spouse is not the only male or female in the interview. Try not to overwhelm the candidate with too many people to meet in the first encounter. If it is important to meet several people at this first visit, consider having more than one gathering with fewer people at each interview. For example, have one interview with the search committee and another with the ministry staff, rather than bringing everyone into the same meeting.

Questions should be free-flowing but intentional. Always begin with personal history and background. Share each other's stories. Then, have five or six important ministry questions written on a small card. Keep it close at hand. If you can manage without reading the questions, give it a try to be warm and personal.

Bottom line, treat your potential candidate with dignity, confidentiality, and care. Remember, this can be a very emotional experience for the potential hire. Don't leave the spouse out of the process. Include children, somehow, and in some creative way.

Sample Interview Questions

The following are sample questions that go beyond personal background and history. They are not intended all to be asked in a single interview or meeting with a potential candidate.

- How did you solve a difficult situation with a volunteer? (Or ask some other open-ended behavioral question.)
- In what ways do you and your current supervisor work best together? (Or ask some other open-ended question about working relationships with former supervisors.)
- If I become your supervisor, how would I best serve you and make you successful and fulfilled in this new role?
- How do you resolve conflicts with others?
- What do you tend to do when you are overwhelmed with a task or role?
- How do you think other people would describe your leadership style?
- Is there anything in the job description that you would suggest be changed?
- In the past three years what have you accomplished outside of your job?
- Who has contributed most to your success in your current role?
- Do you desire any "do-overs"? (Let them talk about it.)
- What are some ways you could contribute to our vision and current ministry?
- What have been your greatest moments and experiences?
- Describe your ministry dreams and aspirations.
- What questions do you have for us?

One good idea with a potential candidate is to have him or her meet informally with another staff member for lunch or dinner. That meeting could also include a participant in the ministry or a volunteer leader. Informally debrief with the trusted employee or volunteer to gain insights and impressions.

Finally, resist trying to compare candidates outside of the search committee. The key role of the search committee is to present the best possible candidate to the ministry. Trust their work. Empower them to do their job. And trust God for the final results.

A letter of offer with an acceptance form from the new hire is a point to thank God for his leading. A letter of offer should include as much detail as possible to assist the new hire in accepting the position (see the list below).

Craft a simple formal and legal document that releases the ministry from certain liabilities in case of unforeseen circumstances with the candidate. While every situation cannot be anticipated, protect the ministry as best you can. Initially, agree on salary, beginning date of employment, and guaranteed benefits. Don't make verbal promises that cannot be fulfilled.

The following items should be included in the offer:

- Job title and job description
- Date of hire
- Base salary
- All benefits
- Vacation weeks and sick days (Your employee handbook may cover these details. Have the employee sign a receipt of the employee handbook. If you don't have such a manual, create a simple document of agreed expectations, or borrow from another ministry.)
- Additional expenses covered by the ministry (List items such as cell phone, mileage, entertainment allowance, educational allowance, and conference or additional training expenses.)
- Moving and other initial expenses
- Probation period (always wise in any hire)

Celebrate. After the offer is made and accepted, plan a celebration. Be creative and ask one question, "How would I like to be welcomed to this ministry and staff?" Have as much as possible in place for the employee's first day on the job, so that their first 100 days can be all they anticipate from chapter 1 in this handbook.

Additional Reading

Burkett, Larry. *Business By the Book*. Updated. Nashville: Thomas Nelson, 1998.

Holford, Trish. *Our Staff: Building Our Human Resources*. Minneapolis: Augsburg Fortress, 2002.

Olsen, Chuck and Ellen Morseth. *Selecting Church Leaders: A Practice in Spiritual Discernment*. Herndon, Va.: Alban Institute, 2000.

Wendover, Robert W. *Smart Hiring, The Second Edition: The Complete Guide to Hiring the Best Employees*. Naperville, Ill.: Sourcebooks, Inc., 1998.

Williamson, Gerald. *Pastor Search Committee Planbook*. Nashville: Broadman and Holman, 1981.

De-hiring a Ministry Staff Member

Whoever loves discipline loves knowledge,
but he who hates correction is stupid.

Proverbs 12:1

A servant cannot be corrected by mere words;
though he understands, he will not respond.

Do you see a man who speaks in haste? There is more hope
for a fool than for him.

If a man pampers his servant from youth, he will bring grief in the end.

Proverbs 29:19 – 21

Drive out the mocker, and out goes strife.

Proverbs 22:10

De-hire the people on our team who are not contributing to our
mission. We know that letting someone go can't possibly be easy.
We're glad we don't have that responsibility. But look around.
A few of the people on our team are killing us!

We've seen you ignore the problem, work around the problem, and
joke about the problem. It seems like you spend more time cleaning
up after them than recognizing our achievements. So get on with it! Be
fair, but let them go work somewhere else.

David Cotrell, Listen Up, Leader!

Richard was shocked. His senior pastor had just said, "Richard, I don't
know how to tell you this, but you are just not a fit here at Faith
Church. We will be asking for your resignation by the end of the
week." It was already late Thursday morning.

The only other thing the pastor shared was information about a two-month severance package that included full salary and insurance. Richard walked out of the church, got in his car, and aimlessly drove around for a few hours, only stopping for a "to go" coffee where he felt assured no one would know him. Bewildered and demoralized, he finally found the courage to go home.

Richard's wife, Vicki, and their two preschool children were playing a favorite board game on the family room floor. Greeted with the usual hugs, kisses, and questions about the day, he avoided the bad news. Later that evening, when they had put the children to bed, he was free to talk.

At last Richard broke down in tears and blurted out that he had been "let go" by the church. He could not get out the word *fired*, it felt so demeaning and humiliating. Indeed, he felt dirty, as if he had committed an unpardonable sin. Richard and Vicki stayed up well into the early hours of the morning rehearsing the past four years of ministry, desperately looking for the misjudgment or gross error in their lives and ministry. They fell asleep empty.

Over the next two days, Richard tried to talk with the senior pastor and other staff. He called a couple of board members to discern the reasons behind the pastor's decision. Richard only became more confused. His record of imperfect performance and a few character flaws were now bigger than life. Until today, those issues had been lightly discussed and bypassed with "you are doing a great job and we really appreciate you as a part of this staff and ministry."

Richard signed the severance agreement on Friday afternoon. He came back on Saturday to clear out his office. Over the next few weeks the phone rang continually with volunteer leaders and people in the ministry expressing confusion and saddened emotions. The calls finally stopped. The senior pastor, staff members, and board members never followed up to see how Richard was doing.

De-hiring May Need to Be a Reality

Not every staff person is in the right job at the right time. When they were hired, they may have been the "perfect fit." Over the course of time, they may have changed, matured, or moved in a different direction. In the same way, the ministry may have changed its direction or there may have been a cultural change external to the ministry. Perhaps differing philosophies between senior leadership and the staff member have rendered them unable to work together. Regardless of the changes, there may no longer be a fit with the ministry staff person and the ministry. Things change.

As discussed in the previous chapter, attitude is one of the keys to an effective hire. Negative, distant, or problematic attitudes may also contribute to a de-hire.

In his excellent audio series *Pastor to Pastor*, H. B. London Jr., vice president of pastoral ministries at Focus on the Family, addresses the inability of a senior leader to coexist with staff members who cannot demonstrate genuine loyalty toward leadership. London says, "The moment a staff member can no longer be supportive of his leader he should leave, regardless of his or her value to the body or enrichment to the congregation. He or she should leave immediately."

London also points out that a senior leader needs to be decisive if a staff member needs to leave. It goes without saying, a difficult or disloyal ministry staff member negatively impacts other staff members, volunteer leaders, and ministry participants. Prolonging an unhealthy staff member's exit is unwise and detrimental to both the staff person and the ministry.

Before Dismissing or De-hiring a Staff Member

Face-to-face confrontation. Don't expect your ministry staff person to be a mind reader. Sometimes, they cannot see the forest from their tree. Or, they cannot see the problematic tree in their forest.

Don't believe your staff person is going to grant permission to dismiss them. If your staff member is not meeting responsibilities in their job description, exhibiting problematic behavior, or becoming an irritant to other staff or ministry participants, it is time to be honest. They need to hear the truth, the specific truth(s).

The staff member's growth and improvement should be your first desire. Calmly and considerately approach the individual. Resist creating or developing a predetermined judgment. Explore the negative behavior or problematic issues with the hope of discovering a solution to redeem the staff person's role and ministry effectiveness. Be clear about the behavior that is obvious to you and others. Share the results of that behavior and how it affects people, the environment, and ministry outcomes — and bottom line, that it is unacceptable. With a focus on future development, you may want to ask your staff member:

- Are you fulfilled in your current role?
- Are there changes you would like to make in your job position?
- Is there anything that was unclear to you about your job or our expectations?
- How do you perceive you are meeting your job expectations as defined in your job description or annual objectives?

- Are you aware of _____ (a problematic behavior or issue); or did you say _____? (Be specific about an observed comment, behavior, or obvious concern.)
- Is there anything in your life that is hindering you from effectively doing your job?
- Is there anything that I can do to help you better do your job?
- Do you think you would be happier doing something else? What would that look like?
- Would you like some time to get away and think about the issues we have discussed?

Where you conduct this type of interview is important. Based on your relationship with the staff member, and the gravity of the current situation, you will need to discern the most effective place to meet. Your office, their office, or a neutral meeting place will be important to the general spirit and tone of the meeting, as well as the staff member's response.

Define certain outcomes. If a staff person is deficient in one or more areas of behavior or ministry performance, there are a number of ways to address such concerns. Begin not by immediately instituting methods of change but by discussing desired outcomes.

Some desired outcomes might be:

Indicators That It May Be Time to Consider a De-hiring Process

- The ministry staff member's ongoing complaints about leadership, other people, and the direction or condition of the ministry (in other words, a negative spirit)
- Lack of growth and ability to "keep up" with the ministry
- Obvious misuse or abuse of time and resources
- Significant lack of commitment, engagement, and participation in routine areas of ministry
- Bad-mouthing the ministry from the inside or outside
- Creating a hostile and toxic environment among other staff, volunteers, or ministry participants
- The job just not getting done
- People leaving, confused about the staff member's leadership
- Regular complaints about behavior from other staff and/or volunteers
- Insubordination

- Change in a particular attitude
- Development of a ministry skill
- Adjustment in job responsibilities or general ministry role
- Renewed vision for the ministry

Some methods to achieve those outcomes might include:

- Additional training or education
- Professional counseling
- One-on-one mentoring or coaching
- Careful rewriting of the job description and reassignment in ministry responsibilities
- An extended sabbatical for the staff member to engage and discover other ministry models (the objective is to return with a renewed vision and objectives that align with the overall ministry)

Conduct formal evaluations. Job descriptions, past performance reviews, and future objectives should be discussed, evaluated, and documented on an annual if not more frequent basis. In addition, staff members need a time to share and vent their feelings and frustrations toward their job or the ministry. It is one more time and place to keep channels of communication open and clear. Evaluations should not be performed only when the staff member is not performing as expected or behaving poorly. However, when that is the case, routine accountability is necessary.

A Little Bit of Legal Advice

The following five points are adapted from Paul Falcone's book, *101 Sample Write-Ups for Documenting Employee Performance Problems* (New York: American Management Association, 1999).

1. The staff member must understand your expectations and the consequences of not meeting those expectations. Both should be in writing.

2. Your performance policy and disciplinary actions must be followed consistently with all employees.

3. Appropriate disciplinary or probationary actions should always be taken before dismissal.

4. The staff member should always have an opportunity to respond to the issues of behavior or poor performance. The staff member must be allowed an opportunity to share his or her story.

5. Always allow a reasonable time to complete reasonable steps toward improvement or change.

NOTE: If a staff member has committed a moral violation or egregious actions (sexual harassment, gross negligence, harmful behavior to a person or the ministry), dismissal may be immediate. However, that action must be clearly articulated, with clear documentation and empirical support.

Some additional questions to ask your staff member may include:

- How are you feeling about your job and the people you serve?
- Is there anything between you and me or another staff member that needs to be resolved?
- Do you feel you need a break from the ministry for a period of time? If so, what would you hope to accomplish?
- Where do you see yourself in the next one, three, or five years?
- How is your health, eating, sleeping, and exercise?
- How is your spiritual walk with God?
- How are you and your spouse (children) getting along?
- Do you have close friends outside of this ministry?
- How can I encourage you?

Process toward Dismissal of Your Staff Member

No matter the size of your ministry, a written de-hiring or ministry staff dismissal policy should be available to all staff in a ministry staff handbook or file. Such a policy should be developed with the assistance or guidance of legal counsel because de-hiring a staff person may create a culpable situation, making the ministry legally vulnerable.

Things Not to Say or Do Before Dismissal of a Staff Member

- Do not make crude personal judgments.
- Do not make threatening remarks or comments.
- Do not say things to incite a quarrel or argument.
- Do not quote others.
- Never lose your cool.
- Resist bringing close colleagues and family into the process.

A written policy allows the ministry staff person to be able to expect certain steps, procedures, and meetings over the course of a disciplinary or probationary time period. If a staff person is genuinely surprised at the point of dismissal, leadership has not done its job in following process or ethical guidelines.

Document a staff member's conduct and ministry performance. Begin with the formal annual or semiannual written evaluations. In addition, as problems arise, develop a written confidential file including summaries of any incidents or face-to-face confrontation(s). On occasion you may need to write an informal observation to the staff person about erratic or unhealthy behavior or performance, which the staff person knows is in their personnel file. This type of soft warning can serve as a preamble to a more formal warning that might come later. Up to this point, the confrontations have been rather low-key, on a more personal level, to inspire, instruct, or encourage growth, change, and renewed vitality in the life and ministry of the staff member.

Formal confrontation follows the informal discussions and dialogues you have shared as a ministry staff leader thus far. If the unacceptable behavior or lack of job proficiency continues, it is now time to consider a formal probationary period to help work through the issues.

The desired outcome is for the ministry staff person to remain in the ministry, not to leave at the end of the probation period. It may be appropriate at this meeting to establish a general time frame to achieve agreed improvements and desired outcomes. An offer of personal help or formal training (described next) should have more specific time frames.

Offer help or training to change the negative behavior or poor performance. This might take various forms. One, you may offer private or professional counseling, paid by the ministry. Two, you may acquire a personal coach or consultant to work with the staff member for a period of time to reach desired outcomes. Three, you may recommend a personal time-out for the staff member to get away to pray, think, and re-create their personal passion and objectives for the ministry. Place any of these possible solutions within a reasonable time frame.

Training may include formal course work at a graduate school or specialized ministry training course, or specific reading and assignments with accountability back to a supervisor or designated ministry coach. Another

Ten-Point Review of the De-hiring Process

1. Maintain formal annual or semi-annual evaluations.

2. Document misbehavior and poor job performance.

3. Establish informal and face-to-face dialogue about behavioral issues and job performance with your staff member.

4. Keep written goals and objectives in the forefront.

5. Maintain consistent, ongoing accountability throughout the process.

6. Offer help to grow or change.

7. Monitor the progress with clear outcomes, adequate time frames, and written summaries.

8. Administer clear warnings and disciplinary or probationary action.

9. If all of the above do not redeem the staff member to effective ministry, then present a fair offer of severance and assistance in writing, to be signed by the staff member and ministry.

10. If possible, seek to help, support, and offer encouragement to the dismissed staff member through the ministry or outside resources.

option is to send the staff person to another healthy ministry to observe their model and style of leadership. Again, set dates for any of these options, granting the staff member permission to say no to some or all current responsibilities to participate in any mutually agreed-upon training.

Present a written summary of agreed-upon outcomes and expectations, including established deadlines. Be sure this document is presented to the appropriate team, committee, or board for additional accountability and placed in a "personnel file" or your confidential files.

Establish intermediate consequences for improper behavior or performance. If you reach the deadline for improvement and the desired outcomes have not been achieved, then consequences must be administrated. Some intermediate disciplinary actions may include:

- Time off with pay, carefully letting others know the reason for the absence
- Time off without pay
- Removal from certain public or leadership ministry responsibilities for a period of time (This also may need to take place during the probationary period.)
- Day-to-day meetings with a supervisor or mentor to monitor performance

This document may or may not be a "last chance warning." However, it does serve as a serious word of caution that the staff member's job is in jeopardy.

A final decision for continuance or dismissal may come after the above process has been fulfilled. One way to handle the decision is to allow a staff person three or four days to consider his or her own decision to resign with one or two severance options. The leader and staff member then meet on that final day to agree upon the dismissal. At that point, determine when the staff person will actually leave and whether the dismissal will come with any type of formal recognition or happen quietly, with appropriate information reported to leadership and the ministry at large.

When offering a severance package, err on the side of generosity for the cause of Christ's mission. Demonstrate grace. Even if the staff member has been guilty of gross misbehavior or engaged in a sin of dire consequences, demonstrate a testimony of mercy and love. Many will be judging and evaluating your response. Regardless of the reason for dismissal, remind the governing leaders that this staff member has a family, a reputation, and a future. Protect what you should and what you can.

Following Dismissal

Conduct an exit interview face-to-face or over the phone. Written questionnaires are cold, impersonal, and ineffective. Wisely determine the best person from your ministry to conduct the interview; that may be you, it may be someone else. If a hostile spirit exists, you may want to schedule this interview at a later time or possibly outsource the exit interview.

Be sure to show thanks and appreciation for the staff member's contribution to the ministry. Ask if there is anything the ministry can do to encourage or help at this time. Even if the outgoing staff member has an unreceptive spirit, it is still important to conduct the interview. This may be a final cathartic opportunity for you or the dismissed employee, a time for closure or healing.

Finally, ask five or six questions during the exit interview, including what the former employee would have liked changed or handled differently in the process. It is important to humbly and sincerely seek their input, desiring the ministry's overall growth and improvement. In addition, you may secure an outside employment agency to assist the person's next career step.

No process is infallible, but certainly the exit interview is a good time to listen.

If possible, pray with the former staff member.

Conduct your own exit debrief. De-hiring a staff person may be hard on you both emotionally and physically and call into question some of your own leadership skills. It is difficult to hear harsh criticisms come your way, fair or unfair. It is equally difficult to know the potential impact this decision may have on a spouse, children, and a family's economic, social, and spiritual well-being.

It is important that you receive wise counsel during such a stressful situation. Talk and pray regularly through the process and outcome with a trusted friend or board member who can maintain confidentiality. It is not necessary for you to carry the entire weight of a de-hire on your own shoulders.

Additional Reading

Burkett, Larry. *Business By the Book.* Updated. Nashville: Thomas Nelson, 1998.

Falcone, Paul. *The Hiring and Firing Question and Answer Book.* New York: American Management Association, 2001.

Julian, Larry S. *God Is My CEO: Following God's Principles in a Bottom-Line World.* Holbrook, Mass.: Adams Media, 2001.

McKay, Harvey. *We Got Fired: And It Is the Best Thing That Happened to Us.* New York: Ballantine, 2004.

Muir, Kevin. *Employee Termination Guidebook.* Cedar Park, Tex.: Turnaround Central, 2005.

Steingold, Fred S. *The Employer's Legal Handbook.* Berkeley, Calif.: Nolo, 2004.

Equitably Honoring Ministry Staff Members

Do not withhold good from those who deserve it,
when it is in your power to act.

Proverbs 3:27

When a king's face brightens, it means life; his favor is like a
rain cloud in spring.

Pleasant words are a honeycomb, sweet to the soul
and healing to the bones.

Proverbs 16:15, 24

Do not exalt yourself in the king's presence, and do not claim a place
among great men; it is better for him to say to you, "Come up here,"
than for him to humiliate you before a nobleman.

Proverbs 25:6–7

How you (the senior pastor) "present" your ministry staff member
is how your people will "perceive" him or her. Savvy leaders create
an environment that recognizes and rewards all employees for
outstanding performance.

Megan Malugani

Story Number One: My wife and I visited a local church a number of years ago on what happened to be the Sunday of the senior pastor's twenty-fifth anniversary. What impressed us most about the service was that it wasn't all about one man and his marvelous accomplishments. It was about others too.

As the service began, a ministry staff member was called to the platform who was celebrating his fifteenth anniversary at the church. He was honored by the board, staff, and senior pastor. Kind words were exchanged, a delightful video was shown, and a generous gift was given. Next, another staff person was asked to come up front and he received similar acclaim for his twentieth anniversary at the church. Finally the senior pastor was honored. A few church members and leaders shared many kind thoughts, showed a video, and gave a gift.

Frankly, it was all very equitable. The spotlight wasn't brighter on one than another. The gifts given were not disproportionate. This church and its leadership got it right. Honor was given openly and equitably.

Story Number Two: I spoke at a parachurch ministry's sixtieth anniversary celebration this past year. Led by a new director, much has been accomplished in his short time at the helm. I know he could have said a lot about what he has done to rebuild a once struggling ministry … but he didn't.

Instead this director honored his staff. Every one! He sat toward the back of the room while one staff member after another got up and shared brief reports on their ministry. What was so interesting is that no one talked about themselves. Each told the story of another person in the ministry. "Like director, like staff." This ministry leader gets it. Everyone is learning from their leader to honor one another.

Story Number Three: Recently I ran into a ministry friend responsible for a large and fast growing ministry. When I asked him the usual conversation opener, "How are you doing?" this man went on for thirty minutes about his staff and their accomplishments. I could not get him to talk to me about his own role and ministry!

Encourage and Build Up One Another

An encouraging environment must begin with leadership. The governing board can become a tremendous source of encouragement to the senior leadership. Supervisors and senior leaders in turn have daily opportunity to encourage ministry staff members. As in verses such as 1 Thessalonians 5:11, the biblical idea behind the word *encourage* is "to invite, to call, and to provide a sense of comfort." I wish I could remember who said, "*Encourage* means to give courage." I like that.

Everyone needs to be included, invited, and encouraged to be a significant part of the ministry's vision and mission. If kept at arm's length, a staff member becomes isolated, independent, and disconnected. After a while the distance is obvious. The next step is a quiet departure. Some staff members simply do not know how to invite themselves into a senior leader's life and ministry, due to past negative experiences or personality differences. That's why it's your responsibility to take the initiative.

Offering encouragement may not be natural for some leaders. Some have never been encouraged themselves. Some have tried and miserably failed in their attempts to draw in others or have been severely burned trying to build a close ministry staff relationship. Regardless of one's experience, ministry staff members who follow a senior leader request a personal occasional gesture that says, "You are important to this ministry and to me."

Encouragement best happens when it is intentional. The following principles may help the leader establish a plan to encourage ministry staff.

Create a Ministry Staff Plan

Think about your staff beyond the present circumstances and current objectives. Consider the big picture and the kind of staff that you need in the future to accomplish the ministry's mission and goals. Also, consider each staff person with his or her unique background, talents, gifts, and potential. Ask yourself what each ministry staff person needs to grow and be fulfilled in this ministry.

Creating a ministry staff plan signals that you are thinking about your staff, and that will soon be obvious to them. Indeed, staff members will be thrilled to know that their ministry leader is advocating and even budgeting time and dollars for their personal growth and development.

When staff feel valued and appreciated, they are more willing to take those many small, incremental steps toward ministry goals with you. If not in actual words, they are responding to your encouragement with thoughts such as, *We want to be included in your ministry and grow in our ministry. Take a risk on me. I would love the challenge and opportunity to achieve and embrace something beyond where I am today. I am motivated to go where I have not been!* Of course, not every staff person will respond that enthusiastically, but you may be delighted how many are quietly saying those words on the inside.

Create training opportunities for your staff to grow and mature as *individuals* (in the next chapter we will talk more about team growth). Especially in today's fast-changing world, cross-training, "multiple hats," and extension ministries are in vogue. Regardless if a person is single- or multi-task oriented, they all want more training to rise to the current challenges. Start with the following:

Ways to Make a Performance Review a Time of Encouragement

The following are suggested inclusions for an annual or semiannual ministry staff review:

1. Review the ministry staff member's job description.
2. Review the staff member's past year's performance, especially as related to the ministry's core values and vision.
3. Present the coming year's objectives.
4. Give your staff member freedom and safety to vent, dream, and contribute.
5. Celebrate your staff member for his or her personal contribution to you and the ministry. (Don't avoid the "personal contribution to you" discussion.)
6. Don't use the evaluation as a time to correct. That can happen at another time.
7. Resist comparing the staff person's performance to anyone else's, including your own.
8. Say "Well done!" not just "Thanks."

- Systematically pray for each staff person who reports to you.
- Attempt to spend some time each week listening to each staff member in order to learn about their lives and heart for the ministry. Ask questions. Let them share their needs and dreams.
- Discern what new or regular experience within or outside the ministry would benefit each staff member.
- Make budgetary and time resources available for staff members to prioritize and pursue these new growth venues.

Training your staff not only helps them become exceptional in the area where they already serve but it helps them grow and expand into other areas of ministry where they may discover equal or even greater giftedness. You may be the one to help them reach their God-given potential. Be a good steward of the gifted people God has entrusted to you.

Take a bold risk with some staff. That may be scary. You may be thinking of potential disasters right now. But consider a risk (or two) someone took with you. How did it turn out? Are you grateful for the opportunity that was afforded you?

In his book *How Twelve Exceptional Companies Are Navigating the Road to the Next Economy* James Citrin, writing about risk-taking with employees, says, "Create experiments, not contests." A contest focuses solely on competition and winning. Experiments may result in the occasional failure, but create learning and growing experiences where learners and leaders can be encouraged to take next steps. Give your ministry staff permission to work out their own problems and blunders.

Questions Ministry Staff "Silently" Ask Their Supervisor

- I know what my job description says, but what do you really expect?
- Do you have any idea how many hours I really worked last week?
- Have you ever thought of asking for my input or opinion?
- Have you ever thought of asking about me and my family?
- Without discussion, do you accidentally overlook me in favor of another?
- Do you realize when and how you leave the ministry staff out of the pictures you paint of the ministry? How do you think that makes us feel?
- Did you hear me the last time I said I am not using my gifts?
- Can we talk about the future and where I might fit in?

Create ways for staff to become involved in your ministry. The number of ways to include staff in what you do is only limited to the amount of time and thought you give to this area of creative opportunity. Something powerful happens when staff members are engaged in ministry with a senior leader or supervisor, intrinsic factors that increase motivation, self-worth, and confidence. In addition, the sense of unity is powerful.

Invite staff to participate in "smaller" areas of service, even one-time or short-term experiences. Have them share their input on some of your ideas and dreams for the future. Pray together about ministry needs or opportunities. Travel together. Go out to lunch and share your heartbeat for the ministry. For the staff person, those brief moments can mean a lot and go a long way to encourage them.

Invite staff into your public arena, giving them opportunity to share "your platform." Among the many possibilities, this might mean allowing someone to coauthor an article for your constituents or to serve as your representative either at a ministry or social event. Certainly, staff members would be encouraged if you openly identified a skill or talent which exceeds your own. Invite them to share that gift alongside you.

Develop Resources for Your Staff

A great way to frustrate people is to require a task and not provide the right tools. Do they have an adequate budget, working environment, and resources to accomplish the job? Does your staff have freedom and permission to discover and find their own resources if the ministry is not currently able to assist?

A Small Reminder Creates Huge Responses

Keep the following three questions on your desk or in a visible place:

- To whom can I send a note or say, "Good job" or "Thank you"?
- Who can I invite to go with me to _____ this week?
- Who on staff would benefit from _____ opportunity?

Budget. Ask the ministry staff person to design and present a budget to your ministry's financial team. Review it together. Understand it. Be an advocate. Doing this does not require a significant amount of time.

Freedom. Establish clear boundaries so the staff person knows when they may or may not raise funds or resources for the ministry. Ministry policies will create some of those guidelines. You will also need to balance what is fair and equitable to other staff and other areas of ministry. One staff person may be a great fundraiser while another staff member may be challenged to find resources.

Accountability with team support. Make sure that your staff member knows who will be available to provide support and assistance to accomplish new initiatives or solve problems that need special attention. That support may be a committee, the staff team, the board, or you. Always assure the staff member that they will never have to struggle through an issue alone, unless they bypass the system of accountability.

"Tool kit." There are many ministry programs that need to be built and others that need to be fixed. Such opportunities can make or break a ministry as well as the spirit of the staff member. Are the "tools" available for new ministry construction or for adequate maintenance and repairs? Does your staff person have a place to go to find the necessary:

- Office support (including supplies, machines, and personnel)?
- Space to do a growing or expanding ministry?
- Time to accomplish the task assigned?
- Other equipment to get the job done as expected (sound system, piano, vehicle availability or rental agreements, video/media systems, computer hardware and software, etc.)?
- Communication channels to get the word out?

Spiritual support. Of course, physical resources can be provided by others. It's even possible for a ministry staff person to be spiritually supported by a host of people both inside and outside the ministry, but *your* spiritual encouragement is needed most. Every staff person needs to know that you as their leader are:

- Praying for them by name
- Holding high the biblical values and Christ-centered mission of the ministry
- Speaking words of faith, love, and hope
- Walking the talk

Become a Giver Rather Than a Receiver

Give Ministry Staff Responsibility and Opportunity

In his article "One More Time: How Do You Motivate Employees?" Frederick Hetzburg writes, "The only way to motivate the employee is to give him challenging work in which he can assume responsibility." While some greater levels of responsibility are earned over a period of time, lighter responsibilities can be granted nearly anytime. When possible, give a ministry staff person a special assignment, challenge, or opportunity. See if he or she excels and responds with positive energy and feedback.

A short-term task with new responsibility can stimulate currently stifled or untapped creative juices. It's a welcomed change of pace for the ministry staff person, giving them cause to believe that you value their work and input.

A long-term assignment may cause the ministry staff member to rise to an entirely new level. Consider an existing staff person for any new role that needs to be filled. Promote up, then hire that person's replacement.

Most ministry staff people value growth as a concept and want to grow personally and professionally. Grant them an opportunity with responsibility to do just that. Give the gift of confidence and trust.

Give Ministry Staff Honest Feedback

When a staff member has accomplished a task, please note it. Even if

---

Extra Encouragement for Those Behind the Scenes

In a healthy ministry, staff members together celebrate when those in the background are honored. Here are a few simple ways (you will think of others) to honor the silent work force:

- Flowers on the desk
- A box (or two) of donuts
- Gift certificate
- Extra time off with pay
- Opportunity to participate in something bigger
- A simple plaque or certificate of honor
- A letter to their children or spouse showing appreciation
- A kind word of acknowledgment at a staff or board meeting
- A "golden coffee mug" that travels each month to the employee honored by their peers

the outcome did not have stellar results, a kind word or short note can encourage a staff person to try again and try harder. Don't leave the faithful and hardworking staff member alone to guess their ministry performance by silence. Give the gift of reassurance.

Even constructive criticism is more appreciated than hearing nothing. At least the staff person knows that a senior supervisor or leader is paying attention, cares, and holds people accountable for the ministry. That is important.

Give Ministry Staff Fair Remuneration

The biblical concept of "double honor" presented in 1 Timothy 5 is not limited to the senior pastor or leader nor is it limited to money. Yes, according to the apostle Paul, it is the responsibility of the Christian community to honor those who "direct (*manage or lead*) the affairs of the church ... especially those whose work (*labor, effort*) is preaching and teaching" (verse 17, italics mine). But in verse 18 he broadens that thought by calling to mind Deuteronomy 25:4, "Do not muzzle the ox while it is treading out the grain," and Deuteronomy 24:15, "The worker deserves his wages." Certainly, the lessons and insights from this text include many ministry staff members, who direct, provide leadership, teach, preach, and work hard for the cause (affairs) of the ministry. The bottom line is: respond with what is appropriate when the job is done.

As a ministry leader, become a strong voice for equitable and fair remuneration and honor for your ministry staff. Resist unhealthy comparisons with yourself, the private sector, and other ministries. Carefully consider the weight of responsibility and ministry the staff member carries, on your behalf and others.

As it relates to honoring a staff person with wages and benefits (and perks), be thoughtful toward education, experience, giftedness, effectiveness, and employment longevity. Weigh in the balance of ministry the needs and contribution of each staff member. This is not always an easy task, especially with a large staff. Give the gift of generosity, fairness, and equity.

Give Ministry Staff Time Away

God is serious about his people getting rest. He designed the Sabbath for us. He encourages us to slow down, be still, and wait. Never do we hear him say, "Hurry up and do more."

In some Christian ministries the "sabbatical leave" is rather controversial. Much broader in scope than in educational circles, it can be offered to build up, prepare, stimulate, refresh, and recreate ministry staff after an extended period of hard faithful labor. Consider it for your staff. Be equitable in providing "away time" to both senior and associate roles.

One of my friends has been a ministry staff member for more than forty years, representing three churches. His current ministry grants him a six-week sabbatical leave every six years, time that my friend uses to rest, recreate, and write. He returns to his ministry refreshed and ready to accept new challenges with fresh, new insight.

Not every ministry can grant a six-week leave. However, extra time away does not need to be expensive or lengthy. A weeklong retreat, a weekend at a retreat center, even an extra day off can provide encouragement to an overworked, overstressed ministry staff person. Be observant of the times when your staff members deliver those "extra" hours and efforts. Notice when they have endured unexpected time constraints or unusual demands on their schedule. Give the gift of rest and renewal.

Give Ministry Staff Honor and Equity

Staff members need to regularly hear the words, "Good job; well done; congratulations on being with us five years, ten years," etc. However, be careful to honor all and not just a few; your staff will be quick to perceive inequities. It is so easy to forget those who work behind the scenes. Likewise, it is easy to take for granted those who are often in the "spotlight." Extend honor and recognition to volunteers as well.

Give your ministry staff the gift of honor and respect. When possible, personalize rewards for excellence and commitment to make them even more meaningful. Enhance ministry staff members' reputations among people in the ministry by lifting up these men and women for special appreciation. Be creative in how you recognize good work and faithfulness. Treat your ministry staff as you would like the governing board to respect you. Give the gift of honor.

> Love and faithfulness keep a king safe; through love his throne is made secure.
>
> **Proverbs 20:28**

Additional Reading

Broadbooks, Bob. *From Pastor to Pastor: Letters of Encouragement.* Kansas City, Mo.: Beacon Hill, 2003.

Jeremiah, David. *The Power of Encouragement: Lift Up the Defeated.* Portland, Ore.: Multnomah, 1997.

Practical Advice for Senior and Governing Leaders

Miller, Calvin. *The Power of Encouragement*. Carol Stream, Ill.: Tyndale, 2003.

Rogers, Tom. *Life in the Fishbowl: Building Up Church Workers*. St. Louis: Concordia, 1999.

Sundberg, JoNancy. *Encouragement for Pastors*. New York: Random House, 2000.

Watts, Robert Jr. *People Are Never the Problem*. Colorado Springs: Cook/Honor Books, 1999.

Wiersbe, Warren W. *Bumps Are What You Climb On: Encouragement for Difficult Days*. Grand Rapids, Mich.: Baker, 2002.

Building an Effective Team

Be sure you know the condition of your flocks, give careful
attention to your herds.

Proverbs 27:23

By justice a king gives a country stability.

Proverbs 29:4

Teams are not built by retreats or creative activities, but by men and
women committed to each other and to accomplishing a lofty goal.

James C. Galvin

If I could solve all the problems myself, I would.

Thomas Edison, when asked why he had a team of twenty-one assistants

In building up others, you build up yourself.

Jim Casey, UPS founder

Ray had just joined the staff at Burgundy Hills Church as minister of pastoral care and visitation, bringing with him eleven years of experience at a collegiate parachurch ministry and seventeen years as minister of education in a church from another denomination. Needless to say, his ministry diversity was considered an immediate asset to the team.

As Ray headed down the corridor toward the conference room for staff meeting one morning, he was embarrassed by two colleagues loudly arguing about an item on the agenda. Jean and Carol were clearly not on the same page.

The quarrelers arrived to the meeting about ten minutes late and sat at opposite ends of the conference table. By then, the executive pastor had opened in prayer, dispensed with a couple of preliminaries, and was launching into the main question before them: "So, do we recommend to the board that we expand the children's wing or the youth center building next year? The board needs a decision by next Monday."

Jean and Carol sat frozen in their chairs, saying nothing. A long, rather uncomfortable silence filled the room. Finally one staff person stated his opinion. No one responded.

At the end of the second period of silence, Jean began to speak on behalf of the children's ministry addition. Carol cut her off in midsentence with a harsh comment and judgmental tone, spouting facts and figures in favor of the youth center. Jean questioned Carol's statistics and their voices got louder, neither listening to the other. Ray twice attempted to contribute his experience and expertise, but was quickly ignored and drowned out.

The debate finally wound down and again there was silence. The executive pastor asked for a vote. The children's wing expansion won 5–3.

Ray sat back in amazement as Carol stomped out of the room, slamming the door behind her. Ray had vast experience in educational ministry priorities. He knew the value of accurate numbers of attendees and alignment with the church's mission statement. He could have had significant input in this decision. He just shook his head.

We Now Call It a Team

Team leadership (whether in secular business or sacred ministry) has been the management style of choice for a number of years, replacing more traditional, hierarchical management systems. Indeed, most of us are very used to the term *ministry team* nowadays.

Whether two horses, a football team, or a ministry staff, a team is a group of two or more committed to accomplishing the same mission, with shared or supportive objectives and goals. You might think of ministry teamwork sequentially as such: (1) biblical core values to best establish and create the foundation for your ministry team (rather than superstars or big projects alone); (2) a common mission to point everyone in the right direction; (3) skilled leadership to keep the team moving in that direction; and (4) different roles and styles to allow each person to uniquely contribute to the final outcomes.

While there are many aspects to "team," this chapter is designed to create a greater awareness of what your ministry staff team can look like and how your team can begin to function most effectively. Each aspect of building a team may take time and develop through various seasons of ministry. Be patient. Remain team-focused. Hire the best people for your ministry staff. Before you realize it, a team will emerge.

The different roles and aspects of an effective team are:

- The team leader
- Team members
- Team members' relationships (accountability) and responsibility to the ministry
- Team objectives and goals
- The decision-making process

Do you have a team? Is everyone "pulling" in the same direction? While a team does not preclude conflict among its members, are they too isolated in their own area of ministry to solidly contribute? Do you realize that the team begins with you, the senior leader?

The Team Leader
Leading a Team Takes Time

In his article "Execution: The Discipline of Getting Things Done," former Honeywell chairman Larry Bossidy notes, "Effective leaders devote as much as 40 percent of their time and energy in selecting, appraising, and developing people." I can almost hear senior pastors and leaders screaming, "I don't have that kind of time to invest in my staff." I hear you. So the next question is, "How much time *are* you willing to invest?"

It takes time to instill loyalty and treat people honestly and fairly. Being consistent is a discipline wrapped up in time management. It just takes time to:

- Be friendly and listen to the needs of your staff members.
- Inform your staff members of "everything." They are invested with their very lives in this ministry and have a deep desire to know what is happening. Resist keeping them on the outside looking in.
- Invest in those who are loyal and exude integrity. You need to do all that you can to encourage and keep them on your team. Guess what? That takes time.
- Train team members. Just because they are on the team, don't assume they can perform at the level needed to accomplish your goal. Most training can be effectively and efficiently outsourced. However, staff members also want to learn from you. Don't deny them your best lessons in life and ministry.

Building the "A" Team

You are the only one who can establish an effective team. Can "team" happen without you? Sure, for a brief period of time. A team of horses will effectively pull a wagon without a driver—until danger appears. A team of good people will have good moments and accomplish some good short-term goals. But is that good enough?

A well-led team generally has greater longevity, works effectively through crisis moments, and accomplishes both short- and long-term goals, confirming and achieving the stated vision and mission of the ministry. The following are a few simple guidelines to establish a healthy team:

- Choose the right people. This will be your most difficult task. (See chapter 31.) Reward team members for good work. In some cases, learn to outsource certain tasks so the team is not distracted by unnecessary functions. Demonstrate the courage to let team members go who cannot contribute to the team.
- Let people know they are on the team. Create clear boundaries for team members to know what they can contribute to the larger ministry outside of their designated division. Bring them together systematically. Lead them consistently. Give them clear definition and purpose. Write out a mission statement for your ministry staff team. Give your team a name.
- Assign real work to the team. If the team only "chats" about getting things done and never actually engages in doing ministry together, it becomes nothing more than a small discussion group. It would be like teaching a football team everything about football and never playing a game. It is important that you are doing something together, even if it means everyone doing their own work between team meetings, knowing their individual work clearly contributes to the whole.
- When your team is together, talk as a team, not just with a few individuals on the team. Ask everyone to share an opinion or idea. Bring in outside guests who address the entire team and the objectives you are trying to accomplish. Go as a team to see what others are doing. Make sure the entire team is engaged in the decision-making process.
- Keep communications constant. Send out an agenda in advance of each meeting. Give everyone on the team a copy of reports, articles, memos, and minutes. Inform them of the governing board's discussions and actions if they do not attend board meetings. (As a

team leader in one church, I worked very hard and long to finally allow the board to welcome the ministry staff team to attend all board meetings with a voice, but no vote. It made a positive difference.)

• Be a good example of a team player. Show "team" in your own life and ministry style of leadership. Let them know you are one of them.

Conducting Staff Meetings

Though occasionally you can get away with an unplanned agenda or good reasons for not being ready for a team meeting, that should most certainly be the exception. Be prepared. Remember, the ministry staff member's time is just as valuable as yours.

Resist canceling a meeting and don't frequently substitute for your leadership role. Both signal to the other members that the meeting is not important to you, so why should it be important to them? If "others" often lead the meeting, staff members will become confused who is really leading. Establish your role and their identity with consistent leadership presence and preparation.

Invite input and include the ministry staff in creating the agenda. Apart from maintaining the ministry core values and keeping everyone focused on the big picture, mission, and vision, your role is to address staff needs and concerns.

> ### Eight Ways a Team Member Can Sabotage Teamwork
>
> 1. Do all of the talking.
> 2. Never ask anyone else an open-ended question.
> 3. Subtly put down or ignore a divergent view or opinion by another staff member.
> 4. Attempt to "save the day" by enthusiastically having the best answer and pressuring the team toward immediate closure.
> 5. Demand that we fix and solve this problem right now.
> 6. Never give up your position or ministry role in the discussion.
> 7. Talk before and after the meeting, not during the meeting.
> 8. Hang on to rigid policies, being sure to say, "We can't do that!"

Paying Attention to Individual Team Members

It is important that you watch your staff member's "life-gauges." Throughout this handbook, the staff member is encouraged to monitor his or her own emotional health, spiritual vitality, intellectual capital, and relationship skills to prevent burnout or unnecessary stress. As a team leader, you need to keep an eye on their gauges as well. Sometimes the staff member cannot see what you see.

I remember approaching a team member who was clearly exhausted and had been sharing stories about relationship crises at home and in the office. I simply said, "Go home and don't come back until Monday." When he started to argue, I became the "tough guy." He went home. The ministry survived the weekend. He was renewed and refreshed on Monday. Though his gauges were warning him of ministry and personal overload, he could not see it that day. I could. I had to be a responsible team leader to a team member.

Being Fair and Consistent

Finally, create and develop a reputation of fairness and consistency. In his book *Association Source* Gene H. Cheatham writes, "Realize that fairness establishes your credibility." Fairness and consistency will serve you well in building your team. While some team members have aspirations to arrive at the "top" of the team, the majority will be most appreciative to know that a genuine spirit of equality is being promoted and demonstrated.

The Team Member

Everyone Is Different

Diversity can be one of your team's strongest characteristics. Each member has a unique background, spiritual gifts, experiences, longevity, and style — and desires to be recognized for his or her unique contribution. The prima donna is out; the blending of talent and experience is in.

Where diversity exists, conflict is inevitable. It is the leader's role to bring conflict resolution skills to the table. However, each team member must contribute to the team's unity and peace. If a team member does not contribute to resolution, he or she is a part of the problem. Apathetic attitudes, derogatory comments, and unhealthy political alliances are not acceptable team behavior. Don't allow that kind of passive or political behavior to continue. Deal with it, now.

Left-brain and right-brain thinkers will sit on your ministry team. That means logic and emotions will flow on each issue, finding collision courses along the way. Learn to celebrate the God-given representation in each discussion. Encourage your team that diversity is working for you and not against you. Remind the ministry team that they represent the body of Christ with their multiple feelings, insights, gifts, and dreams.

Expectations

Make your expectations clear. You may even put in writing a list of basic assumptions and expectations. Your expectations of a team member may include:

- Being on time with their presence and communication tools
- Encouraging and respecting other team members
- Giving open and honest feedback on issues and reasons for failure
- Fulfilling agreed-upon assignments and meeting deadlines
- Giving their best to the glory of God
- Committing to pray, participate in team dialogue, and partner in team projects

Make clear what your team member can expect of you. This may be the second half of your one-page list of expectations. Think through what your staff really needs and hopes you will deliver to them, personally and as a team. Consider items such as:

- Accepting and encouraging differing ideas and opinions
- Never embarrassing a staff person in a team meeting or a public arena
- Having well planned agendas exhibiting forethought and afterthought
- Committing to pray, encourage, and provide available resources for the success of both individual team members and the team as a whole
- Practicing open, honest, and godly communication

The above lists are very general and represent only the expectations staff members have of their senior leader and vice versa. However, expectations can make or break a team if they are not clearly defined. Take time for each team member to create and compare their own list of expectations.

Some Misunderstandings of the Team's Purpose

A ministry team is created to accomplish the ministry's stated mission. Some staff members or leaders may have other purposes in mind, purposes that only serve to distract or detour. Teams are *not* created to:

- Abdicate responsibility from doing one's job by hiding inside the team. (Think of the person on the back of a tandem bike not pedaling.)
- Provide all the relational "warm fuzzies" that are not being nurtured or initiated through healthy relationships. (Think about the differences between an effective team and a caring community.)
- Establish job security or feel significant and important. (Think of the feelings after being accepted on your first sports team or musical ensemble.)
- Accomplish one's agenda that could not be accomplished alone. (Think about the big picture and mission of the ministry.)

Relationships and Responsibility

Though *accountability* is not always a favored word in working environments, a healthy team knows how to hold one another accountable. There is open and free exchange of ideas, long after the team meeting has ended. It is clear what everyone's job (and responsibility) entails. There is little to guess and much to invest.

Some team members look for the "silver bullet" in the meeting. They believe that something "magical" or "special" is going to happen in the team meeting itself, creating a powerful *kumbaya* moment and instant team effectiveness. While the meeting is important, it is the integrity and engagement of each and every team member that make a team work. If the football team's center does not hike the ball at the right time in the right way to the right person, the entire team suffers. Ministry teams are no different.

While team members do not need to be best buddies to work well together, everyone needs to learn how to get along. Often the "elephant" in the room is the tension between two or more team members. Everyone knows it, can explain it, and can feel it. When nothing is done, the elephant takes over and the team mission is never accomplished.

Team members carry the responsibility to work with each other. That begins with good old fashioned "talking to each other." Get out from behind the computer. Quit leaving voice messages. Instead of sending a memo, walk to that person's office or find a cup of coffee and talk.

A good team values every member of the team and recognizes each individual contribution. Everyone knows what they can expect of one another and thus are free to give ministry away. Ministry ownership and results are not in question. And all glory goes to God alone. People see the accomplishment as "ours," the team's, not any one person's.

Team Objectives and Goals

There is no one answer to the question, "What should be our team objectives and goals?" because it is tailored to every team within every ministry. The answer may be performing a task or developing a mission statement under which everyone develops their own area of ministry. The main issue is: are we on the same page and are we striving toward the same objectives?

Objectives are important to team building. Objectives are those things we will strive to accomplish that align with our mission. Goals are the small accomplishments needed to meet the objective. If the objective is to win a baseball game, a goal is to get a run this inning. If the objective is to reach Toledo by dinnertime, the goal is to leave Chicago by noon.

A ministry team may spend a lot of time together, yet if nothing is observably accomplished to fulfill the mission, a team doesn't really exist. It won't be long before people sense they have no purpose or reason to come together. The objective of a baseball team is to win the game. They should not really care who hits a homerun or how many runs they score as long as it is one more run than the opposing team. A ministry team should have the joy and celebration of "winning a game."

Establish realistic objectives and goals. Share the assignments and give freedom to everyone to accomplish their task, in their own way, within an agreed time frame. Celebrate the results. Share a team victory.

Making Decisions as a Team

"If we need to run this ministry project through the team it will take forever and may never get done" is a statement occasionally repeated by team leaders or some members. Sometimes it is just easier to make a decision and go with it. However, we all realize (if we are honest) that the team will always make a better decision than any one person. Why is that?

A team decision involves all of the collective gifts, personalities, experiences, and greater diversity of the team. No one person can make that great of an investment in one decision. The team leader must be committed to shared ownership and promote shared decision-making by the team. Everyone needs to participate. How is that best done?

The greatest single issue to great team-making decisions is getting everyone to share their diversity of gifts, talents, and background. Some people are simply quiet and don't talk in the meeting. Others monopolize the meeting with strong personality to get the decision they think is the best. Neither member has contributed well. The following are a few suggestions to engage and gain every team member's input:

> **Why Do Teams Fail to Meet Objectives?**
>
> - Fuzzy objective
> - No goals
> - Too many goals or objectives at one time
> - Individual agendas
> - It is unclear who is responsible to do what is requested
> - A leader is not following up on assignments
> - Passive responses to team members not doing their part ("It's okay, Bill, you will do better next time. Don't worry about it.")
> - One person or a secondary group/committee having to manage and approve every step of the goal

- Go around the room and ask every staff member the same question.
- Write the responses where everyone can view them.
- Divide the team into groups of no more that three staff members. Give each group an assignment (the same or different assignment is okay). After a time of discussion have them report back to the entire team.
- Give each team member an assignment for the next team meeting, asking them to give a verbal and written report of their findings or personal conclusions.
- Give each member a red and green card to hold up when you ask, "Is this a good idea?" or "Is this the direction we need to go?" Green, of course, means "Go forward!" and red means, "Slow down or stop." The point is, everyone weighs in on the discussion.
- Ask your team members simple, focused questions. Try not to ask a question that involves so many different issues that it cannot be answered. For example, do not ask, "*What* should we rename our ministry?" It is better to ask, "Should we rename our ministry? If so, why? If not, why?" Now you have a discussion, with input and worthwhile opinion. So, carefully think though the questions you ask your staff team. A clear, well thought out question can make all the difference in the final discussion.

To move toward a higher level of team performance, consider the size and makeup of your team. If the team is too large (more than twelve members), it is going to always be difficult to gain everyone's input. Streamline the team if needed.

Make sure that the ministry team is representing the entire ministry before making final decisions. If your ministry includes 150 ministry participants, did the six team members spend time in dialogue with the 150? Are the voices of the ministry being heard? What about the voices and diverse input from outside the ministry? Has that been accurately recorded without bias or prejudice? The decision-making process needs to attempt to include all those who will be affected by the decision. Hard work? Yes!

None of us is as smart as all of us.

Peter B. Graziert

Additional Reading

Cladis, George. *Leading the Team-Based Church.* San Francisco: Jossey-Bass, 1999.

Ellis, Lee. *Leading Talents, Leading Teams.* Chicago: Northfield, 2003.

Forman, Rowland, Jeff Jones, and Bruce Miller. *An Intentional Strategy for Developing Leaders in Your Church.* Grand Rapids, Mich.: Zondervan, 2004.

Gangel, Kenneth O. *Team Leadership in Christian Ministry.* Chicago: Moody Press, 1970.

Herrington, Jim, Mike Bonem, and James H. Fur. *Leading Congregational Change.* San Francisco: Jossey-Bass, 2000.

Orsburn, Jack D. and Linda Moran. *The New Self-Directed Work Teams.* New York: McGraw-Hill, 1999.

Trent, John. *Leading from Your Strengths: Building Close-Knit Ministry Teams.* Nashville: Broadman and Holman, 2004.

Working with One Ministry
Staff Member

For acquiring a disciplined and prudent life, doing what is right
and just and fair; for giving prudence to the simple, knowledge and
discretion to the young—let the wise listen and add to their learning,
and let the discerning get guidance.

Proverbs 1:3–5

The role of the pastor is determined by their calling, gifts, and needs of
the church and the gifts of others on the leadership team.

Pastor George Cladis, Brentwood (Tenn.) Presbyterian Church

When Jason accepted an administrative position at Evangel Church
he considered it a wonderful chance to exercise and nurture all of
his ministry gifts in a well-established body. The administrative
role was only a means to that end.

Tom now had his first staff member, the administrative relief he needed
for his fast-growing ministry. From Jason's interview and reference checks,
it didn't take long to realize he was a bright and talented young man, one of
those "most likely to succeed" types. The church was privileged to hire him.

Within months, Jason wanted to preach and finally got that opportunity
when Tom went on vacation. Jason was well received by the congregation.
They loved his sermon. Jason loved the experience.

Preaching and teaching the Bible quickly became Jason's greatest joy in
ministry; in fact, it was soon evident to the congregation that he was a more
effective communicator than Tom. However, with only two people on staff,
Tom needed Jason to do the job he hired him to do, so he started limiting

Jason's pulpit and teaching opportunities. Frustrations and small tensions began to separate the two ministry leaders.

Jason finally went to another church as senior pastor and Tom struggled to replace him. Today both churches have multiple staff members and are vibrant outreaches into their communities. Jason and Tom learned valuable lessons.

One on One

My first full-time ministry experience was with Pastor Bob Savage, a veteran missionary in Ecuador and stateside pastor, now in heaven after a courageous battle with cancer. I served for three years as the youth pastor under Bob at a semirural church near Muskegon, Michigan, the first paid ministry staff member other than an administrative assistant.

When it came to pastoral ministry, it was just Pastor Bob and me. I was twenty-two years old, married to Donna for one year, and finishing my baccalaureate degree from Cornerstone University. I can honestly say those first three years could not have been a better introduction to ministry.

As the only other pastoral staff member, I observed, participated in, and experienced every aspect of pastoral ministry by watching him. From board meetings to family brawls, from the hospital emergency room to the pulpit, I had a full induction.

Bob took me everywhere. Then he would spontaneously ask me to participate. I will never forget the first summer when he went on vacation, he quietly said, "Next week, you're in charge." What? Me? I can't do that! But God was gracious as he matured me quickly through a church family member's fatal motorcycle accident. That week I conducted my first funeral, and so much more.

More Than One

We've all heard it said, "There shouldn't be any 'lone rangers' in ministry. Even the Lone Ranger had Tonto." Well, as juvenile as that sounds, the day of the solo pastor is indeed rapidly fading.

Even some rural pastorates are working in tandem, with some level of ministry partnership. I know of one ministry in the Midwest, where three churches were for decades shepherded by one pastor. Today a team of two ministers serves the semirural congregations.

When a ministry has the resources and opportunity to hire the second ministry staff member (beyond an administrative or clerical role), a significant shift will take place. Once there was one leader who was responsible for the ministry, now there are two. Two offices, two phones, two health insurance policies, two more of everything now need attention and consideration.

By the same token, the opportunities can double (almost) and the responsibilities are halved (not quite). Yet there will be more freedom, greater focus, and increased flexibility for each ministry leader. The options have just increased. So should the ministry.

Shifting from a solo pastorate or leadership ministry role in a parachurch ministry to a dual role with a full-time paid associate will require some adaptations. The changes do not need to be difficult, as some would suggest or predict. With a new way of thinking through ministry needs and responsibilities, a smooth transition can be made. First of all, your associate is *not*:

- A ministry gofer
- A substitute when the senior leader is gone or overloaded
- Someone off in another part of the ministry, seldom seen or heard
- Competition
- Your successor (normally not, but may be)
- Cheap labor or a hireling
- A clone

Hopefully, you have hired someone who is called to ministry, whose personal background, spiritual gifts, training, and style are ready to merge into a meaningful and significant role to touch and shape lives. As a ministry leader, you have the opportunity to create a place for the associate to grow, to be their greatest encourager and example at the most teachable time in their ministry lives. You can:

- Provide multiple opportunities to discover and share spiritual gifts.
- Create new occasions for exploring talent and learning new skills.
- Develop and expand your associate's strengths.
- Gently and honestly point out weaknesses and prevent unnecessary failure.
- Model a godly ministry and begin leaving your legacy in the life of another.
- Discover your own strengths and weaknesses.

Your associate can be a wonderful blessing and gift from God. Learn to value and invest in your ministry partner, to be a giver and not a taker. The blessings and rewards may last a lifetime.

Parent, Counselor, Best Friend, Spiritual Director, or Boss?

As you consider your role as senior leader in the ministry, you may ask what your role is with this new associate you have just hired, particularly if this is your first experience leading another. Don't worry or be overwhelmed. God will give you everything you need to address the needs of your team member.

Some leaders believe they need to assume all five roles—parent, counselor, best friend, spiritual director, and boss—with the new associate. Indeed, during some weeks, you may experience all five roles ... or maybe just one or two.

Your governing board may expect you to exhibit leadership and management skills not previously required. You may feel or have already felt some sense of panic and added responsibility for the life and future of another. Again, relax! First of all, you need to be you. Besides which, be godly, be faithful, and be available. Let God lead you through the rest. Consider the insights of the following assumed roles:

> ## Opportunities to Extend to Your Associate
>
> - Allow them to experience every aspect of the ministry, at least one time.
> - Allow them to discover and grow their personal area of giftedness, even if it is the same as yours.
> - Provide them leadership responsibility.
> - Help them equip people to discover and use their God-given gifts.
> - Give them the joy of seeing God work miraculously in people's lives.
> - Expose them to the real pain, suffering, and agony of those placed in your care.

Parent. You are not your associate's father or mother. While everyone needs that role fulfilled in their life, that is not your job. Even if your associate exhibits parental needs, set clear boundaries and redirect your staff member to a senior volunteer in the ministry to be a surrogate parent. Helping a staff person get their life together, personally mature, or develop life skills is not your responsibility. You will help them grow. But you don't need to take responsibility to help them grow up.

Counselor. There are times when you will give good, wise counsel to your associate staff member. Even if your background is counseling, resist being a counselor to work through your associate's pathologies. That is not why they have been hired. If they need professional counseling, have the ministry provide that through someone other than you.

Best friend. Of course, I hope you are friendly and that your associate will look back to you as a good friend and personal colleague in ministry. But again, you need to set boundaries. You are not their best friend. The staff person needs to learn how to develop a personal life outside of their ministry life. Proverbs 25:17 warns about spending too much time together, because in the end you may not like each other very well. I have seen some senior pastors and associates become best friends, and the ministry has flourished. But those are exceptions, not the rule.

"Why Can't We Be Friends?"

The following story was told by Nadine Heintz in *Inc.* magazine:

"When P.B. founded National Bankcard Systems, he hired his friends for key positions and socialized regularly with his staff. He figured that his friends would work harder for him than others would and that being a buddy rather than a boss would help the business grow. It didn't. His friends grew complacent, and he ended up firing two of them."

Spiritual director. Pray, read the Bible, and share your spiritual journey with your associate staff member. Be transparent in your struggles and victories. However, you cannot begin to take complete responsibility for your associate's relationship with God. While you will be responsible to point out your protégé's behavioral traits and character flaws, you cannot be in charge of their personal walk with God. Leave it at modeling godliness and consistent, Christlike behavior.

Boss. In some ways you *are* the boss. There is no getting around the fact that the buck stops at your desk. However, you are most likely a shepherd or ministry director concerned more about the mission of seeing lives changed. Be responsible, but do not feel the weight of corporate America. While good biblical management practices are valuable and should be exercised, don't try to be boss of the year. It is not necessary. Consider the coaching or mentoring concept instead. Read on.

Coach or Mentor?

Coaching and mentoring are two rather popular roles among leaders in our current culture. It is helpful to know the difference between the two, though perhaps you may fill both roles with an associate. Consider the following definitions and role descriptions:

Coach. A coach directs, supports, and encourages a team (or individual member) toward maximum potential. Standing on the sidelines, he or she uses background, experience, wisdom, and insights to provide leadership.

Good Gifts for Your Associate

While the following are good gifts from every senior leader, whether their staff is large or small, they are most useful for an "only" associate.

- Positive spirit and relationship between the two of you
- Open and honest communication
- Assignments and opportunities to remain active and productive
- Embracing the big picture and purpose of the ministry
- Ability to adapt and adjust to ongoing change
- Networking with other ministries and ministry leaders
- Treating as sacred your weekly "staff meeting" with just the two of you
- Shared resources (books, magazines, conferences, etc.)

Often a football player will call a timeout and run to the sidelines to ask a coach for advice and wisdom. But it is the player, not the coach, who goes back onto the field to execute the next play.

Coaches grant freedom, permission, and responsibility. They train and place each player in the right spot. They ask questions. They evaluate and extend advice. But they also allow maturing players to think, reflect, respond, and make their own decisions. A mature coach takes the loss, or grants the win and celebrates the victory with the players.

Mentor. A mentor trains, provides resources, and invests personal time and interest into the skills and gifts of a protégé. While mentors don't overlook or ignore weaknesses, their primary goal is to identify a protégé's strengths in a particular area of life or ministry and to help develop those to the next level of excellence and effectiveness.

Mentors know the cost of mentoring. They realize their commitment to the life of another. They dare not limit or hold back a person from exercising their gift and abilities. Mentors will often be on a journey with their protégé. Together they will take a **TRIP**—involving **T**ime, **R**esources, **I**nvolvement, and **P**rayer, each of which is given openly and freely.

Mentors step aside to grant unusual opportunity, perhaps giving an associate a portion of their own job and role. That requires maturity on the mentor's part, but what tremendous confidence and courage that gives an associate. Indeed, as the mentor displays personal security in his or her own role, the associate also learns the value and cost of investing in another for the future. The protégé then becomes a mentor. Reproduction has taken place

At the End of the Day

As a final word of encouragement, determine upfront that the partnership with your staff member be one that glorifies God in every aspect of the ministry you share. Each day you will have choices to share and partner or remain alone and isolated. Remember, there once was one (you); now there are two. You can place high value on your staff member by considering the following principles and insights.

- *Prayer.* Will you be able to pray together at the end of the day? Will you initiate prayer throughout your shared ministry?
- *Vulnerability.* Will you be able to share your heart and life with your associate? Will you be able to go to one who is younger and less experienced and ask for their advice and direction? Will you be able to believe in their ability to make a worthwhile contribution to your life and ministry?
- *Celebrate.* Will you give credit where credit is due? Will you enhance the honorable reputation of your associate minister? Will you be able to take the backseat from time to time?
- *Courage.* Will you demonstrate the courage to confront and carefully point out weaknesses and failures? Will you resist being liked at the moment? Will you show your associate what is most important today and make the tough choices?
- *Story.* Will you create a story that others will tell? Will you both become supporting characters to the main character, God? Will your story be an exciting victory or a solemn tragedy?
- *Identity.* Will ministry volunteers and participants call you a team? Will they see you as examples of Elisha and Elijah; Moses and Joshua; Paul and Timothy; Naomi and Ruth?
- *Growth.* Will the people in the ministry say they have grown today? Will your associate say he or she has matured in life and ministry because of you?

Rejoice and celebrate the associate staff member God has given to you!

Additional Reading

Callahan, Kennon L. *Small, Strong Congregations.* San Francisco: Jossey-Bass, 2001.

Collins, Gary. *Christian Coaching: Helping Others Turn Potential into Reality.* Colorado Springs, NavPress, 2001.

Dawn, Marva and Eugene Peterson. *The Unnecessary Pastor: Rediscovering the Call.* Grand Rapids, Mich.: Eerdmans, 2000.

Palmer, Parker. *Let Your Life Speak: Listening for the Voice of Vocation.* San Francisco: Jossey-Bass, 2000.

Scazzero, Peter. *The Emotionally Healthy Church.* Grand Rapids, Mich.: Zondervan, 2003.

Stanley, Paul and Robert Clinton. *Connecting: The Mentoring Relationships You Need to Succeed in Life.* Colorado Springs: NavPress, 1992.

Wright, H. Norman. *Helping Those Who Hurt.* Minneapolis: Bethany House, 2003.

Name and Subject Index

Name and Subject Index

Name and Subject Index